SOCIAL THEORIES OF THE PRESS

—— PEOPLE AND COMMUNICATION——

Series Editors: F. GERALD KLINE   *University of Minnesota*
PETER CLARKE   *University of Michigan*

Volumes in this series:

Social Theories of the Press

Early German & American Perspectives

Hanno Hardt

Foreword by James W. Carey

 SAGE Publications   *Beverly Hills   London*

For information address:

SAGE PUBLICATIONS, INC.
275 South Beverly Drive
Beverly Hills, California 90212

SAGE PUBLICATIONS LTD
28 Banner Street
London EC1Y 8QE

Printed in the United States of America

Library of Congress Cataloging in Publication Data

Hardt, Hanno.
    Social theories of the press

    (People and Communication; vol. 6)
    Bibliography:
    Includes index.
    1. Communication—Social aspects. 2. Mass media —Social aspects. 3. Sociology—Germany—History. 4. Sociology—United States—History. I. Title.
HM258.H357   301.14   78-31588
ISBN 0-8039-1236-6
ISBN 0-8039-1237-4 pbk.

FIRST PRINTING

CONTENTS

To fulfill their tasks, or even to state them well, social scientists must use the materials of history. Unless one assumes some trans-historical theory of the nature of history, or that man in society is a non-historical entity, no social science can be assumed to transcend history.

C. Wright Mills in
The Sociological Imagination

FOREWORD

That usually reliable source of intellectual guidance, the late Alfred North Whitehead, may have led us astray when he admonished, in *Science and the Modern World,* that no science is mature until it has forgotten its founders. The past, the history of science, holds only an antiquarian interest; it is merely prologue and not a source of understanding of contemporary practice or inspiration toward future work.

Perhaps Whitehead's observation is correction for the physical sciences. In the common view, those sciences exhibit a progressive, orderly, and cumulative development—knowledge that increases in clarity, power, and scope. However, we are entitled to be skeptical of even this claim since Thomas Kuhn's *The Structure of Scientific Revolutions* demonstrated that the history of science could teach us something of the nature of science. It could teach us, above all, something about the nature of conceptual change in the sciences: the moment when scientists give up one set of concepts for another and the special forms of rationality that are exhibited at these moments of paradigm switch. The resulting view of science is less a picture of cumulative development than of a multi-layered group of "geological strata," one piled on the other in a process of radically discontinuous development.

Whitehead's admonition never applied with much pertinence to the human or cultural or social sciences and hence the critical force of the word "mature." In the human sciences a knowledge of history is absolutely necessary to a critical understanding of the nature of current practice and theory. However, historical knowledge of these sciences does more than increase the power of self-reflection. It can also make a major contribution to the substantive development of the human sciences. The history of the human sciences reveals significant problems that have been lost or defined away, concepts of power and scope that have been trivialized or thoughtlessly abandoned, methods and concerns that need to be rejuvenated and not merely picked over like the remains in a historical museum. In short, one of the avenues of progress in the human sciences is a thorough and continuous reinspection of the history of the intellectual enterprise.

This project is particularly necessary in mass communication research. However, the history of thought and scholarship concerning mass communication reveals a significant impasse, an impasse found in much of the historical writing about the human sciences in America. That impasse can be illustrated with a little story that bears a lesson about the effects of communication technology as well.

Among the glittering array of intelligence sent into a modern diaspora by the fall of the Weimar Republic was the political philosopher Franz Neumann. Reflecting on his plight from his new home in America, Neumann contrasted his situation with that of the migrant scholar of the Middle Ages. Neumann was viewed in America as a political scientist, yet his own thought and work did not fit comfortably into American categories and departments. Had he been in migration in the Middle Ages, the same language of scholarship would be spoken and written across the map of Europe. He would have been part of a universal culture, Christian in content, Latin in language, which would have allowed the itinerant scholar, were he Christian, to be at home anywhere. The emergence of printing, for whatever spectacular gains it contained, illustrates a principle: improvements in communication narrow the possibilities of communication. The rise of printing, which emphasized the vernacular, was concomitant with the decline of Latin. Subsequent developments in scholarship were along national rather than universal lines, and we come to speak, though the phrases merely express a tendency, of German idealism, French rationalism, British empiricism, and American pragmatism—distinctive national variations in scholarly outlook. The differences are not merely linguistic as anyone who has attempted translation knows. The linguistic differences attest to differing underlying structures of thought and interest and create extreme difficulties in, though they do not defy, bringing together and negotiating these discrepant frames of reference.

As I argued a few years back, the situation is particularly grave at the moment for the American scholar in the humanities and social sciences. In the years after World War II the ability of such scholars in foreign languages declined, for it seemed for a moment that English would be enough. Actually, the perception was but a temporary artifact of the war itself. From our comfortable distance we failed to grasp the ruinous effect of the war on European scholarship: a major part of a generation lost, universities in disarray, publishing houses disbanded, research traditions fractured. In the 1940s and 1950s a kind of intellectual Marshall plan grew up that led to the widespread exportation of American scholarship and an unprecedented, though temporary, influence for American ideas. The situation is different now, and it is necessary for American scholars to regain intimate contact and familiarity with European scholarship.

However, American scholars need to be in touch with something more than contemporary European scholarship. Many of the originating impulses behind research on mass communication were German, and Hanno Hardt's work succeeds in making this scholarship accessible to us by negotiating the discrepant frames of meaning of German and American traditions. It was not until the twentieth century that journalism and the mass media became subjects of scholarship in the United States in any significant way. Up to that time the nature of the media, their relation to society, their consequences, were taken to be relatively unproblematic. Anglo-American scholarship was devoted almost exclusively to the problem of the nature of freedom of expression. It was in general agreement, however, that if the conditions of freedom were maintained then the consequences of mass communication were relatively automatic—an invisible hand leading the will of individuals to the maximization of the social good.

Operating within a different national tradition of scholarship, a tradition with much more skepticism concerning the doctrines and consequences of the Enlightenment, German scholars found the press a problematic institution—its consequences unclear, its contribution to freedom and enlightenment far from automatic, its relationship to the state, to the capitalist economy, to the social order generally, to be troubling, sometimes menacing. For these reasons, the press became an object of scholarly concern earlier in Germany than in the United States.

We are familiar with the work of the towering and dominating figures of late eighteenth- and nineteenth-century German scholarship—Herder, Kant, Hegel, Marx, Dilthey—though we are not necessarily always aware of the implications of their views for the study of communications and the mass media. We are also familiar with those figures who migrated to the United States and published in English—Cassirer, Adorno, Horkheimer, Lowenthal—for they sometimes made an attempt to translate their work into terms congenial to American understanding. But of other German scholars who were concerned with the press and mass media over the past hundred years or so we know little. Professor Hardt has corrected a major part of this deficiency by presenting the work of these scholars and bringing out the contrasts in sensibility and intellectual position between their scholarship and ours. Of the figures he treats, only Max Weber and Ferdinand Tönnies are known on sight. Weber's work on the press is, however, the least known portion of his work, and so little of Tönnies has been translated that his work is known more in caricature than substance.

We have here a curious chapter in the transatlantic migration of ideas on mass communication. Many of the greatest American scholars of the late nineteenth century were trained in Germany, if for no other reason than there was not at that time an adequate system of graduate education in the United States. On their return, they brought with them the model of what a graduate school should be and many of the ideas of the German classical tradition: ideas loosely grasped by notions such as the materialist theory of history, the distinction between Naturwissenschaft and Geisteswissenschaft, of hermeneutic understanding, of the necessity of a reconstructive imagination or Verstehen in understanding human action. But they returned with more than a few foreign concepts. Because the German tradition of scholarship is grounded in philosophy, they also learned to examine society and its institutions in a synoptic rather than a disciplinary frame; to see, that is, the mass media not in the narrowed context of psychology and the small group but in the larger framework of politics, economics, and culture.

Three of these figures—Albion Small, E. A. Ross, and William Graham Sumner—are the subject of the concluding chapter. But it is well to remember that nearly all of the major figures in early American scholarship on mass communication—John Dewey, Robert Park, George Herbert Mead, W. I. Thomas, Franklin Giddings—were either educated in Germany or (Dewey is a good case) struggled all their life with the German intellectual tradition. In making certain German ideas accessible to American audiences, these men had to convert this scholarship to an American idiom. In doing so, it was inevitable that distortions would creep into the exposition. However, it is impossible to understand these men, to understand the problems they were setting before us, the tacit meanings of their arguments, the significance of the concerns they were announcing without recognizing the German background—the absent presence in their work like the sky trail of a vanished aircraft.

To complicate all this coming and going, the scholarship of some of these Americans has recrossed the Atlantic in recent years and important aspects of the American pragmatic tradition are found in recent German work, particularly in the critical theory of Jurgen Habermas. Moreover, recent German work on mass communications has absorbed some of the spirit and techniques of American behavioral science, though it has absorbed it critically and conteniously. These American and

German traditions must now be understood in a full historical relation to one another and not as independent streams.

One constantly hears in Professor Hardt's chapters echoes of arguments announced later by Robert Park and John Dewey and even the Canadian economist Harold Innis. But one hears those echoes against a background of many things which American scholarship in mass communications has lost: a thoroughly critical attitude towards its subject, a sense of the larger social framework of social theory within which our studies must proceed. This book is not merely a history of pertinent German thought on mass communication; it is much more. It reminds us of valuable ideas from a vital tradition of scholarship that can vivify our own work.

—*James W. Carey*
University of Iowa

PREFACE

The history of mass communication theory and research in the United States has yet to be written. This book represents a contribution to the rediscovery of the historical dimension in communication and mass communication studies.

The development of mass communication as a field of study has had a pronounced European phase which contained a number of suggestions from economic and sociological studies of an emerging industrial, urban environment. These ideas also included some specifically German contributions which found their way into early American scholarship.

The migration of ideas, their modification and adoption in the American context provide a fascinating area for historical inquiry. Also, contemporary perspectives of mass communication can be explained as results of particular concerns involving communication in specific economic and social contexts.

This book reflects my encounter with the German tradition of *Publizistikwissenschaft* and my interest in the transfer of ideas as a central problem for the study of cultural communication and the ensuing questions of domination and power of communication in international settings.

After two generations of scholars and considerations of communication and mass communication as important aspects of a study of society, a number of basic issues remain unchanged and a challenge to the imagination of contemporary scholarship. An awareness of the rich intellectual tradition may provide us with an alternative perspective on the role and function of the media in society. This volume attempts to suggest the necessity for a different approach to the study of communication and mass communication.

I would like to thank a number of individuals and their institutions for advice and support—specifically, my colleagues at the University of Iowa School of Journalism, and Sam Becker (Iowa), Jerry Kline (Minnesota), and Jeremy Tunstall (City University, London) who provided additional feedback and encouragement. The University of Iowa granted me a leave of absence during the winter of 1976; and the following individuals and their institutions supported my work in Germany: Professor Roegele, Institut für Kommunikationswissenschaft, München; Professor Lerg, Institut für Publizistik, Münster; Professor Schmolke, Institut für Publizistik und Kommunikationstheorie, Salzburg, Austria; and Professor Koszyk, Institut für Zeitungsforschung, Dortmund.

In addition, I want to thank George Gerbner, editor of the *Journal of Communication,* with whose permission I used parts of two articles published earlier. Also, I want to thank my students who shared an earlier draft in one of my seminars at Iowa, Carolyn Carlyle, who helped with the bibliography, and Nancy Parizek, who typed the final manuscript.

Finally, I owe much to a most understanding family, Ursula, Nicole, Katreen, and Nina, who are part of my personal history.

—Hanno Hardt

Iowa City/Berlin

January 1979

1

Introduction

THE HISTORICAL DIMENSION

The coming of age of a field of study is accompanied by questions about its past to help establish its identity and to secure its position among the arts and sciences. The history of communication and mass communication theory in the United States emerges as a chapter in the history of philosophical, social, and political thought in Europe and North America during the last hundred years. The present account concentrates on aspects which deal with the reflections of early American sociologists and their German colleagues or teachers who may have contributed to the development of communication and mass communication studies in this country and elsewhere. At the same time, the following pages are intended as a suggestion and a reminder that the intellectual history of this field may also yield theoretical insights concerning the relationship between communication and the advancement of society which may have consequences for the development of communication and mass communication research today.

Based upon the contributions of individual scholars during the late nineteenth and early twentieth centuries rather than on major themes of German or European intellectual history of that time, this has been a subjective and rather intuitive selection, guided in part by explanations of academic kinship, theoretical proximity, commonality of interests, and social-political involvement in contemporary issues.

The social thought of this age was dominated by the writings of Spencer, Comte, and Marx, in particular, which shaped the work of others or prompted a response to their theoretical propositions. By the time the nineteenth century came to a close, the spirit of social criticism had been firmly established. The observation of social life had led to the Spencerian view of freedom through competing religious or philosophical doctrines, the Comtean realization that religion had to be replaced by a new scientific philosophy which would help organize the political and economic conditions, and a Marxian position which foresaw the growth of science and technology and the rise of an egalitarian society as a reaction to capitalistic forces. The work of these theorists was supported by others who engaged in closer observations of specific conditions, who conducted surveys and reported the failures of society in a scientific manner, e.g., in objective descriptions. They were not always dispassionate, and they were often supported by socialist thought and reformist ideas that surfaced in the journalism of the day. At times, social science theory and social criticism appeared to flow simultaneously from the work of committed intellectuals. While it was mainly an ideological force that dominated the social criticism of German scholars, it was an engagement in social reform which provided the focal point for the American social sciences. This means that sociology and the study of mass communication as a social phenomenon came into being in the United States as part of an expressed need for the improvement of social conditions and in Germany as a variation of philosophical and political thought. In both instances, however, the developments were caused, at least in part, also by the rapid transformation of society which had resulted in economic and political inequality. Most important for this study, however, was another recurrent notion throughout this period: the tracing of the development of social consciousness through communication as a definition and explanation of the rise of modern society. It was Marx who formulated the idea that the social structure must evolve out of the life-process of individuals, suggesting a way for the social sciences to investigate the workings of society:

> The production of ideas, of conceptions, of consciousness, is at first directly interwoven with the material activity and the material intercourse of men, the language of real life. Conceiving, thinking, the mental intercourse of men, appear at this stage as the direct efflux of their material behaviour. The same applies to mental production as expressed in the language of politics, law, morality, religion, metaphysics, etc.—real, active men, as they are conditioned by a definite development of their productive forces and of the intercourse corresponding to these, up to the furthest forms. Consciousness can never be anything else than conscious existence, and the existence of men is their actual life-process.[1]

This meant that the study of history must include language, public opinion, and the press as necessary elements in any explanation of the material or intellectual and spiritual growth of society. As a matter of fact, they provide central themes for the discussion of those social, economic, and political processes that help shape the human environment.

One of the strongest suggestions that emerges from the work of these early social scientists is that a theory of society, or any attempt to explain the coming of the modern age, must be based upon some understanding of communication as a basic social process involving individuals. In fact, communication becomes the sine qua non of human existence and the growth of society. Consequently, considerable attention is paid to the role and function of language as a socializing and integrating mechanism, as a tool or instrument for the construction of everyday realities as well as for scientific or political world views.

The production of symbols is crucial for the exchange of ideas; without language, man's ability to function as a social being is impaired, he is abandoned to live in a state of ignorance and isolation. Language, then, is the foundation of knowledge, it functions to preserve traditions, and it marks the beginning of civilization.

Communication implies the presence of language and the existence of dialogical relationships; it also fosters the idea of exchange. At the same time, language and communication are effective instruments or tools for individuals or groups; their use involves manipulation of different symbolic forms to effect individual or public opinions.

Therefore, any understanding or human progress from communal relationships to urban societies must be predicated upon an appreciation of the fundamental role of communication in this life-process of society.

The communication of ideas, the importance of preserving and transmitting knowledge as prerequisite for the growth and survival of society called for the creation of communication media that were not only accurate and efficient, but also fast and durable and therefore superior to oral modes of communication. These results were achieved almost instantaneously with the invention of the printing press, the publication of books and pamphlets, and the circulation of newspapers in modern times. The expression of facts and opinions on a large scale had the potential, if not the effect, of social and political integration through democratizing access to knowledge and to the media of dissemination.

The newspaper press rises to a powerful institution in the development of Western civilization: it is the medium for the exchange of ideas and it facilitates the time- and space-binding activities of society. The press as a technological invention or a political medium plays a major role in the definition of reality for the individual as well as for a nation; it supplies identification and formulates public opinions; and it supplements industrial and economic progress as an indispensible organizer of public sentiments.

The history of the modern press reflects the rise of liberalism, the reign of democracy and capitalism, and the growth of urban society. The daily press is a child of the city, and the process of public communication must necessarily be filtered through the economic and political interests that are identified with the concerns for urban development.

Throughout this period the work of political economists supplies a strong bias; thus, the role and function of the press receives a critical treatment that stresses economic aspects. These views range from an interpretation of the press reminiscent of Harold Innis' later work which produced a unique communication and mass communication perspective of world history, to assessments of the traditional, and unavoidable, ties between politics and business that effect the workings of the modern newspaper.

The press is central to any discussion of the production and dissemination of symbols, either in the form of political facts or opinions or in commercial messages. Newspapers sell either information or space for appropriate messages; in all cases there are economic interests at stake that cannot be ignored. As a capitalistic enterprise, the press not only serves other businesses, but by itself represents a capitalistic concern. Thus, the press helps coordinate production, transportation, and exchange of wealth; it aids in the search for ways of disposing of surplus and of promoting territorial divisions of labor; but it also promotes knowledge and education and provides political information.

Press criticism, therefore, focuses upon the real or potential conflict between these functions of newspapers: as an independent institution of society that produces and disseminates information, and as a medium of special interest groups that serves particular business and political segments of society. The difficulties of this position that characterizes the modern press are described in terms of the problems of a journalistic work ethic, the ideas of political as opposed to commercial newspapers, or the consequences of a press system that is recognized for what it is: the effective protection of an economic status quo.

This latter position can be explained also in terms of ideological differences regarding the treatment of leadership, the press, and public opinion. Specifically, the German position frequently reflects an elitist-aristocratic view which upholds the leader-masses dichotomy in the discussion of social, political, or cultural developments. Thus, it extols the intellectual qualities of a minority and delivers a rationale for its position vis-à-vis the masses which are capable of understanding and reflecting the ideas of their leaders but unfit to assume a creative and innovative role in the rise of modern society. The idea prevails that newspapers serve social and cultural elites in their communication with the masses. Even journalists are often reduced in their functions to mere objects through which the transmission of knowledge and information occurs without distortion. Although the press may reflect the opinions of the masses, it is not independent thought or creative insight, but more frequently a reaction to the opinions of the leaders that is reported. In this sense, the press assumes a rather fixed role in its relationship with society. The idea of the "average man" as a participant in the process of social communication is seriously reduced to that of a cooperating consumer of information in the context of describing the forces of history and the distribution of decision-making powers in society.

The views represented by the American position as it evolves in this study reveal the tendency to treat the press as a forum for the review of *all* ideas. Although the concept of authority may appear and suggest expert knowledge or special interest that will make itself felt in the communication process, there is no suggestion here that this precludes others from gaining similar access to the society through the newspapers, for instance. The press offers access to all kinds of commercial or political thoughts; and despite its economic interests, it is basically seen in the context of a classless society. This approach also suggests a concept of communication that fits the idea of a participatory democracy; in what is really a political process, all information is considered equally important, with the result that anyone may advance propositions which either support or oppose individual or special interest group goals.

Since newspapers do not just present windows on the world, but make or affect the opinions of their readers, the uses of the press by intellectual, political, or capitalistic elites present a serious problem. Indeed, control over the media of dissemination may suggest control over the mind of society.

Throughout the history of the press, criticism has assumed an inherent power in newspapers to change attitudes and to corrupt minds and has treated it as a particularly alarming aspect of a mass medium. Indeed, the workings of cultural and political forces in society are said to become transparent in the process of public communication where the communicator's purpose and intent are revealed and expose the nature of his ideology. The suggestive power of the press lies in its position as an institution *and* in the content of its messages. Thus, readers will follow the dictates of the press, because newspapers have gained their respect, are credible, and deliver facts and opinions convincingly. For this reason, newspapers are thought of as even more powerful instruments of communication than conversation, although, generally, greater effectiveness is attributed to face-to-face communication. Specifically, communicator effectiveness is also related to types of communication; the use of pictures (or films), for instance, offers still another argument for the persuasive power of the media.

But even the possibility of corruptive influences of mass communication does not result in an advocacy of drastic changes; instead, there is an implicit belief in the corrective influence of other types of communication which allows for comparison and intelligent choice. This position, in particular, is close to a definition of man as an educated, intelligent individual who participates in the societal process. The effects of the press are described, then, at a societal level where newspapers as institutions of society contribute to the political decision-making process, and at an individual level, where the press may change attitudes and the perception of reality. How this is accomplished and what the long-range effects would be for society were key questions that stimulated the suggestions for empirical research.

Thus, the origins of a modern study of the press are bound up with the rise of social criticism. It seems appropriate, especially in the light of the problems of contemporary communication and mass communication theory and research, to point to these beginnings and to renew the effort to embark upon a critical assessment of the role and function of the mass media in society.

This is so despite the fact that it could be argued, as Stuart Hughes has suggested, that social thinkers following Marx "were haunted by a sense of living in an age of merely derivative philosophy and scholarship"; and that their major contributions lay in the fact that they "narrowed the range through which such general theorizing might operate and cast doubt on the future usefulness of intellectual operations of this type."[2]

THE AMERICAN TRADITION

Specifically, today the tradition of American mass communication research is confronted by the crisis of the social sciences and the emergence of a critical approach to a theory of society. This situation is reflected not only in reactions to specific theoretical and methodological suggestions as they are being formulated and discussed by other disciplines, notably sociology, but also in acts of self-reflection and in a reappraisal of mass communication studies after a generation of research activities has had a profound effect upon the views about media activities and the way in which research is defined and executed.

The current dilemma of mass communication research is neither new nor unique; rather, it is the result of a historical development of a social-scientific enterprise that grew rapidly as a reaction to a number of social problems and as an attempt to treat specific conditions of society in a historical setting. This development also suggests the strength and weakness of the field. The immediacy of mass communication, its relevancy in everyday life, and the promise of research activities to help solve considerable social and political problems, provided the reasons for its prominence and initial success in academic and commercial contexts. Thus, mass communication studies received attention and built a strong rationale for their position among other disciplines and fields of study, particularly after World War II. At the same time, however, they neglected the larger, more meaningful contextual relationship that exists among media, communication and society, namely, the role and function of communication and mass communication in the process of civilization and the growth of society.[3]

Questions about the role and function of the mass media in American society are as old as the press itself. However, the interest in the phenomenon and the necessity for a systematic treatment of mass communication are relatively new. They seem to coincide with two major recent events, the invention of broadcasting technologies and the outbreak of wars. Both created specific demands for the social sciences: to summarize the effects of new technologies and to provide knowledge about the relationship of communicators and their audiences, about messages, and about the effects upon the political and economic lifestyles of society. The introduction of new types of media was accompanied by what Paul Lazarsfeld once called unanticipated consequences[4] which had to be identified and taken into account systematically for a complete understanding of real or potential uses of the mass media.

Not only did broadcasting cross continents and bridge oceans, but it was also envisioned as penetrating the minds of people more than other, older media and, therefore, expanding its influence as a tool of mass persuasion in the service of commercial or political interests. As a result, questions concerning the effects of mass communication were legitimized through economic and political support of research activities.

Similarly, the outbreak of a major conflict like World War II focused attention upon communication as a means of organizing national defenses, and also as an offensive weapon, in the field of psychological warfare, for instance. Consequently, the study of communication techniques received attention and continued encouragement—from government, in particular.

Lazarsfeld concluded quite correctly some years ago that communication research is a legitimate task of the social sciences and, although new, "it is, so to speak, the academic and intellectual shadow of the great changes which have come about in the world."[5] Thus, society became the laboratory and much of the initial research concentrated upon how to reach large numbers of individuals efficiently and effectively through the mass media. This was quite consistent with one of the prevailing definitions of mass communication as an activity directed towards a relatively large, heterogeneous, and anonymous audience.[6] Furthermore, much of the work that was completed treated society as potential or actual consumer of commercial or political messages at the expense of considering other, perhaps more critical perspectives on communication as a societal force.

There is still another reason for this development of the field. As we know, modern mass communication research has its roots primarily in the work of Harold Lasswell, Paul Lazarsfeld, Kurt Lewin, and Carl Hovland. Their interests in political power, audience effects, small group communication, and psychological analyses of communication effects, respectively, have been shaped by their disciplines. Their work provided important points of departure since the 1930s for several generations of communication and mass communication researchers. Nevertheless, this period of innovative ideas and the implementation of research designs was relatively short; it remained identified with the work of these principals in the field whose concerns with communication or mass communication phenomena, by the way, were rather peripheral to their major professional interests. Their students and followers, as is often the case, were less successful in generating and advancing new ideas; they were more successful in sustaining interest in those approaches with their particular methodologies and disciplinary frames of reference. There have been some exceptions, perhaps, but even so, the continuity of mass communication research often suffered, since little attention was paid to potential contributions to a mass communication theory. Instead, the collection of information became a preoccupation that raised some questions about the accumulation of unintegrated data that soon flooded the mass communication research field.

Nevertheless, a definitive perspective for an inquiry into mass communication activities was established and emerged from the early encounters with empirical communication research as a dominant way of looking at the world of the media and society. There was always an economic or political context, however, which mass communication research shared in the United States and which affected the investigation of media behavior. Specifically, the work was frequently conducted in an environment that was highly sensitive to the expert criticism of social scientists. Lazarsfeld observed as early as the late 1940s that "we academic people always have a certain sense of tight-rope walking: at what point will the commercial partners find some necessary conclusion too hard to take and at what point will they shut us off from the indispensable sources of funds and data?"[7] Not much has changed since that time; it is safe to assume that many of the most recent mass communication research projects have been sponsored by official or private sources rather than by academic institutions.

The shaping of a research perspective, then, rested upon the influence of economic and political environments as well as upon the theoretical and methodological orientations of a number of academic disciplines. Sociology, psychology, and political science, in particular, played a major role in the formation of research questions. They also introduced intra- and interpersonal communication aspects as part of a necessary condition to help explain causes and effects of mass communication, to understand differences between oral and written modes of communication, and to define traditional and modern systems of communication and society.

Most important, however, was the fact that mass communication research continued to operate within the prevailing philosophical mode of social-scientific research. Veikko Pietilä identified and described the influence of empiricism, behaviorism, and psychologism in the development of American communication research, for instance.[8] Consequently, not only was the search for mass communication causes and effects generally conducted with methodologies that generated knowledge based upon the interpretation of quantitative data, but also the search for an understanding of the consequences of mass communication activities was based upon various models of communication which provided a schematic diagram that identified major components like communicator, message, and audience as focal points, if not agendas for research.

The encounter with functionalism in its sociological and anthropological approaches, which postulate a system of society with stable relationships among its individual elements, meant that mass communication phenomena were treated as sources of information about the current state of exchange of information within a social system. Thus, functional analysis of mass communication suggested guidelines for the study of mass communication as an activity that contributed to the support and maintenance of the social system.

Functionalism as it emerged from its psychological roots provided mass communication research with its stimulus-response model; based upon a behavioristic theory, the approach led to a view of the mass media as deterministic stimuli with direct, cumulative effects upon the members of society.

THE GERMAN EXPERIENCE

The history of mass communication as a field of scholarly study is considerably older in Germany than in the United States. Recent encounters with the tradition of the American social sciences may help illustrate the pervasive influence of mass communication theory and research in Germany. The following reaction against unreflected adoption of theoretical or methodological premises may help define a framework for criticism.

The "discovery" of empirical social research for mass communication studies in Germany roughly coincided with the return of members of the Frankfurt Institute from the United States who began to promote the use of empirical techniques in the early 1950s. Thus, Adorno argued in 1952 for abandoning the idea of sociology as a *Geisteswissenschaft* and suggested the study of social phenomena with the methods of administrative research.[9] A few years later the widespread use of social science research methods resulted in a polarization of empirical and dialectical methodologists. The latter ones were represented by members of the Frankfurt Institute and Jürgen Habermas, who now exposed the dangers of a strictly empirical approach to the study of society. Adorno's warning that empirical social research is not "a magic mirror that reflects the future, no science-oriented astrology" did not prevent a *Positivismusstreit* among German sociologists. The clash occurred over the meta-theoretical foundation of sociology as science and involved representatives of critical theory (Adorno, Habermas) and critical rationalism (Karl Popper, Hans Albert). The outcome was not clear, not even to some participants; but the problem of the dialectical position focused on "how to integrate those techniques [of empirical social research] with a truly critical approach stressing the primacy of theory."[10]

It was not only Habermas' *Strukturwandel der Öffentlichkeit*, published in 1962, that focused the attention of *Publizistik-wissenschaft* on the problem of critical theory, but also the availability of most of the American mass communication and communication literature, and the rise of a postwar generation of young social scientists whose commitments were to the development of a contemporary theory of mass communication which brought about a drastic change in the direction of *Publizistikwissenschaft*.

The introduction of functionalism as an American contribution to the development of postwar studies of communication and mass communication at various institutes of *Publizistik* also included a particular view of society. Based upon a sociological tradition represented at that time by Parsons, Merton, and Davis in the United States, the functional or structural-functional approach suggested a view which describes a tendency of society towards stability, value consensus, and equilibrium. The problems of sudden and profound changes, conflict and revolution, for instance, could be taken into account only in terms of "deviations," "variances," or "dysfunctions," that is to say, without departing from a "static" picture of society. Although critics, like Ralph Dahrendorf,[11] pointed out the necessity of studying social change in postwar German society and, therefore, the need for rejecting the functional model of society, their ideas remained largely ineffective, particularly with respect to the work on communication and mass communication problems.

At another level, functionalism could be seen as a conscious alternative to Marxism. Without characterizing it as a political ideology that rose from the structure of American capitalism, it was, nevertheless, a product of modern American social thought. Specifically, the activities of a group of Harvard scholars, among them George Homans, Parsons, and L. J. Henderson, perhaps described how sociology in the United States searched for "a theoretical defense against Marxism"[12] in the 1930s when it became a new perspective brought into sharp focus by the collapse of the American economy. Functionalism projected a politically and ideologically neutral image, while it supported values of order and stability. Thus, supporting change within the context of a status quo did not alter its position vis-à-vis social criticism or efforts of radical social changes.

In addition, the end of World War II also brought along a new style of scientific inquiry described as "abstract empiricism." It provided social scientists in postwar Western Europe with a powerful and compelling description of their function and added to their definition of sociology at the same time. Paul Lazarsfeld, in a paper delivered in 1948 to a group of social scientists in Sweden who wanted to set up research institutions, explained the work of the sociologist as the methodologist of the social sciences. He said,

> This then is the first function of the sociologist, which we can make fairly explicit. He is so to say the *pathfinder* of the advancing army of social scientists, when a new sector of human affairs is about to become an object of empirical scientific investigations. It is the sociologist who takes the first steps. He is the bridge between the social philospher, the individual observer and commentator on the one hand and the organized team work of the empirical investigators and analysers on the other. . . . Historically speaking we then have to distinguish three major ways of looking at social subject matters: social analysis as practiced by the individual observer; organized full-fledged empirical sciences; and a transitory phase which we call the sociology of any special area of social behavior.[13]

The promise of empirical methods as they had been developed in the United States was turned into a stream of mass communication studies at a number of institutes in West Germany. The method, it seemed, gave status and respectability to the field of mass communication research by providing an instrument for the collection of data and by supplying the scientific context for the interpretation of communication phenomena in modern society. The results were less than encouraging, however, because German mass communication researchers missed asking relevant or significant questions from the point of view of aiding society in its new beginning, politically as well as morally. When Dröge and Lerg observed a lack of theory development in American mass communication research as it had developed up to 1965, they failed to comment on an identical trend then visible in West German social science research. [14]

What Hans Bohrmann and Rolf Sülzer have called the "reformed" *Publizistikwissenschaft*[15] was now in a position of legitimizing its own role in the context of the university, but also vis-à-vis the professions and industry through a close identification with a respected empirical research tradition.

It is more than a coincidence that the end of World War II marked the beginning of a process of reorientation that has led to the exploration of other fields, including sociology, social psychology, philosophy, and political science as related areas and as fields of study that have recognized the importance of mass communication in their definitions of social and political processes. The challenges of contemporary life could be met only after understanding the relationship among various social forces in society; there was a need for a comprehensive view of society in order to develop a theoretical base for the study of social phenomena. Therefore, the process of democratization of postwar Germany resulted also in a breakdown of the traditional barriers around *Zeitungswissenschaft* through the introduction and acceptance of theoretical and methodological frameworks suggested by other disciplines.

Finally, since the late 1960s *Publizistikwissenschaft* has entered what could be called a critical or reflective phase in its approach to problems of social research as well as to questions of its own position in society. The controversies in sociology as well as the demands of students and faculty for relevance of research and teaching helped accelerate the process of internal debates and forced discussions into the open. In addition, there was the realization that the mounting number of independent, empirical studies could neither solve the problems of Germany's mass communication system with respect to questions of monopolization and freedom of the press, for instance, nor satisfy the demands for a comprehensive theory that would bring about the necessary or desired social or political changes in the mass media system. It was never so much a question of whether to reject empirical methods or not as it was a problem of interpretation of what empirical social research could and should do *within* a theoretical framework. The limitations of empirical techniques became more obvious: empirical methods provided a mirror for the curious mass media researcher; they satisfied the demands for an accurate picture of a particular media situation and thus provided immediate feedback; they were unable, however, to suggest a theory of society that takes into account the mass media behavior.

The critical approach to the study of mass communication as a social phenomenon has received support from writers like Hans Magnus Enzensberger, Horst Holzer, Friedrich Knilli, Dieter Prokop, and Franz Dröge. They seem to agree with Dröge's remark that "it cannot be the task of science in a late capitalist, alienated society to deal with single social phenomena."[16] And there is general agreement that communication research must develop methodologies that will allow drawing conclusions about the interdependence of communication phenomena and society.

It may be well, however, to remember Adorno's words that "the applicability of a science to society depends in an essential way on the state of society itself. There is no general social issue which some scientific method of therapy could treat universally."[17] Thus, a critical communication theory must not rely on speculations but be based on the condition of society and knowledge about communication in society.

REALISM AND UTOPIA

The current dilemma of mass communication studies is a result of these developments in the social sciences; although variations or adjustments to these perspectives exist, there prevails a spirit of realism which continues to dominate and control the field. Its major characteristics are an emphasis upon facts combined with the search for causes and an explanation of their consequences for the social system. At the individual level this approach translates into the exploration of communication as a process of adaptation to the irresistible forces of the social system. Such a perspective is opposed by what could be called a utopian outlook that views the role of communication and mass communication in terms of creating a possible or desirable social environment; it is based upon theories or visions of a better society in which mass communication performs a major task.

The antithesis of utopia and reality, so to speak, reveals itself in a division between a critical-intellectual and an administrative-bureaucratic view of mass communication. The critical position seeks to make practice conform to theory; it is more interested in general principles and based upon certain human values. Lazarsfeld's description of critical research is quite useful as an explanation of this view. He said that critical research "develops a theory of the prevailing trends in our times, general trends which yet require consideration in any concrete research problem; and it seems to imply ideas of basic human values according to which all actual or desired effects should be appraised."[18] The administrative view, on the other hand, is characterized by its empirical basis. Practice, or action, is more important than any consideration of theoretical propositions; there are strong ties with the existing economic and political powers in society and with those forces which support the established order. This perspective also aims to provide a meticulous account for mass communication phenomena, their role and function in the dominant social and political system, and it tends to lead to conclusions about adaption rather than conflict or revolution.

There is a tendency for the critical-intellectual position also to coincide with a politically liberal or radical perspective, whereas the administrative-bureaucratic position tends to lean toward a more conservative view concerning mass communication and its role in society.

Both positions contain unsatisfactory elements, however. The critical approach fails to translate theory into practice and, although intellectually convincing in its arguments, it remains relatively ineffective as an alternative to the present mode of thinking about mass communication research. It is an idea that is based upon what Lazarsfeld described as the need "to do and think what we consider true and not to adjust ourselves to the seemingly inescapable."[19] This task is demanding, however, and it may seem easier to follow the lead of an administrative approach that supports routinized research activities instead of sharing the fascination of new theories and the flow of ideas. The force of the latter position may produce undesirable results in the long run, however, and it may help to introduce a critical dimension to mass communication studies in order to provoke ideas hitherto neglected or undiscovered in the discourse about mass communication in contemporary society.

One of the best examples of recent years and a source of challenging ideas has been the work of the Commission on Freedom of the Press. Based upon notions of democracy, freedom of expression, and freedom of the press, the authors embarked upon a vigorous critique of the American media. They demonstrated by their work how the academic community can bring to bear upon society its expert observations concerning one of the most important institutions in a democracy. The commission concluded in its report, about 30 years ago, that the mass media were the single, most powerful influence in modern society. The document also noted the failure of other agencies of society suggesting that "if the schools did a better job of educating our people, the responsibility of the press to raise the level of American culture, or even to supply our citizens with correct and full political, economic, and social information would be materially altered."[20] The commission was particularly interested in the flow of ideas; it stated that a "civilized society is a working system of ideas. Therefore, it must make sure that as many as possible of the ideas which its members have are available for its examination"; because of the great influence of the media it is "imperative that the great agencies of mass communication show hospitality to ideas which their owners do not share."[21]

Specifically, the study of mass communication can make sense only in the context of a theory of society; thus, questions of freedom and control of expression, of private and public spheres of communication, and of a democratic system of mass communication must be raised as part of an attempt to define the position of individuals in contemporary industrialized Western societies. It is vital for an understanding of the importance of mass media research as a social and political force to comprehend the relationship between economic and political powers in society, their use of communication research as a source of knowledge, and the effect of this relationship upon defining the role of the media. It is equally important to address individual concerns for identity and self-respect in the process of societal communication.

This approach also implies that the study of communication and of the institutions of societal communication must be placed in the realm of a cultural and intellectual history of society. The mass media play a major role in the creation and perpetuation of cultural and social-political traditions. At the same time, they can be understood and explained only in relation to other social institutions, particularly education and religion, and in the context of economic-technological patterns of control.

Concerns about the press as a societal institution had a place in the writings of American sociologists who acknowledged not only the importance of communication, but who were equally involved in discussing the role of the press as it emerged as a powerful agent for the collection and dissemination of information in society. The following chapters may help contribute to the writing of a more complete history of communication and mass communication theory and research as it emerged from the works of sociologists in the United States and in Germany, whose universities provided in many cases a cultural and intellectual environment for American scholars at the beginning of their careers. It seemd important for that reason to deal more extensively with the contributions of German scholars who are among the major sources of a German tradition of *Zeitungswissenschaft*, to demonstrate the nature of their arguments, and to illustrate the character of their work as it concerned questions of communication and the role and function of the press in society.

The contributions of Albert Schäffle, Karl Knies, Karl Bücher, Ferdinand Tönnies, and Max Weber as they relate to the field of communication and mass communication studies are synonymous with the rise of the social sciences that included the first theoretical discussions of the mass media. Although primarily known for their scholarship in economic and sociological thought, their ideas concerning communication and the press appear as integral parts of any contemplation of societal issues; they suggest the need for a study of communication and mass communication in social and economic contexts, and they reflect, in an autobiographical sense, their own knowledge and experience with the press and public opinion as political and economic forces in the Germany of their own times. As teachers, colleagues, or contemporaries of American sociologists, they are among the most important sources of communication and mass communication theories emerging from German scholarship. The following chapters may provide some insights into the richness and originality of their thought. Since little is known about these individuals, with the exception of Weber and Tönnies brief biographical introductions will focus on their major contributions and their backgrounds as they relate to the issues under discussion. Most of the original material will appear for the first time in translation.

Among American scholars whose ideas appeared to be similar to those of their German colleagues are Albion Small, Edward A. Ross, and William Graham Sumner. They stand as representatives of a number of early American sociologists whose training or background included encounters with the German tradition of the social sciences and whose scholarship, labeled "American science" in Germany, included similar notions concerning the importance of communication and mass communication in a modern society. Not only does their work reflect the influence of German or European social thought, but it also represents a first attempt to integrate some foreign ideas into uniquely American social, economic, and political conditions. There are long-standing and recognized differences in the social thought of the United States and Germany, for instance, based upon the nature of political and cultural movements that created different premises for arguments concerning the role and function of societal institutions, including the press. Hawthorn characterized these differences when he concluded that "philosophical, social and political thinking has proceeded within what are by comparison with Europe extremely narrow bounds, the bounds of an established liberalism. In Europe, liberalism was at first a critical principle, and no sooner had it been established . . . than it itself began to be undermined by what has there generally been understood as socialism. In the United States, on the other hand, liberalism was only ever a critical principle in arguments against Europe. It was established with the new republic, ideologically, if not in fact, and criticisms of the progress, or not, of that republic have always been in its own terms."[22]

A review and comparison of these critical approaches to the study of communication and mass communication should include an awareness of these roots of sociological thought. In this sense, the tradition of social criticism in the United States, particularly as it includes the role and function of the press, has never been a strong one, because it never overcame the limitations of its own peculiar development as an intellectual exercise within an established social and political system. The following pages, finally, may suggest that turning towards a critical-intellectual tradition in the study of communication and mass communication must begin with an understanding of its history.

NOTES

1. Karl Marx and Friedrich Engels, *The German Ideology*, edited by C. J. Arthur. (New York: International Publishers, New World Paperbacks, 1970), 47.

2. As quoted in T. B. Bottomore, *Critics of Society: Radical Thought in North America* (New York: Pantheon Books, 1968), 132.

3. This is a point at which historical and sociological interests meet to form a necessary alliance of shared research questions. The debate concerning the relationship between history and sociology has continued for some years. See, for instance, H. Stuart Hughes, "The Historian and the Social Scientist," *American Historical Review* 66 (1960), 20-46; A. S. Eisenstadt, "American History and Social Science," *The Centennial Review* 7 (1963), 255-272; C. Vann Woodward, "History and the Third Culture," *Journal of Contemporary History* 3:2 (1968), 23-35.

4. "Mass Media of Communication in Modern Society," reprinted in *Qualitative Analysis. Historical and Critical Essays* (Boston: Allyn and Bacon, 1972), 110.

5. Ibid., 112.

6. Charles R. Wright, *Mass Communication, A Sociological Perspective* (New York: Random House, 1975), 8.

7. "The Role of Criticism in the Management of Mass Media," in *Qualitative Analysis*, 124.

8. *On the Scientific Status and Position of Communication Research* (Tampere: Institute of Journalism and Mass Communication, Monograph No. 35, 1977), 34-44.

9. Martin Jay, *The Dialectical Imagination. A History of the Frankfurt School and the Institute of Social Research, 1923-50* (Boston: Little, Brown, 1973), 346.

10. Ibid., 251.

11. *Pfade aus Utopia: Arbeiten zur Theorie und Methode der Soziologie* (München: Piper, 1967), 263-277.

12. For a discussion of these developments, see Alvin Gouldner, *The Coming Crisis of Western Sociology* (New York: Basic Books, 1970), 149.

13. Lazarsfeld's paper is discussed by C. Wright Mills, *The Sociological Imagination* (Harmondsworth, England: Penguin Books, 1970), 70.

14. Franz W. Dröge and Winfried B. Lerg, *Kritik der Kommunikationswissenschaft* (Bremen: B. C. Heye, 1965); reprinted from *Publizistik* 10:3 (1965), 251-284.

15. "Massenkommunikationsforschung in der BRD. Deutschsprachige Veröffentlichungen nach 1960. Kommentar und Bibliographie," in Jörg Aufermann, Hans Bohrmann, and Rolf Sülzer, eds., *Gesellschaftliche Kommunikation und Information*, Band 1 (Frankfurt: Athenäum, 1973), 101.

16. *Wissen ohne Bewusstsein—Materialien zur Medienanalyse* (Frankfurt: Athenäum, 1972), 1. Also, Horst Holzer, *Gescheiterte Aufklärung? Politik, Ökonomie und Kommunikation in der Bundesrepublik Deutschland* (München: Piper, 1971); Hans Magnus Enzensberger, *Einzelheiten I. Bewusstseins Industrie* (Frankfurt: Suhrkamp, 1962); Friedrich Knilli, *Deutsche Lautsprecher. Versuch zu einer Semiotik des Radios* (Stuttgart: Metzler, 1970); Dieter Prokop, *Materialien zur Theorie des Films* (München: Hanser, 1971).

17. Frankfurt Institute for Social Research, *Aspects of Sociology* (Boston: Beacon Press, 1972), 126.

18. "Administrative and Critical Communication Research," in *Qualitative Analysis*, 160.

19. Ibid., 161.

20. Robert D. Leigh, ed., *A Free and Responsible Press. A General Report on Mass Communication: Newspapers, Radio, Motion Pictures, Magazines, and Books By the Commission on Freedom of the Press* (Chicago: University of Chicago Press: Midway Reprints, 1974), vii.

21. Ibid.

22. Geoffrey Hawthorn, *Enlightenment & Despair. A History of Sociology.* (Cambridge: Cambridge University Press, 1976), 194-195.

2

The Nerves of Society

Albert Schäffle on Symbolic Communication

SCHÄFFLE: A BIOGRAPHICAL NOTE

Albert Eberhard Friedrich Schäffle (1831-1903) was the most important German contributor to an organismic theory of society that had its roots in the writings of Spencer and Lilienfeld. His work as a social theorist reflects a variety of personal and professional experiences in business, politics, and academic life that marked his career.

After formal schooling in his native Württemberg Schäffle became a journalist at age 19. In the course of his duties as a foreign affairs editor for the *Schwäbischer Merkur,* he felt a need to further his education, specifically to engage in a systematic study of economics, law, politics, and technology. Subsequently he read the works of List, Hildebrand, and Rau (economics), v. Mohl, Bluntschli, Zachariä, and Zöpfl (constitutional law), Köstlin and Hufnagel (criminal law), and Payen, Karmarsch, and Hartmann (technology).[1] In his autobiography Schäffle admits that his newspaper career provided him with the best possible education. He was forced to express himself in writing promptly and on a wide range of subjects, which led to an extensive knowledge in a number of academic disciplines and to the mastery of reading French and English sources. He left his editorial position with the *Schwäbischer Merkur* in 1855 rather critical of publishers who did not seem to recognize the intellectual capabilities of journalists and their expertise in particular fields. But he remained active as a publicist through his acquaintance with Johann Georg von Cotta, whose *Deutsche Vierteljahrsschrift* became the forum for his ideas on economic and fiscal matters.

In 1860 Schäffle accepted a call to Tübingen to serve as a professor of political economy. Shortly thereafter he became editor of the *Zeitschrift für die gesamte Staatswissenschaft,* a position he occupied until his death. He also continued to publish regularly in academic and popular journals and newspapers; many of his contributions consisted of reactions to specific political events or were meant to be of a practical nature.

In addition to his teaching and his work as an economic and political publicist Schäffle served as a state representative to Württemberg's Chamber of Deputies, and he contributed to the work of the European tariff union. He left Tübingen in 1868 to accept a similar position at the University of Vienna, Austria. After three years he resigned to join the Graf Hohenwart cabinet as a secretary of commerce, a post he held for less than a year, when the government collapsed.

At age 40 Schäffle returned to private life. Unable to secure a position in government or a university appointment, he devoted his time to writing and speaking on economic, financial, and political issues until his death. He had returned to his native Württemberg, from where he participated in the political life of Germany.

Schäffle's major work is *Bau und Leben des Sozialen Körpers,* which was first published in four volumes between 1875 and 1879; a two-volume edition followed in 1896. It represents his attempt to conceptualize sociology as a complete description of reality. Considering organizational, functional, and developmental aspects of society, Schäffle tried to convey a systematic view of social life that could provide a starting point for the explanation of social phenomena. In this light, *Bau und Leben des Sozialen Körpers* became the basis for his life-long involvement in economic and political problems. He viewed contemporary developments in the context of his theoretical statements, thus combining practical experiences with theoretical insights.

Bau und Leben des Sozialen Körpers reflects Schäffle's conviction that a discussion of political and economic affairs cannot proceed without an understanding of the complete system of human interaction. Therefore, he offered an organismic approach which tried to explain social conditions through a series of analogies. He acknowledged the differences between social and organic bodies, however; and he rejected the criticism that his contribution toward the development of a science of sociology was an attempt to reduce a social phenomenon to a biological fact. He cited Espinas, Ratzel, and Small among those contemporaries who understood and appreciated his intentions.[2] Schäffle considered his work on *Bau und Leben des Sozialen Körpers* as a liberating experience and as a successful way of dealing with the formulation of his later ideas. He expressed hope that others would find this work equally stimulating, and he admitted that at times he may have appeared strange and difficult to identify among his contemporaries.[3]

Schäffle recognized the influence of Comte, Spencer, and Lilienfeld on his work, but he never identified society with an organism, or social movements with the biological struggle for survival. In his discussion of the function of political economy, for instance, Schäffle emphasized the importance of psychological and moral considerations. Defining socialization as a process of production and consumption of external goods, he also stressed the idea that central to any economically controlled processes is the person with his moral life who must not only satisfy material wants but also attempt to realize his potential as a human being. He felt that

the personal self-preservation and self-development of human beings, i.e., their conscious moral life, is very comprehensively dependent upon acquisition and use of such external goods as are not furnished gratuitously by nature. Either universally, or at all events for particular members of human society, many goods are accessible only in consequence of human co-operation, i.e., only mediately and, in comparison with human want, in a limited, i.e., insufficient, degree.

This limited availability of means of satisfaction or use is the occasion of a peculiar regimen of production and of use. The aim of the same is: with a minimum of personal sacrifice to secure a maximum of realization of human purposes; in other words, at minimum cost to obtain a maximum of utility, and thus to insure the amplest possible provision for the *entire personal life*.[4]

In other words, people instead of goods became the focal point of his economic theory; and this way of thinking provided a guideline for the subsequent treatment of social, political, and economic problems. Schäffle became known as a reformer who searched for a more equitable solution through propositions for the development of public property and a planned economy, but who never joined in the socialist cause.

The basis for an understanding of the systemic nature of social life and the complexity of the social system can be found in an essay entitled "Güter der Darstellung und Mittheilung," published in 1873.[5] In it Schäffle showed an appreciation for the importance of symbols, tradition, and communication in society. He described these elements as constituting a psychic mechanism of the social body which mediates collective sensations, collective stimulations, and the internal relationships of a collective consciousness.[6] It is in this context of an anti-individualistic approach to the study of social systems that Schäffle's views on communication and on the press must be appreciated as an explanation of the existence and the survival of society.

Consequently, a discussion of Schäffle's contribution to the study of communication and mass communication phenomena concentrates on his discussions in "Güter der Darstellung und Mittheilung" and on the elaboration of his thoughts in *Bau und Leben des Sozialen Körpers*.

COMMUNICATION AS A BINDING FORCE

Schäffle did not present a unified theory of communiction, but throughout his writings he returned to the fundamental importance of communication as a binding force in society. His statements concerning the process of communication and the activities of the press reflect his concern and express the importance he attached to these social phenomena.

In the development of his organismic conception of the social environment, Schäffle compared the nervous system in the animal world to the communication system in human societies. He described the existence of nerve cells, ganglions, and nerve centers as forming an extensive network throughout the body, and he suggested that a similar organization exists in the social world. He differentiated between individual and institutional elements which comprise the communication system. The first element resembles "cells," according to Schäffle, represented by individual members of society and their nervous systems with which they receive, internalize, and disseminate impressions and suggestions. In this role the individual functions as an observer and reporter of events, as a disseminator of value judgments, and as a participant in the public decision-making processes. He added, "Individuals and entire corporations, councils, public authorities and meetings function as professional organs of knowledge through observation, research, reporting, supervision and control—as social organs of consciousness through evaluations, valuations, criticism, judgments of taste, appreciations and condemnations—finally, as executive organs through decision-making processes, orders, instructions, prohibitions, agitations, etc."[7] The second element, which approximates the function of nerve centers, is made up of the institutions in society which disseminate ideas. Schäffle referred to them as the external institutions for the communication of ideas with their presentations or symbols. In this context he suggested, "The presentation, the production of symbols and their acquisition belong to individuals, who are capable of thinking, feeling and acting. Only the finished product of the presentation falls into the realm of communication."[8]

The activities of creating and internalizing symbols result in messages which consist of a variety of symbols, such as oral presentations, gestures, songs, musical productions, signs, drawings, writings, printed matter, art exhibitions, stage and opera productions, pictures, paintings, and other works. But symbols, according to Schäffle, can be only carriers of ideas; they still must be transmitted. This means that "the path, the space through which this carrier of ideas will take its course and flight must be prepared in the most appropriate way as an institution for external communication and transmission."[9]

Thus, Schäffle identified two basic elements in the communication of ideas, the production of symbols and the means of external communication or transmission through appropriate institutions. Connected with them are technical and economic, as well as other, protective measures which surround the process of social communication, not unlike muscles and bones which protect nerves that run throughout a body. He mentioned, for example, that a library besides books, catalogues, and librarians, also needs "technical-mechanical installations and a labor force, regular support, accurate safety devices and a solidly constructed building."[10]

Schäffle concluded that all social "nerve centers" consist of professional and nonprofessional intellectual workers, of symbols, and of translators and other technical means concerning the physical plant of these enterprises.

Specifically, in his discussion of the individual as a contributor to the intellectual output, Schäffle stated that the results of all intellectual activities in a society consist of the sum total of individual efforts to contribute to the intellectual atmosphere. Everyone to some degree, at least, adds to the final outcome. Each member is in touch with others and with the social environment in general through many avenues of communication. At the same time, each individual serves as a collection point of communication networks, tied into the social structure in a variety of ways depending upon the degree of versatility developed by the individual. Schäffle referred to the "multipolarity" of each individual in society. This notion suggests that with the rise of civilization man confronts an increasingly denser and more integrated communication network. Schäffle argued, "Each new book, which is read by an individual, each newspaper which he subscribes to, each social circle, which he joins, increases his participation by dozens and hundreds of connections—and often from one day to the next."[11] He pointed to the importance of language as a prerequisite for the participation in society; language becomes the instrument of intellectual growth and permits the development of relationships with others and with the social environment in general.

According to Schäffle, individuals are capable of acquiring a vocabulary which will increase with their intellectual goals and which may be extended to include foreign languages and cultures.

Turning to the discussion of symbols, Schäffle described symbols and the process of symbol making as unique features of human civilization and of man as a social animal. Symbols are to be divided according to their personal or material nature. The former category includes words, sounds and gestures, language, songs, and facial expressions, for instance, whereas the latter category involves writings, prints, pictures, monuments, and sculptures. All symbols are external reflections of internal processes.

The external presentation of ideas through the means of using one's own body is the common characteristic of all personal symbols. Schäffle described, for instance, the symbolism of language, song, dance, and gesture as forms of personal, subjective presentations of ideas. They culminate in language as the most powerful and most influential means of social communication. The spoken word as the "Ur-symbol" of ideas will always remain the most important and, at the same time, the most immaterial and inexpensive means of achieving intellectual cohesion in the daily affairs of society. Language, according to Schäffle, is the outcome of a historical process that reflects a world of ideas; it also is the shared property of all members of society. This suggests certain ways of thinking and feeling that must be common to all individuals in order to gain a sense of understanding of each other. As a result, certain words, sayings, songs, and sagas elicit similar emotional and intellectual responses from all members of a particular society. The importance of language as the most treasured possession makes any suppression of a native language or dialect, for instance, a crime. Schäffle compared such incidents to murder and mayhem committed against a people and its culture.

Gestures, according to Schaffle, as forms of nonverbal communication, can also be defined as expressions of ideas. He called them a language for the eye, not for the ear:

> The slightest movement of the body is enough to produce this type of personal symbol. The medium of communication is the light which surrounds us, according to the hypothesis of the natural science, the vehicle for the communication of these thoughts are the ether waves. In terms of its simplicity, cheapness, as well as originality and durability mimicry resembles language. . . . However, mimicry is as unique as language is universal. A collection and publication through mediating objects, analogous of written and printed words, is impossible. . . . But the individuality of mimicry makes it most useful for artistic presentations and for the communication of idealistic feelings and values.[12]

Theatre and dance represent forms of artistic communication of feelings and values that have an almost universal effect upon society as expressions of commonly shared experiences. But the spoken word remains the most effective means of communication which is capable not only of arousing feelings but also of engaging the mind.

Concluding his discussion of personal symbols, Schäffle added that the production and consumption of symbols often occur alone and in isolation, but also sometimes in the company of others. He recognized the potential effectiveness of personal symbols in terms of their "intimacy, ardour and immediacy," and he acknowledged their disadvantages in the communication over space and time.[13]

He felt that a high degree of motivation, pressure by peers, and the small size of a group are important elements leading to effective communication, regarding not only the production but also the consumption of personal symbols. This type of communication becomes less effective, however, with large audiences which are distributed over wide areas. Nevertheless, personal communication became institutionalized in the form of regular events or festivities in communities with the establishment of markets and fairs, the activities of schools and churches, and the work of artists and musicians who traveled throughout the country. But Schäffle indicated that indeed, the beginnings of civilization encounter great difficulties regarding the establishment, protection and technical assistance of personal symbols. Language and the art of speaking are hardly developed. Knowledge and the art of presenting knowledge belong to the few. There is little receptiveness for talks and presentations with religious or scientific messages among the people. There are no external means to assist in the presentation and in the joining of the audience for the benefit of the presentation. The travels of actors for the purpose of repeating their presentations everywhere run into such obstacles as prejudice, legal uncertainties, difficulties of transportation, and differences of languages and dialects.[14]

THE DEVELOPMENT OF MATERIAL SYMBOLS

Turning to the discussion of symbols in their material form, Schäffle observed that the increasing number, variety, and use of material or "real" symbols marked a tremendous advancement in the cultural sphere and significant economic progress. These symbols, according to Schäffle, are capable of being collected and widely distributed. Specifically, "the invention and introduction of the alphabet, mathematical representation, chronometric representation of time, money as the symbol of value . . . contributed to leading mankind to the fine arts and crafts, to technology and business, and to knowing and feeling in the context of a moral and religious life."[15]

This development established a tradition that was documented in a variety of material symbols which now could be gathered and transmitted for the benefit of future generations. Personal symbols (like words) could be equated with material symbols (like letters), gestures with pictorial languages of paintings and sculptures, and numerous works in the arts and sciences with material representations of specific ideas and decisions. Communication with the aid of material symbols, then, becomes more or less permanent and capable of wide circulation. Scientific knowledge, for instance, now can be gathered and disseminated; and the same process of committing one's ideas to a fixed form of writing or printing governs the private and social affairs of man.

In scrolls and in printed works knowledge becomes the content of a thousand-year-old tradition. Schäffle saw press and literature as

> organs of criticism of contemporary activities. Large nations can be united in their will through the same organ. Writing, reading and arithmetic . . . become the first element of universal education to an extent that the training of oral presentation and communication of ideas, feelings and intentions are often neglected due to false educational methods.[16]

Material symbols contain the possibility of providing a remarkable efficiency in terms of production, communication, and consumption, although original production is less economical than the mass production of symbols. Schäffle remarked that, as a rule, an original production of a material symbol becomes a highly individual effort. Whether a personal effort to record a private experience or a business transaction, there is always the unique, individual cooperation necessary to create the message or to describe the situation. This is a stage in the communication process that cannot be done collectively or by one for the benefit of the many. But once beyond this point of individual creation, the art of mechanical reproduction gains the highest degree of effectiveness and quality of reproduction in the processing of material symbols. Schäffle saw the original work almost as the raw material for the communication industry: "These industries reproduce the manuscript in literary publishing houses, drawings, designs, pictures, models, prints and photographs in art publishing houses. Often with the intention of making available for the consumption only the reproductions."[17] At the same time, increasing education and wider distribution contribute to a lowering of costs for the production of originals as well as the process of copying and reproducing originals in large numbers. This development has the effect of attracting even more consumers.

Schäffle added that perhaps the most fundamental and obvious difference between symbolic goods, such as described above, and material goods, such as food and clothing, must be seen in the fact that the former can and will be reproduced and disseminated without raising economic problems of the kind that befall the production and consumption of material goods in society. He referred to the potential for increasing the amount of "intellectual" food and its distribution at any time, whereas the production of food, for instance, may encounter certain economic difficulties through increases in the population or limitations in the production cycles.

He emphasized the importance of traffic in communication and cited the advancement of communication technology, the institution of postal services, and the exchange of material symbols among individuals and organizations as conditions that enhance the development of the use of material symbols in society. On the other hand, Schäffle warned that it would be a mistake to ignore the meaning of personal symbols in the context of these technological developments. He said,

> The spoken word and the gesture apply to what is by far the largest part of the communication of ideas, namely the communication in small circles and for short-term purposes. Most of the expressions of ideas occur and end within a smaller circle and belong to the moment. . . . the need for material symbols of longer lasting quality and with wider distribution is added . . . with a rising civilization.[18]

And he urged that the sociologist must recognize the importance of material symbols, because the production, consumption, and adoption of material symbols are keys to an understanding of the "tremendous effects of social communication on one hand, and the growing simplicity of its means, on the other hand."[19]

Schäffle called the system of personal and material symbols and their interconnections the psycho-physical mechanism of the social body, and he argued that those who do not understand this communication mechanism will be unable to grasp the ideas of the function of the social and intellectual life of society.

Summarizing his discussions, Schäffle pointed out that

> each individual as a receiver and as a sender is woven into the social body through thousands of communication links each day and each hour of the

day. . . . The daily press as just one nerve center which connects the readers, is comprised of a complete system of conduits which run back and forth endlessly among the audience. This texture of the social nerve centers displays—at least in an educated society—infinitely more communication links than an organic nervous system. Each of the numerous words of a language creates at least a community of two, or perhaps of millions of people through the reading of a newspaper or a book, in thoughts, feelings and decisions. The white conductive mass of animal nerve centers and their unknown internal workings is surpassed by that mass of social communication and tradition which occurs in oral, written and printed form, in all kinds of artistic productions, in social circles, and in business relationships with a tremendous consumption of paper.[20]

Schäffle had engaged in a concentrated and rather specific discussion of the symbolic process and communication in the context of dealing with the production and consumption of goods in an essay published in his own journal a few years earlier.[21] In the article which became the basis for his presentations of personal and material symbols in *Bau und Leben des Sozialen Körpers,* Schäffle acknowledged the fact that the material goods of society which represent its morality and its economic wealth can be divided into

presentations, representational goods, signs, symbols, which are, because of the social nature of man, often also the means of presentations for others, goods of expression and communication—and, in a real sense, useful goods, organs, instruments which are not signs or mediators of ideas, but means of production and consumption and of symbolic, but not purely ideal use.[22]

He lists speeches, books, and art as examples of symbols; food, clothing, and shelter as means of sensual pleasure; and means of production with a mechanical or chemical effect. Another way of differentiating between these types of goods, according to Schäffle, is a classification system of means of entertainment and means of subsistence. He expanded the definition of symbols to include any kind of external presentation ranging from material to personal expressions in order to engage in a wide-ranging and complete discussion of communication and the means of communication in a society.

Schäffle stressed the definite need for communication, which goes hand in hand with a need for *Gemeinschaft* and for the continued development of community as a spiritual and political idea. Since human knowledge, values, and plans of action can only be communicated through symbols, it becomes necessary for communities to develop their communication technology, enhancing the quality of symbolic goods as well as fostering the growth of all forms of communication. There is an increasing need to communicate in society and to enter into dialogical relationships concerning not only scientific or factual matters but also feelings, phantasies, and matters of personal taste. Schäffle also included the growing need for decision making in the process of social communication. A community demands such a continuous communication of ideas, because only through the production and consumption of symbolic goods will it be possible for a society to grow as a cultural, religious, artistic, scientific, or economic entity. He said,

> The progress of association among people, the development of cultural community, specifically, the development of moral community in the ideal cultural areas depends upon the development of a symbolizing technique and upon the adequate supply of steadily improving symbolic goods, upon the development of all forms of communication for intellectual intercourse involving knowledge, appreciations and decisions.[23]

Schäffle added that the discussion of symbolic goods must include not only intellectual matters but also expressions of feelings, appraisals of ideas, and criticism.

SYMBOLS AS BASIS OF SOCIAL SYSTEMS

He demonstrated the necessity for coordination and control of communication in the production process of advanced societies, pointing out that only with the aid of symbols could it be possible to create a social system in which tradition, transportation, and commerce are fully developed. He said,

> Indeed, the business of collecting, storing, transporting and communicating, commerce of any kind, exhibits a great demand for attending

symbol-using work and for means of presentation; because the transmission
of goods from everywhere into any direction, from one time to another . . .
only works through mediating presentations, through communication,
exchange and distribution of symbolic means of expression. . . . That is
why commerce leads to the development of the art of presentation and favors
those places where this art has been mastered.[24]

In stressing the need for an understanding of the symbolic processes in society Schäffle suggested that economists must increase
their knowledge pertaining to questions about symbolic goods
and their fundamental place in any social system. He referred to
the fact that symbolic goods with their "communistic definition
of uses and their extremely individualistic creation result in
significant consequences for the economic reaction of symbolic
goods in the societal processes of production, transmission,
compensation and consumption."[25] Schäffle provided a listing
of examples for the multitude of symbolic goods that are involved
in the successful conduct of commerce and industry, where communication is the key to efficient and profitable business transactions. With the development of human cultures, the production
and consumption of symbols increases simply because of a better
utilization of time and space. That is to say, literature as a time-
binding force contains the traditions of a society, which are
preserved and carried into the future, at the same time that
similar and other devices such as public lectures or newspapers
bridge distances with the transmission of ideas. In effect, he
commented upon the power of the printed word: "The press and
literature become an organ of criticism of contemporary affairs.
The minds of many peoples can be united through the same
organ."[26] And finally, Schäffle suggested that the economics of
material symbols also affect the way in which personal symbols
are used in society. Since the latter are based upon books, newspapers, and similar representations, man is able to reproduce
the teaching of his truth and the expression of his feelings many
times and almost everywhere.

The production of symbols, then, important to any development of civilization, can be studied in terms of the production
of original symbols and their reproduction for mass consumption.

Schäffle argued that the production of original symbols is closely tied to the growth of society, which, in turn, will support the development of talented individuals. The creative act must remain a personal contribution, and therefore cannot be treated under at theory of mass production. The creation of original material symbols, however, necessitates the existence of scientific and artistic talent and the training and education of those whose talents emerge in and through society. Schäffle stressed the importance of collecting and disseminating literature and art that has survived the ages as economically meaningful for the education of artists. Since only material symbols can be transmitted and preserved over time, either in their original form or as reproductions, the development of material symbols itself becomes a prerequisite for progress and future development.

Newspapers, on the other hand, may serve as examples of a variety of symbols reproduced for the benefit of their readers. In this case questions of reproduction must be treated in terms of devising ways for the most useful consumption. The publishing industry represents an organization that tries to organize the reproduction of symbols in a number of economically feasible and profitable enterprises. It must be the goal of society to reproduce original symbols in such a way that they can be preserved and circulated for the purposes of the general public. The creative process, as it turns out, is stimulated by fame and financial rewards with the result of increasing the production of original symbols for the specific purposes of wide circulation through mass reproduction. The task of reproducing material symbols, however, does not require unusual talent. Schäffle described the purpose of elementary education with its emphasis upon reading, writing, and arithmetic as providing the foundation for the preservation and transmission of symbols. He said that, from the standpoint of political economy, elementary schools become most useful institutions. They create "through the teaching of writing a prerequisite for the most fruitful production, through the teaching of reading the prerequisite for the most prolific use of material symbols for everyday life, and through both a mediator for productive creation and acquisition of useful goods."[27] He added that, in this sense, schools are another example of an economic interpretation of an aspect of life which is not based mainly on a question of profits.

Since the content of most symbolic goods can be understood, e.g., consumed, their use tends to be maximized through the reproduction and dissemination of original material symbols. Schäffle insisted that the reproduction is a necessity for achieving an economically most useful level of consumption. He concentrated his discussion on the publishing industry as a phenomenon of modern times which combines efforts of promoting original works and their reproductions: "Economically speaking, the production task of publishing industries consists of bringing forth the best possible products in the best possible form for preservation and dissemination at the lowest cost."[28] In this connection, Schäffle paid some attention to the question of traffic in symbolic goods; and he suggested that the discussion regarding material symbols, such as mechanically reproduced presentations, should be considered under the aspects of tradition, transportation, and personal transactions.

The collection and storage of symbols are essential activities of societal institutions, such as museums, schools, and universities, as well as private or public libraries. They are the result of a realization that the preservation of symbols is a prerequisite for the development of a tradition that lasts over many generations. Schäffle cited the difficulties of preserving information during the early days of mankind to point out the importance of contemporary efforts to maintain continuity. Furthermore, he contended that "a tradition once existing through symbolic goods in public collections, destroys any esoteric doctrine and any acquisition through *arcana*."[29] And he added that the advantage of public collections, from an economic point of view, could be observed when looking at such institutions as "the British Museum, the Glyptothek in Munich or the Gallerie in Dresden."[30]

With the improvement in man's ability to collect and store symbolic goods also came better ways of transmitting symbols. Schäffle mentioned the postal system as a good example of a useful and most efficient organization for the transmission of news and information among members of society. Commenting on a variety of ways in which symbolic goods are disseminated among organizations, groups, and individual members of society, Schäffle added that the technology of transporting symbolic goods in turn has led to economic considerations concerning the consumption and use of symbolic goods.

Finally, personal transmission of symbols, as well as the commercial activities of publishing houses or free publications, are additional means of transmitting symbols from one person to another or to large numbers of individuals. As a matter of fact, books, newspapers, and public announcements, among others, are carriers of important information, organized for the purposes of successive use by large audiences. Schäffle added, "Such presentations, which can be used only by one or few consumers at any time, or by many successively, receive economic consideration through the organization of successive use."[31]

Symbolic communication, finally, may also be the object of commercial speculations. The newspaper industry and publishing houses, for instance, offer manifestations of such speculative aspects in the form of their business practices, such as consignment of goods, advance payments, or on-approval purchases.

COST AND COST EFFICIENCY OF COMMUNICATION

The discussion of production and distribution of goods raises questions about their cost and cost efficiency. Schäffle pointed out that it would be impossible to assess costs at the level of private exchange of information, conversations, or personal messages. A cost-benefit argument should be directed at the degree of personal satisfaction gained through communication with others rather than any monetary value established by this type of exchange. The highly personalized nature of communication precludes any standardization of values attached to interpersonal exchanges. Schäffle also listed another type of communication connected with the normal conduct of business that receives no attention except in connection with business transactions. He mentioned planning, correspondence, bookkeeping, and similar communication activities that are subsumed under the general expenses and become part of the sales price of a product. On the other hand, the communication of symbols can be tied into an economic system at the level of institutional involvement. For instance, theatrical productions, books, or newspapers may be utilized as sources of information or entertainment only after payment of a set price or an admission fee. As a matter of fact, many symbolic goods are offered in the marketplace, often in competitive situations, as commercial properties or as objects of commercial speculation by institutions that specialize in the reproduction of symbolic goods and in their distribution in society.

A unique phenomenon in the marketplace of symbolic goods is the dissemination of so-called free symbolic goods. Schäffle referred to education, religion, and politics as sources of symbolic goods that are often advertised as being available at no cost to members of society. He said,

> The mission and the church disseminate their symbols, sermon, religious instruction, bibles, tracts, hymn books freely or at very low cost. But it also happens with the profane symbolism of political life: appeals, posters, etc. are distributed free to the masses during political agitation. The real or assumed intrinsic value of the communication must be appreciated only through the communication itself.[32]

In fact, it can be stated that these symbolic goods bear indirect costs of production which must be absorbed by individuals, groups, or organizations. In the field of education, for instance, the question always remains whether state, community, or individual citizens will cover the cost of producing symbolic goods; and it frequently becomes an important issue with serious political consequences. Schäffle admitted, however, that a substantial amount of symbolic communication is produced with a commercial interest and direct and full remuneration in mind. He cited specifically those symbolic goods with private or personal value, among them some university-level lectures, musical productions, and literary and artistic publications. He observed that here, too, the effects are peculiar because of the communicative-communistic nature of symbols: "Once published, the publication allows for widespread acquisition of its intellectual content; private 'property' of this content ceases to exist with the first copy. This means . . . that the imitator is freed from the cost of producing an original, of experimental presentations, and of an honorarium."[33]

At the same time, Schäffle stressed the idea that the production of symbolic goods must not be viewed solely as a speculative venture, based on the initiative of business interests, but also as a public effort aimed at advancing culture and society.

Since the consumption of symbolic goods remains the key to the development of a society, Schäffle argued for a communication system that maximizes the use of symbols by individuals. He envisioned a system in which the access to information and the establishment of regulations for the use and protection of symbolic goods become a priority. He pointed out that any good administration of libraries, collections, or schools follows these two economic considerations of maximum consumption of symbolic goods. And he stressed, again, an earlier suggestion that schooling through private and public education must help perfect the capacity of individuals to produce and consume symbols, emphasizing certain activities, such as reading, writing, drawing, and mathematics. But aside from the type of symbolic communication that is represented in the spoken and written language and in literature, Schäffle identified another form of symbolic activity in which symbols and technology are joined in a "symbolizing-organizing" manner. He cited architecture and the applied arts industry as examples of activities that contribute substantially to the satisfaction of societal needs, concluding that the rise of education will result in more aesthetically designed goods for daily life. Thus, he argued, "Since each product represents the realization of a prescribed idea, once they circulate, useful products of some originality can become symbols, whose ideas can be imitated and generally acquired."[34] Schäffle ended his discussion of the economic aspects of communication as the exchange of original or reproduced symbols in the context of societal needs and gratifications with the statement that an

> increasing cheapness, simplification and distribution of a rational, linguistic use of symbols—in oral form during earlier cultures, in written-typographical form culminating in the present culture and rise in population—had to and will continue to exert an influence that is most radical and most beneficent for the moral, intellectual development of the societal organism.[35]

COMMUNICATION AND PERSUASION

Schäffle returned to the problem of communication and mass media influences in the context of providing a social-psychological explanation for the relationship between the masses and their leaders. His ideas are based upon the premise that a social organism must be coordinated around intellectual centers which represent the leading elements in society. Thus, he differentiated between an "active side of authority," namely leadership and domination of the masses, and a "passive side of authority," which consists of the reaction of the masses to their leaders.[36]

According to Schäffle, all intellectual and spiritual activities of social organisms occur through symbolic interaction between leaders and masses. The question of authority is typically settled by birth, tradition, or intellectual superiority. Individuals, families, rank, class, or professional institutions act as carriers of authority. But they are only one part of a spiritual and intellectual activity which leads from individual to collective movements. Schäffle regarded the discussion of public opinion and media influences, among others, as part of a reactive mechanism used by the masses. He singled out public sphere, public, public opinion, and press, but commented upon the necessity to see these elements as a whole. Insisting upon the existence of certain conditions under which the system will function properly, Schäffle stressed the fact that the power of a collective mind emerges only from the mutual exchange between leaders and their followers. Thus, the quality of leadership, as well as size, intensity, and skill used to trigger appropriate reactions to influence the masses are equally important. A prerequisite for this success, however, is the existence of a vivid, intellectually and spiritually strong people, capable of releasing new energy upon appeals to their feelings and convictions. A favorable international climate and the advancement of mass communication technology provide ideal conditions for increasing the size of mass appeals; the spread of socialist propaganda around the world suggests the magnitude of political campaigns in modern times. Also, to arouse the masses requires skill in selecting the appropriate themes and techniques; the official press and the opposition press, for instance, demonstrate the high art of arousing and guiding the reactions of the masses and the degree of perfection with which it is practiced. He added,

> All these phenomena form a homogeneous whole. What else is the much debated public sphere, but an intellectual openness for social knowledge, appreciation and decision mediated symbolically through words, writing and print to the masses or at least to interested, special circles? What else is the public but a social mass, open, receptive, and reactive to the organs of social and intellectual activity with whom they share in the knowledge, appreciation and decision-making? What else is public opinion, but the expression of opinion, value and disposition of a general or special public? And finally the press—is it not the real transmitter in the intellectual exchange between the leading organs of society and the public?[37]

Referring specifically to the press and the public as being of universal importance to the intellectual life of society, Schäffle warned that it would be a mistake if the social sciences would neglect to study these phenomena.

Schäffle defined the public sphere *(Oeffentlichkeit)* as a sphere created by an exchange of personal and material symbols over longer and shorter distances in the social body. A prerequisite for the public sphere is openness, that is, the possibility for the dissemination of ideas beyond the boundaries of certain groups or organizations. It is absolutely necessary to preserve the public sphere; it serves as a battleground for ideas and ideologies and as a source from which social and political decisions flow as an expression of an active, participatory community. Positive law and other regulations secure the existence of a public sphere; and basic rights, such as freedom of the press and speech, the right to petition the government, and rights bestowed by open records laws and open meeting laws, provide the possibility for an exchange of information and for assistance in the daily activities of social and political organizations. He suggested,

> Often publicity is seen as an evil, and its most effective form, a free press, as an arbitrary concession of liberal legislation. Even though one deeply despises the contemporary corruption of the press, one would have to say that such a statement is confining and completely untrue.
> The public sphere, per se, except where degenerated and abused, is neither an evil nor a necessary evil, but a social-psychological necessity.[38]

In addition, it seemed to Schäffle that it would be impossible to completely suppress the public sphere:

> Prohibit all newspapers, the public sphere will choose public streets; scatter all groups gathered for small talk in public, the public sphere will move into restaurants; close them and the necessary exchanges of symbols will take place in private salons, in family or in business circles among naturally cooperating masses of society.[39]

The abolishment of the public sphere is a task which Schäffle compared to the removal of the nervous system from a body, an impossible condition that would result in the mutilation of the social body. Church and state, according to Schäffle, have yet to be successful in their attempts at such an operation. The consequences of any suppression of the public sphere would be a weakening of the spiritual powers of the people, a removal of the bonds of spiritual unity between leaders and the masses, followed by a general decline of society, which grows passive and becomes unable to react to crisis situations.

On the other hand, Schäffle agreed that there are situations which must lie outside the public sphere and should be regarded as strictly private matters. Marriage and family affairs, for instance, are the concern of·those directly involved; laws that restrict the press in its coverage of private matters and that suppress profane or obscene publications provide the necessary regulations for the protection of individuals. Even within the realm of the public sphere, however, there are occasions or stages of thinking and planning which often remain undisclosed; not all thought processes are constantly exposed to public scrutiny. For instance, Schäffle wrote, "Neither governments, nor parliaments, nor courts, nor parties, not even newspaper offices work like publicly displayed machines under glass covers, nor do they place themselves behind a megaphone to think, feel, reflect and plan constantly in a loud voice."[40]

The public *(Publikum)* consists of all of those who appear "publicly" on streets and public thoroughfares; but public also refers to specific groups of people, without legal or organizational boundaries, who participate in an intellectual exchange with specific individuals. Schäffle insisted that the idea of the public must embrace the notion of people interacting freely and without force with those who provide intellectual and spiritual stimulation. Implicit in this suggestion is the idea that there is more than one public at all times, the number depending on the variety of groups and associations and social institutions. The characteristic of each public differs depending on the particular identification with the leadership. Thus, there are specific publics surrounding scientists, writers, poets, preachers, journalists, and politicians. He continued that the "essentially free and intellectual relationship between the public and the other public for whom it represents the public, is established through an informal exchange of personal and material symbols, namely through the press."[41] For Schäffle the public is basically passive, receptive; it is an object for outside stimulation rather than an aggressive or giving force. There is one exception, however; the public reacts to express a mood which will, in turn, provide feedback for those who utilize these expressions for the formulation of additional strategies. Typically, public speakers, politicians, and speculators are among those who investigate the public mood before they embark on their campaigns.

Public opinion *(Oeffentliche Meinung),* according to Schäffle, is the reaction of the public to specific ideas, decisions, or feelings expressed by the leadership in society. Despite the fact that public opinion has often been held in low esteem, Schäffle considered it an extremely important factor in any discussion of social action; it seems almost impossible to act without or against public opinion, if the participation of the people is important for the success of a plan. The same goes for the daily press, which represents

> the most powerful means to influence public opinion by intellectually
> active elements. In this role the press is a super power. Belletristic
> literature, the tribunal, the forum, the eloquence of profane and
> sacred language, even the social conversations of salons, clubs and pubs as
> a psycho-physical foundation of public opinion must yield to the
> daily press and take up the second or third position.[42]

Schäffle saw the value of public opinion not in the fact that it represents the opinion of the masses, but in the idea that it corresponds with the true necessities and the pure nature of the social body. As such, a good opinion which is a public opinion has real power, whereas private opinions, even if they are also good ones, cannot become as powerful. Consequently, to be effective it is necessary to act "through the people for the people." At the same time, Schäffle warned that public opinion is not always a single, unified reaction, but could and often does consist of a multitude of reactions, some commonly running counter to others, depending on the seriousness of national, class, or religious differences within a society. Also, it is possible that public opinions are manufactured through clever use of the press and to a point at which the public believes in what it hears and adopts those ideas as its own creation. Nevertheless, Schäffle warned not to underestimate public opinion: "Those who want to be effective must count on public opinion to replace an artificial or falsified public opinion with a natural, widely popular and healthy public opinion, in any case."[43] The importance of public opinion does not decline only because it cannot be fully grasped or measured, according to Schäffle. This, in effect, often leads to various claims to know and understand the opinion of the people, claims which are often presented by members of the leadership elite without substantial proof.

Schäffle defined public opinion as a backdrop; he spoke of it as a choir in the social drama set against the leading role played by individuals or small groups that comprise the leadership in society. Public opinion deals with matters already developed in the minds of others; it is incapable of producing innovative ideas, even of recognizing them before they are presented for their reaction by those who popularize the discoveries. He added that people who

> cheer earlier accomplishments and who erect monuments to honor
> past achievements, are often those who face the aspirations of their
> contemporaries with indifference or with hate. At the same time at
> which they lay wreaths at the feet of older martyrs of human
> progress, they keep a rock ready in their other hand for the struggling genius
> of their own age. As a rule, public opinion in its role as a choir is
> neither appointed nor able to completely understand the first signs of new
> ideas at the threshold of public consciousness.[44]

THE PRESS AS TRANSMITTER

The daily press *(Tagespresse)* represents the most powerful institution in society through which the exchange of ideas between the people and their leaders takes place. Schäffle characterized the press and its journalists not in terms of a creative or leading intellectual or political power, but rather as an instrument that modifies and transmits messages. As a "conductor" or "condensator" of intellectual currents, the press seeks the company of government, political parties and organizations, on one hand, and contacts with the public on the other hand. However, Schäffle also recognized that the press operates in competitive situations; and although there may be some influence by prestigious newspapers on segments of the leadership or the public, more often than not newspapers suffer from a loss of credibility. But newspapers need feedback to gain some measure of their editorial position vis-à-vis the masses; therefore, the press constantly looks for justifications, which it hopes to find in the coverage of mass meetings and other events which may help measure the amount and type of public support of its own position. Elections, in particular, seem to offer a chance for a periodic public measurement of opinions regarding a host of political and practical questions.

In its various manifestations ranging from special interest journals to local newspapers and the prestige press, these media represent a large interconnected system for the collection and transmission of ideas and as such serve as an organ of public opinion. Although there are other media, such as tribunals, stages, and public forums, which serve a similar function, the press remains without competition when it comes to the regularity of its service and success in reaching specific publics. Schäffle added that

> this instrument does not only stimulate mass movements, but
> records them also with the aid of a network of regional and special
> interest journals. From the smallest home-town paper to
> the world press, from journals of knowledge to comic books, the daily
> press is a large, connected system of cells which collect and
> reproduce ideas, and as such it is an "organ of public opinion."[45]

Schäffle described the power of the press to identify and define contemporary movements and ideas in society as a function of its regular and frequent access to the public and its use of suitably prepared material to fit the intellectual requirements of its readers. Not public speakers, preachers, or teachers reach as large an audience as frequently and with such a variety of material as the press.

Schäffle regarded the influence of the press on scientific work as negligible and added that it did not contribute to great new ideas; instead, the press had emerged as the strongest means of stimulating and regulating its social environment on a daily basis. The press, in his view, is an indispensible instrument for the destruction, change, or creation of public opinion, and a necessary forum for those who want to preach, lie, judge, terrorize, excite, or alarm the masses. Consequently, the press becomes a target for political parties with their good or bad intentions, politics, financial speculations, and religious propaganda. He added, "With the help of the press one 'makes' public opinion at least for the day."[46] As a "maker" of public opinion, the press becomes the first power in the state, because "the domination of opinions, judgments and dispositions of various social masses and classes is the key to the success of social action and of exerting power."[47] Therefore, it must not come as a surprise that governments purchase newspapers and thus encourage the corruption of the press, even on an international scale. Financial interests own newspapers and pay them for their services, and any political party which hopes for success must support its press. And finally, those who want to profit in the marketplace must influence the buying and consumption habits of the masses. It is obvious, according to Schäffle, that

> the benefactor and saviour of the people is compelled to use this
> instrument for the most general innervation of the social
> body as much as the most powerful demon who pulls his people into the
> abyss of despotism and militarism, civil war and world war, and
> moral, legal and economic deterioration.[48]

Schäffle concluded his discussion of the role and function of the daily press with the observation that all avenues of public opinion, including the press, are subject to corruption and falsification, a fact which suggested a number of additional observations concerning press behavior.

Referring to a series of comments made by Lasalle, Goethe, Schelling, Fichte, and Hegel, Schäffle considered the influence of a corrupted press system upon the spiritual and psychological well-being of a society. He was convinced that the degenertion of the daily press was related to some of the social-psychological dysfunctions in society. As an example, he used Fichte's description of the "ideal reader" whose reading of book reviews instead of books had a narcotizing effect upon his mental disposition; he lost his powers to think, but he gained an opinion which gave him the needed security.[49] On the other hand, Schäffle recognized also that it was not the press alone or the journalists who were to blame for immorality or mental decline in society. He said that under current conditions "there are two circumstances which are the real major causes of a corruption of the press that affects the roots of a nation's health—one-sided mechanical centralization in the state and monopolistic exploitation of the daily press for purposes of speculation by financial interests."[50] The press is an easy victim, according to Schäffle, who characterized the journalist as one who thinks, feels, and lives with the day, often not used to or incapable of serious intellectual work. He added that "except for some stylistic skills the journalistic trade requires just a minimum of thorough education.[51] While this condition may aid those who seek to corrupt the press, Schäffle placed the blame also on those leaders who misdirect the press and abuse its facilities and on the people who choose to tolerate a bad press. He said that "in the long run, a nation will have the press it deserves and will be responsible for its own downfall, if it continues to put up with a poisoned press."[52] Neither police intervention, however, nor protection under the ideas of freedom of expression as a universal right will contribute to the improvement of press activities. Schäffle felt that the causes of a weak or inferior press are based upon the general deterioration of society. This condition leads to increasingly mechanical, as opposed to natural, reorganizations of society. As a result, centralization must breed central powers which use the press and thus exert a corrupting influence on newspapers and journalists.

Still, for Schäffle the press remained the most pervasive instrument of communication; it covers all areas of social life, and it invades the privacy of individuals under the guise of exploring the shape and content of public opinion. In this context, journalists fulfill two major functions: they transmit information from their sources, and they provide leadership for the public through the publication of information and opinion. But journalists are not originators of creative ideas or political opinions; they occupy the role of modifiers and mediators positioned between the leaders in society and their followers, or the public. Schaffle admitted, however, that journalists continue the creative process in society through their own work; but he rejected the notion that they are directly involved in intellectual activities as sources of ideas. Instead, journalists are in constant need of contact with those who furnish new artistic or intellectual stimuli as well as with the public, whose support they seek for their work. Throughout his discussion of the role and function of the press Schäffle suggested the dangers of abusing the press, since the organization of the press in the social system lends itself easily to such activities.

Schäffle concluded that the press is corrupt, a fact which he traced to the economic organization of society, not to any particular political problem. He claimed that for the most part the influential big city press is in the hands of banking and stock market interests and has been turned into a profitable investment; and he expressed fears that the situation could easily result in complete enslavement of the press by financial powers. He said, "This primary cause of press corruption must be attributed to the control of a degenerated form of capitalism. The evil is intensified by the fact that the profitableness of speculative newspapering depends upon advertising and its readers."[53] Schäffle observed that these developments must also have a devastating effect upon the work of individual journalists. They will become members of a proletariat, degraded and for sale as intellectual slaves to press baronies and those stock exchange and banking interests that operate behind them.

SUGGESTIONS FOR PRESS REFORM

Schäffle's suggestion for an improvement of the newspaper industry was part of a general economic reform. In that context, the press would be freed from the influence of financial speculation and from advertising control to regain its freedom and to operate independently. He rejected ideas of government monopoly or centralization of journalistic activities under official supervision, but aimed for an economic reconstruction of society that minimized or destroyed the potential for corruption.

His reform ideas seem radical, nevertheless. He advocated that the press be removed from the influence of private capital and suggested a takeover by publicly owned corporations. Organized into production and delivery systems with specific duties, the press would operate free from financial speculations and advertising pressures. Schäffle considered this arrangement absolutely necessary to keep literary and journalistic activities free from governmental influence. He also pleaded that in a socialist state attempts should be made to avoid centralization of printing industries. On the contrary, there should be all types of production facilities that would offer their services to any organization, party, or individual—and for the same price. Specifically, he advocated that "It should be up to any organization or party to maintain their own printing plants. The production and delivery of manuscripts, as well as the establishment of the exchange value of the copies, would be a matter for private individuals, parties, and organizations, such as public [scientific and other] institutions."[54]

Freedom of the press and freedom of expression can be guaranteed only if the production and dissemination of ideas remain absolutely free and undisturbed by capitalist or bureaucratic efforts to organize these activities for purposes of financial gain or political control. In that case journalism would regain its natural form, and it would flourish with renewed vigor. He said that journalism without advertising constraints would once again become a subject of "parties and organizations, and of scientific, political and religious propaganda."[55] Schäffle thought that profits made from the sale of press products would be distributed among the writers and would benefit those journals and newspapers for which they work. Under such a system, he was convinced, journalism would rise to new heights. Thus, "an end would be put to the official clap-trap of a centralized-communistic state which narcotizes the people, and to the liberal bunk of the monied aristocracy which has the same effect."[56] He considered advertising a waste of economic resources, although he advocated the establishment of advertising sheets, or shoppers, financed by the large institutions in society, while political debates would dominate the party press. In general, he envisioned a better-educated public able to follow arguments presented by experts and critical minds; and he hoped for a general improvement of the image of journalists and their morale. At the same time, however, he realized that these developments should be viewed as historical processes, necessary for the welfare of society. For his own time, Schäffle had a more pessimistic outlook when he concluded, "On the basis of the current social order, the corruption of the press will increase rather than decrease. . . . Nowadays the journals are and must be business enterprises and speculative ventures, if they want to survive the competition without subsidies."[57] In support of his assessment of press activities, he quoted a cultural historian, v. Hellwald, who had suggested that

> the press is a simple business, aimed at maximizing material gains, for whom the sentence holds true that all's fair for the trade. . . . Nobody thinks of defending a principle which could be injurious to the money bags, because one wants to do well and make excellent profits; great newspaper publishers who think of themselves as businessmen must know the advantages of supporting A or of fighting B; for the good of the newspaper these roles are changed very calmly over night.[58]

The degeneration of journalism, according to Schäffle, must also be traced to the condition of the social sciences. He argued that the social sciences have been unable to provide necessary insights based on the kind of evidence that the natural sciences, for instance, make available to the public. He was convinced that if the social sciences had been able to offer "such sound, positive insights . . . this would have put an end to charlatanism of government, to the cult of verbosity in the press, to the deception of the audience, to the contamination of journalism with literary scum, and to the paid sophistry and rhetoric."[59] Schäffle echoed Comte's hope that with the progress of the social sciences the corruption of the public spirit could be ended. At the same time he warned that "sociology, because of the nature of its subject matter, can never attain the positive reliability of the natural sciences in the treatment of objects."[60] He realized that the nature of human beings and the organization of society contribute highly subjective elements to a systemic approach to life which would never preclude the communication of false or deceptive materials for the benefit of smaller groups or individuals in society.

In summary, for Schäffle *homo symbolicus* represented the key to his organismic theory of society which treats communication as a necessary condition for the development of civilization and the progress of mankind. Personal and material symbols and their interconnections comprise the mechanism of the social body which directs social and intellectual activities in society. Schäffle stressed the importance of individual, creative contributions while acknowledging the economic environment with its own demands of production and consumption of symbolic goods; thus, communication emerges as a central concern of economic theorists and their discussions of societal developments. The press as a transmitter of ideas and a leader of the public plays a major role in the advancement of society, despite the dependence upon economic and political forces which corrupt or misdirect the activities of journalists. Schäffle recognized the need for a substantial reform of the daily press; he suggested the separation of advertising and information and opinion functions to improve the quality of newspaper coverage and the professional ethics of journalism. His presentation reflects not only a vast knowledge of the natural sciences, economic theory, and history, but also an understanding of contemporary events, particularly as they relate to the use of mass media, including the press, in the political process of his times. Although pessimistic about immediate changes, he proposed a type of press system that would help maximize the communication of information most beneficial for the advancement of society.

NOTES

1. Albert E.F. Schäffle, *Aus Meinem Leben* (Berlin: Ernst Hofmann, 1905), Vol. 1, 43.
2. Ibid., 131.

3. Ibid., 132.

4. Translation is taken from Albion W. Small, *Origins of Sociology* (Chicago: University of Chicago Press, 1924), 299.

5. "Ueber die volkswirthschaftliche Natur der Güter der Darstellung und der Mittheilung," *Zeitschrift für die gesammte Staatswissenschaft,* Heft 1 (1873), 1-70.

6. Albert E.F. Schäffle, *Bau und Leben des Sozialen Körpers* (Tübingen: Verlag der H. Lauppschen Buchhandlung, 1881), Vol. 1, vi.

7. Ibid., 353.

8. Ibid.

9. Ibid.

10. Ibid.

11. Ibid., 355.

12. Ibid., 358.

13. Ibid., 359.

14. Ibid., 361.

15. Ibid., 362.

16. Ibid., 363.

17. Ibid., 364-365.

18. Ibid., 367.

19. Ibid., 368.

20. Ibid., 369.

21. "Ueber die volkswirthschaftliche Natur."

22. Ibid., 1-2.

23. Ibid., 6.

24. Ibid., 9.

25. Ibid., 14.

26. Ibid., 23.

27. Ibid., 26.

28. Ibid., 34.

29. Ibid., 40.

30. Ibid.

31. Ibid., 42.

32. Ibid., 45.

33. Ibid., 46.

34. Ibid., 66.

35. Ibid., 69.

36. *Bau und Leben,* I, 433.

37. Ibid., I, 444.

38. Ibid., I, 447.

39. Ibid., I, 448.

40. Ibid., I, 449.

41. Ibid., I, 451.

42. Ibid., I, 452.

43. Ibid., I, 455.

44. Ibid., I, 456.

45. Ibid., I, 459.

46. Ibid., I, 460.

47. Ibid.

48. Ibid.
49. Ibid., I, 462.
50. Ibid., I, 463.
51. Ibid., I, 464.
52. Ibid.
53. Ibid., I, 465.
54. Ibid., III, 520.
55. Ibid., III, 520-521.
56. Ibid., III, 521.
57. Ibid., IV, 69.
58. Ibid., IV, 69-70.
59. Ibid., I, 466.
60. Ibid.

3

The News of Society

Karl Knies on Communication
and Transportation

KNIES: A BIOGRAPHICAL NOTE

Karl Knies (1821-1898) was one of the founding fathers of the German historical school of economic thought. He joined Wilhelm Roscher and Bruno Hildebrand in their criticism of the classical school and in attempts to describe the economic behavior of man in terms of his association with diverse groups in society while stressing the limited applicability of generalizations based upon observations of man's varied economic activities.

He was born and raised in Marburg, Hesse, where he became a *Privatdozent* in 1846, lecturing on history and political science. After a teaching assignment at the polytechnical school in Kassel, he left for Schaffhausen, Switzerland, in 1852 and became a teacher at the *Kantonschule*. Three years later Knies was appointed professor of cameralistic sciences at Freiburg. During his career at Freiburg he headed a committee to reform elementary and middle schools, and in 1861 he became a member of the lower house of the Baden parliament. From 1865 until his retirement in 1896, he was a professor of political science at Heidelberg.

Throughout his career Knies published widely, mostly monographs and books on economic and political topics, but also articles in scholarly and popular journals. Among his most important works are *Die Statistik als selbständige Wissenschaft,* 1850; *Die politische Oekonomie vom Standpunkte der geschicht-*

lichen Methode, 1853, 1883; *Der Telegraph als Verkehrsmittel,* 1857; and a two-volume work, *Geld und Kredit* 1873-79.

In general, Knies' work reflects the concern of German writers on political economy for the protection and development of the state. Thus, questions of economic policy within a larger study of the social environment were often raised in the context of an assessment of technological advancements and their effects upon society. His monographs dealing with railroads (see *Die Eisen-bahnen und ihre Wirkungen,* 1853) and the telegraph are examples of treating specific economic problems in this light. Members of the historical school stressed the unity of social life; they described the interconnections of individual social processes and regarded an organistic view of society as the basis for their development of theoretical propositions.

Gustav von Schmoller, a later representative of the historical school, described Knies and his approach:

> The most essential thing from his point of view is war against mere
> abstraction, against premature and false generalization, such as were
> common among older economists. . . . The connection between national
> economy and the other departments of national life, the dependence
> of economic systems upon the intellectual and material elements of
> the periods in which they arose, the emphasis upon the collective
> character of all social phenomena, for him these are the main things.
> In this connection also he displayed rare foresight, calmness, prudence.[1]

Knies regarded the historical realities of the economic world as the object of the study of political economy; he stressed the interdependency of economic and cultural spheres of society and suggested that the sum total of all economic subsystems does not constitute the economic structure of society since it omits social and societal processes. The task of economists includes the observation of a variety of historical manifestations. Knies pointed out that the historical existence of a nation yields information about the common features of a variety of social and cultural developments; and he said "Also, the economic conditions and developments of peoples may be regarded only as one link which is closely connected with the total organism. In reality political economy is not isolated, complete in itself, but it is the economic side of the life of the people."[2] Knies also suggested the notion of society as a growing and developing organism; he recognized the importance of process as a definitional aspect of society and its consequences for the development of a scientific approach to the study of economic questions: "Economic conditions, too, participate in the general and uniform movement and development. . . . In a continuing movement—because the evolution of life is a continuous process."[3]

Knies also addressed the difficulties of historical research, which he described as ranging from a lack of data to the problems of interpretation of statistical materials and the limitations of comparative analyses. He said,

> Unprejudiced critical research must admit, or stress, that mistakes and deceptions easily occur during the collection and arrangement of economic facts . . . because so much material must be obtained from "interested parties," who can make not only wrong judgments, but who also may act under the spell of an "optical illusion." Thus, the immediate task of verifying and completing factual accounts is made more difficult by the fact that the experiment of the natural scientist fails, direct insights into the "position and movement" of the intellectual-personal elements of those interested in economics are impossible. . . . Therefore a considerable dispute arises and continues concerning the facts themselves which should have been gathered reliably and almost completely, before one proceeds.[4]

His observations are based upon an understanding of economic facts as a combination of material and personal factors. Specifically, Knies recognized that man's environment, his material world, as well as his intellectual and spiritual dimension, his personal world, interact to produce particular economic results. In this connection he cited Albert Schäffle, who had suggested that "without a psychological explanation there is no truth to political economy or politics."[5] Knies concluded that this was a flat admission that a theory of "an evolution of society based upon a mechanism of external events, which is a logical consequence of a positivistic sociology, must lead to showings and results which are objectively false."[6] As an economist, he was particularly interested in the observation and discussion of those developments, which, according to his methodological premises, can be sufficiently identified and defined. He knew that qualitative differences could not be described numerically, and that the spirit of movements or traditions could not be reflected or explained adequately by mere numbers. His appreciation for an understanding of contemporary situations in the light of past experiences provided the basis for the use of statistical materials combined with historical observations. In a sense his work reflected his own dictum that

> the method of investigation, reasoning and conclusion which is used by an academic discipline, is closely related to its overall character. It is for this reason that the progress of a science, in general, affects its current methodology, in particular, while on the other hand, any more significant improvement of a method of investigation has a most profound influence upon the science.[7]

Knies' interest in communication or symbolic interaction remained ill defined, however. His *Geld und Kredit*, a work of considerable theoretical importance for contemporary economic thought, recognized the symbolic nature of money in the context of interpersonal communication, used here in the widest sense of the word, without attempting to develop a theoretical framework for symbolic transactions. In this framework money is defined by Knies as serving particular economic conditions in which a commodity "turns into 'money' because it is used to function as a 'measurement of values,' a 'means of exchange,' and a 'legal tender.'"[8] His *Der Telegraph als Verkehrsmittel,* on the other hand, provided an elaboration of the impact of technology on symbolic communication with emphasis upon the economic problems of the press. The advancement of technology, the expansion of a national economy, and the developments in transportation and communication in Germany served as a catalyst for the discussion of the role and function of mass communication. He recognized the impact of technological changes, and concluded that "to enable and to facilitate communication is synonymous with eliminating the earlier degree of isolation of a country."[9]

Consequently, Knies' discussion treated the press as a means of transporting information through time and over vast distances; he provided an interpretation of the press that stressed the vehicular functions of the medium at the expense of other, more commonly expressed notions of the role and functions of newspapers in society.

COMMUNICATION, NEWS, AND TRANSPORTATION

Knies based his discussion concerning the development of technology and the progress of transportation on the idea that men need and seek contact with others, in fact, that most of the early efforts of education and training were aimed at perfecting man's ability to function as a social being. He said, "From earliest childhood on our efforts are directed at making ourselves proficient in social intercourse, to accept others and to communicate to others; these efforts, big or small, presuppose a mutual exchange of means with which to satisfy human needs."[10] Thus, man has always tried to overcome natural barriers that prevented his intellectual growth and his physical expansion. In this context Knies looked at communication as any process that helps break down the isolation of individuals. This definition embraces not only "the celebrated inventions of the alphabet, printing, etc., but nearly everything that coincides with the history of man as a social being."[11] The idea of transportation became a special, important aspect of this definition and most appropriate for Knies to introduce his economic approach to an understanding of the processes of socialization and acculturation. He defined transportation and the means of transportation in this way: "We call transportation an act of moving objects from their original place to another place with the aid of force, and means of transportation the sum of all necessary instruments to bring about the move."[12] Knies observed that different types of material goods need particular types of vehicles for their transportation. For instance, he pointed to the differences among objects, people, and news, to the necessity for different means of transportation, and to the time requirement associated with the transmission of different objects. Thus, experience has taught us that "faster transportation is desirable for persons than for goods, and it must be even faster for news than for persons. This situation has always found its expression in the institutions for transportation."[13]

The history of the transmission of news finds its beginnings in the person-to-person contact, where information is passed directly from the originator to the intended recipient. Knies observed that this form is perhaps the most accurate way of communicating ideas, since content and audience are controlled solely by the sender of news. Furthermore, this type of personal communication may lead to a dialogical relationship, in which the mutuality of receiving and dispatching information could result in decision-making processes without delay. Face-to-face communication also lends itself to instant manipulation of messages, depending on the reaction of the recipient and the intentions of the sender. Knies felt that the peculiar nature of the direct communication link continued to make it most appropriate for some kinds of news dissemination, even under modern conditions of an advanced communication technology and even though it may be time consuming and disadvantageous with respect to a division of labor.

A more advanced system of transmitting news and information was the employment of messengers, whose oral presentations replaced the intimacy and accuracy of the person-to-person approach. Although freed from the physical constraints of direct communication, the sender also sacrificed some advantages. Knies pointed out that "The intellectual and moral qualities of the messenger, the confidence in the personal loyalty, are all-important as soon as more significant news is involved. . . . The gates are opened to misuse when news meant for a second person is also communicated to a third one."[14] But even under the most favorable conditions, this system of news dissemination could not be considered a substantial change from the earlier approach; such change came about only with the invention of optical and aural systems of communication capable of covering great distances. These systems, which could be defined as forerunners of the telegraph, provided a genuinely new dimension. News could now be received by many individuals, as long as they were within the reach of the signal, replacing the necessity for personal contact with originators or messengers of information. Knies thought that this type of news communication served well in those instances, in which relatively few pieces of information needed fast and widespread dissemination. Also, he argued that the importance of the systems increased with their use as public communication systems, as opposed to private or restricted systems, whose messages could only be deciphered by certain groups or individuals.

With the introduction of written communication, the dissemination of news could be organized according to a number of principles which combined the advantages of earlier systems with the progress of technology. For instance, news could be kept secret; and the task of transmitting messages could be left to intellectually less qualified individuals, which made it also less expensive. Knies said that

> The use of the written word provided the same accuracy and security which oral communication guaranteed all participants for the dissemination of news. In one respect even more so, since what is offered is not only an exact formulation of the respective expression, but also a durable and fixed one. Littera scripta manet.[15]

The invention of printing added to the advancement of news dissemination for and among large numbers of individuals. Knies agreed that the

> significance lies in the fact that the invention of the means to let news reach all and everyone without special efforts, partly resulted in the new development of this special type of news transmission and partly in its boundless growth. Also the more distant developments in the art of printing have found an application in the field of news dissemination.[16]

He mentioned lithography, for instance, and the use of pictures on handbills and other types of communication.

At this point in the history of news and its dissemination, the question of transportation became significant enough to lead to the development of occupational roles, such as news carriers, and to the establishment of institutions, such as the postal services. But no other technological advancement had greater influence on the need for faster and better news service than the railroads. Knies suggested

> that particularly the railroads themselves have promoted in many ways a faster means of transportation for the traffic in news, indeed, they initiated it. . . . The goal was reached with the invention of the electric telegraph. It turned out to be suited for the transmission of news with a speed that surpassed by far the efficiency of a locomotive.[17]

Knies saw the invention of the telegraph as a series of related scientific discoveries over a long period of time. He pointed to the advancement of science as a stimulus for economic progress when he described the development of technology to provide inexpensive telegraph lines and the use of a code "language" which allowed for the expression of words and ideas in the most precise manner. Thus, technology supported the need of men to remain in communication.

News provides the vehicle for ideas and becomes one of the forms in which individuals express their relationships. According to Knies, news "belongs to intellectual, thought-communication which occurs between persons. It differs from other forms of communication by being thought-communication between persons who are physically separated. . . . One could also say that news is the communication of an event which occurred away from the location of the recipient."[18] He added that actual distances were immaterial; the conditions would be met when news was actually transmitted. More important, however, was another criterion: Knies differentiated between books and newspapers, counting the former as part of an educational mission, whereas "news follows the daily events; is part of the events, part of the day with attendant occurrences.[19] Since he intended to separate historical accounts as events of earlier days from contemporary phenomena, his definition of news promotes the idea of surmounting spatial rather than temporal obstacles in the way of social communication. He said,

> News itself is short-lived, its purpose is not like that of a book with its written instructions aimed at the continuous satisfaction of lasting needs— once announced its traces are lost again, or its account becomes history, a registered fact, or its vehicle becomes a document for argumentation, a means for refreshing one's memory of past experiences.

Knies suggested further that with an increasing variety in the means of transmitting news, ranging from oral communication to the telegraph, the purposes for the use of these communication vehicles have increased as well. A myriad of events needs presentation; not only events affecting the lives of individuals or organizations but also moods and feelings want to be expressed. He added,

> There are events to be reported, events of a person's life, of a family circle, involving communal-local phenomena, of church and of state; moods want to find their expression and feelings, problems and suspicions, happiness and sorrow, love and hate . . . who can count all the forms in which men search for each other and meet![21]

Knies remarked that news satisfies the needs or interests not only of the recipient but also of the originator or the source of information. He cited news presentations in the press and advertisements as shifting the center of interest in the communication process. The exchange of business correspondence, on the other hand, served as the example of a communication system in which both or all parties involved share an equal interest in the outcome of the process.

Knies commented upon the importance of literacy in the development of communication systems, and he suggested that decreasing illiteracy must result in an increase in news communication. Literacy statistics would help determine limits on a participation of society in the exchange of information. Societies with an advanced culture, according to Knies, present a more cohesive and well-developed system of news communication. The reasons are found not only in the ability to read or write but also in the advanced technological stages of such a society, whose efforts will also be aimed at perfecting its system of transmitting news and information. Knies added that such systems were based upon economic considerations, that the transmission of news was a service used and paid for by those who needed to satisfy their curiosity, perhaps, or those whose social and economic livelihood depended upon the successful communication of news. It followed, therefore, that "not only those who cannot write or read, but also those, who cannot pay, e.g., the extremely poor as those who lack disposable goods for such relatively superfluous service, are excluded from the communication of news."[22]

Knies proposed that the number of individuals affected in such ways differs with the degree of poverty or wealth found in a society. He added that a rise in prosperity, the availability of income beyond the poverty level, and access to reasonable or cheap means of transmission would also help improve the conditions needed for an increase in the communication of news.

Knies supported his arguments also by pointing to psychological or internal needs as prerequisites for the increase in communication among individuals who are physically separated. Without such needs, separations alone would not necessarily fulfill the conditions for communication. He cited emigration as a phenomenon that had brought about an increase in communication over long distances based upon family ties or close personal relationships. Letters were often exchanged by members of certain social classes, who under normal circumstances would never have resorted to this type of communication. Thus, the arrival of a letter signaled a special event in villages, and everyone acted as if there were a communal right to share its content. Knies added that similar observations could be made about the communication concerning individuals who had left their homes temporarily to live abroad and others who had traveled and who not only returned to tell about their experiences but also remained in touch with their communities through letters. Finally, he mentioned war as an occasion when the flow of written communication had increased significantly.

Knies came to the conclusion that modern civilization had revealed ways of life that had to affect the communication patterns of individuals not only within cultural or political boundaries but also in different nations. In particular, Knies saw life during the Middle Ages as relatively isolated; people lived in their communities removed from the events of the outside world. Government, too, operated at a distance, so to speak, and did not seem directly related to the people. Only later and with the improvement of the communication systems did all of the parts of a nation become interrelated, even inseparable to many observers. These developments also led to considerations of individual states not as independent single units, but as parts of larger groupings of states closely connected with each other. It became natural, therefore, to experience events in distant parts of the world and to be interested in the fate of other nations. More important, perhaps, was the effect of information networks on the organization of the bureaucracy. Knies mentioned that international news had become a considerable item in the exchange of information between governments and their representatives. And he said that one must not forget "the modern 'centralization' of government bureaucracies as a lever of internal news communication! Small mountains of official news accumulate from towns to county seats, from county seats to provincial capitals, and from provincial capitals to the capital."[23] He observed that with the modernization of social and political life came the need for public information and with it the development of forms of dissemination. In this context newspapers gained recognition and began to play an important role in the news communication processes of public life. Also, as a result of the increased flow of information, the postal system had developed as an official support system for the fast, efficient, and inexpensive dissemination of private and public communication. The press, among others, came to rely upon these services and established a dependency which could be regarded as a potential threat to its freedom.

Knies proposed that the improvement of postal services, for instance, was in itself an indication of the demands for more frequent communication with other parts of the world, and that it had a positive effect upon the dissemination of newspapers. The low postal rates helped secure a fast and regular stream of information between editorial offices and their correspondents; it also enabled newspapers to be distributed without delay and at reasonable rates. Knies warned that any changes in the official policies pertaining to newspaper deliveries could result in serious setbacks for the press. He said that "besides the real death penalty, namely the suppression of a paper, there is a milder form of 'death penalty,' the lifting of postal privileges. We wish that this will never be put to use against a paper whose reading is not prohibited by the state."[24] Knies described the post office as a public institution whose service should be available to all newspapers, not to just a few, and he felt that any removal of postal privileges would undoubtedly be regarded as a restriction, if not a prohibition, of that particular newspaper. His recognition of economic factors as being crucial to the survival of the press, including its freedom of expression, however, was not confined to the relationship between private and public interests.

THE PRESS AND COMMERCIAL MESSAGES

Knies paid considerable attention to the discussion of advertisements, which became a major factor in the discussion of the roles and functions of the press in modern society.

The press had become the most important vehicle for the transmission of commercial messages, according to Knies. Advertisements explain circumstances under which commodities are bought or sold; they also stimulate business by suggesting the availability of goods in the marketplace. The role played by the press in the dissemination of commercial announcements is reflected in the following observation: "'Knowledge is power' according to the men of politics and science—'knowledge is sales,' according to the one who offers material goods, personal service, etc., 'knowledge is production' according to the one who senses a need, but who can't see the source to satisfy it."[25] Knies saw the importance of advertising in the context of supply and demand as the guiding principles of a market situation, and he addressed questions of production and consumption of industrial commodities in the framework of communication principles that allowed for the speedy and inexpensive dissemination of information concerning particular goods. But Knies considered the advertisement also as a source of information about the economic and cultural conditions of society, and he urged that advertisements be used not only by historians but also by politicians who wanted to learn more about the conditions of their local communities, their towns, or regions. He said,

> The advertisement according to type, number or form is an excellent guide to knowledge about economic and cultural-historical conditions and developments, and even more so, except in cases where it is restricted, to the communication of acknowledged facts, because it appears naive and not conscious of its power as historical evidence while submitting to contemporary controls at the same time.[26]

But advertisements do not only inform about the supply or demand of goods; according to Knies, they also lead interested parties directly to the source. Thus, advertisements save time and effort. Knies thought that they must be considered a major force in a competitive situation, in which the advertiser appeared on a public platform to exhibit his commodities and to compete against others: "The advertisement is really a competition in many cases, and it provokes more competition; whoever enters it must be confident to win or to hold the goodwill of the target audience on an open field of battle against his competitors."[27] At the same time, Knies realized that advertisements could also be abused by those unwilling to submit to fair play and honesty in business transactions. But even in these situations, advertisements served as a control function; since they insisted upon the publicness of the transactions, for instance, they would force prices to remain in a competitive framework.

In addition, advertisements stimulate consumption and production. Knies suggested that the effects of commercial communication were considerable and thus of major importance to the economic system. He explained, "The goods which we see before us in our thoughts stimulate us in a manner similar to those times when we walk through warehouses and stores unwilling to buy anything, but leaving the place finally with heavy shopping bags."[28] This, in part, explained the amount of attention that business had paid to advertising. He mentioned that millions were spent on the dissemination of commercial information.

Knies also recognized the importance of advertising support for newspapers and magazines which lacked financial independence. He said, "The experiment has been made repeatedly to deliver newspapers and handbills to many thousand of customers without charge relying on advertising revenues, if one could only succeed in raising confidence in the fact that the delivery was really made to thousands of recipients at no cost."[29] Since advertising competed with other advertising for space, it became important for businessmen also to consider such strategies as the type of media or the place within a newspaper, for instance. Knies suggested that "locally limited purposes can only be served through local newspapers; advertising for world-wide communication, however, can only be meaningful in newspapers with large circulation."[30] He also added that advertisers must pay some attention to the fact that advertisements are communication events of rather limited significance. He explained that advertising is bound by considerations of time, e.g., seasons in which certain goods may be demanded more than others, and by economic conditions, e.g., availability of financial resources to execute purchasing functions.

Knies felt that the press shared a basic problem with advertising, the need to accomplish the widest possible distribution with the goal of reaching "all of the public," thus saturating the market. However, he also recognized that readers had to pay for the news, or share in the cost of gathering it, and he compared the sale of news to other business arrangements where commodities are sold on a regular basis to an identifiable group of buyers, customers whose regular purchases form the basis for any production and marketing considerations.

Since news is short-lived, a fact in which one could find its principal value, it can be delivered only on the basis of standing orders. Knies pointed out that "even the largest increase in customers raises the total labor and the production costs only by a very small margin, while the expenditure for 100,000 or 100 customers remains the same for the rest."[31] This meant that publishers and editorial staffs prefer to operate on the largest possible base, a fact which invited considerations of forming industrial concerns for fast, cheap, and efficient service.

Knies acknowledged that the transmission of news had become an important business in society, and a way for many individuals to define their careers and to earn their livelihood. He also recognized the special nature of a profession that fed on the need for individual recognition, on the excitement of being involved in the daily affairs of a society, and on feelings of power and influence. He added that in

> question here is a sphere of activity which can receive a large part
> of its rewards from the intellectual satisfaction of personal interests.
> For this very reason it is also possible for third persons to pay owners
> of workers of the press—regularly or in isolated cases—for getting
> certain news items before the public.[32]

Knies suggested that the reception and reading of news alone can be of tremendous importance to sources or originators of news items, since news not only described the daily events, but also could influence the mood of the readers and their decision-making power. He proposed that the selection process in newspaper offices could provide clues to how journalists tried to manipulate the way in which readers perceived the world around them. While the most important events of the day could hardly be omitted, other occurrences, however, often received different treatments. "Not only books can receive the 'silent treatment,' but also news which is forgotten sooner or later."[33] Knies observed that news could be presented in a variety of shades and colors, quite apart from the editorial comments; and he added that "all this does not really diminish the truth even when the editors should follow their own moods without any further reflection."[34] He expected a partisan press and thought that readers would be able to recognize the different treatment of public events by the press. At the same time, the wide dissemination of news and the possible effects of newspapers on their readers must challenge the moral responsibility of the business managers of the press. Knies felt strongly about the professional responsibilities of journalists, and he argued that men whose business it is to communicate regularly with large audiences should certainly be among the most educated and most conscientious men in society. He added that the moral responsibility of those in charge of the press must increase in times of unrest, when public opinion and the influence of the masses are felt by the government. The existence of party newspapers with their biased, one-sided reporting of public events made it even more necessary to insist upon a high degree of professional ethics. He said "The moral responsibility of the leaders in news communication can only grow with the fact that the recipients, the subscribers, stay with the papers of their leanings, in many cases with the papers of their party. The known one-sidedness makes a balancing reply impossible."[35]

Newspapers, according to Knies, must carry items which touch upon the interests of their readers. However, the final decision and the definition of what constitutes matters of public interest remained in the hands of journalists. On the other hand, journalists were dependent upon their readers; and Knies pointed out that editors may find it more convenient to yield to public taste and to give readers what they want than to follow the dictates of their own taste or intellectual preferences. Still, in all cases and even in different cultural environments, one could observe a mutual influence, flowing from readers to newspapers and from journalists to their public. In addition, Knies proposed that obvious differences existed in the type and form of news communication in different countries and during different periods of history. He said, "La gazette c'est le peuple, c'est le temps, etc., one can still say in view of the contrasts between present and past, between German, American, English and French newspapers, although powerful and regular worldwide communication has led to some adjustment."[36]

A prerequisite for the dissemination of news was the interest of people in public affairs. While in earlier years and throughout the Middle Ages the isolation of individuals and their communities provided limitations that had an unfavorable effect upon regular news dissemination, the beginnings of the modern states in Europe saw the rise of the press. Newspapers became important elements in the formulation and perpetuation of public policies and ideologies. Again, Knies referred to the fact that the treatment of newspapers, their numbers, and circulation were defined by cultural conditions. He explained that "in England, to read a newspaper belongs to the category of 'necessary expenses' for the manual laborer, in the North-American Union there appear more German newspapers than in our beloved fatherland, etc."[37]

NEWSPAPERS AND THE CREATION OF NEEDS

Newspapers fulfilled still another function, according to Knies; not only did they satisfy particular needs and teach their readers to satisfy their information needs through the daily press, but they also helped create needs. The state in its modern democratic phase could hardly tolerate citizens with no interest in public information. By reporting regularly about public life and the events of the day, newspapers had become part of the foundation of the state. He argued that most countries with large populations distributed over wide areas and with cities and metropolitan areas as centers of the political and cultural life of a state need communication networks that will enable everyone to participate in the affairs of the state. Thus, newspapers became the carriers of such information and the means by which individuals could share in the life-process of society. Knies believed that "Our countries would not be able to tolerate the local concentrations of official actions in Paris, London, etc."[38] Unless newspapers reversed their original roles, one could always observe how the press worked almost instinctively towards achieving the goal of publishing information about matters of public importance concerning the state.

The production of newspapers also reflected the prevalent system of developing large-scale concerns to keep up with the times. Knies saw these changes as a result of increased sales and business considerations to increase production costs in order to improve current offerings, such as more and improved news services and specialization among reporting staffs. Consequently, world news coverage in smaller newspapers was more selective, taking into account the extensive coverage by larger newspapers. Thus, the local press with its primary interests in community affairs and regional events retained its unique position as well. But newspaper readers developed additional demands for other types of information. Knies mentioned the *feuilleton* as a widely read section in many newspapers, offering novels, anecdotes, and feature material; the creation of special sections and the inclusion of review articles on literary and artistic matters; and finally the demands for expertly written editorials, morning and night editions, and extras. Knies thought that the people demanded "much, very much for little money."[39]

In general, newspapers confronted conditions similar to those faced by any other sale of commodities. Knies observed that "the higher the price for one copy without increasing its quality appreciably, the smaller the circle of customers must get."[40] If, indeed, one of the major concerns of newspaper enterprises was the distribution of its products to all segments of society, including low-income groups, prices had to be kept down. The treatment of newspapers differed, of course; Knies mentioned that according to customs or to historical developments newspapers were sometimes considered dispensible, or maybe even unknown in some countries, and welcome, even necessary means of survival in other parts of the world. If an individual

> reads a newspaper once a week, like he eats meat once a week, it will happen on his day of rest [with a Saturday or Sunday edition] It is curious to see how much the different tastes of readers, the diversity of needed spices . . . remind us of bearing an analogy to the consumption of material food.[41]

Another relationship seemed to exist for Knies between the rise in newspaper circulation and the creation of information needs.

He suggested that during times of political and social stress subscriptions to newspapers must increase, and that during times which lacked conflict or disorder newspapers tended to lose sales.

Underlying any of these descriptions of the role and function of newspapers, however, was the fact that news communication must be defined as an ephemeral service. Knies wanted his readers to understand that yesterday's newspaper was practically worthless. On the other hand, he recognized the value of newspaper collections as sources of important information and as documents, perhaps, for future historical research. He added that if "news is a commodity, it must have a certain value, an intrinsic value. But the intrinsic value alone is not inherent in the object itself, it can only be there if and as long as a human need exists for the news."[42]

Following this explanation, Knies developed reasons why the press changed its content over time, why it yielded to the demands of the public and produced newspapers that reflected the taste or preference of the masses of readers. He listed the inclusion of religious news, for instance, economic and business reporting, and the fact that some of these developments have led to the creation of newspapers that catered exclusively to special interests. Once institutional participation was assured and the prospective readership considered large enough, many business enterprises engaged in the publication of their own papers or journals to report on their activities.

So far Knies had viewed personal relationships between senders and receivers as a crucial point of departure for an understanding of any theory of news communication. Now he added another element, a material one, to the discussion, based upon his observation that "all inter-local exchange of commodities tends to be accompanied by news communication, even demands it."[43]

THE USES OF THE TELEGRAPH

While personal contacts with customers, the visits to markets in different parts of the world, as well as the attendance at regional or local conventions or fairs were common during earlier times, contemporary conditions required different methods of approaching potential customers. Knies observed that newspaper advertising and business correspondence, in particular, became primary means for the dissemination of information about productions and cost of consumer items. As a result, contacts were established and sales completed without face-to-face communication. The importance of this development increased with the expansion of markets and the establishment of business ties with distant countries. Competition and the fluctuation of market prices provided additional stimuli for the exchange of written communication. Knies also felt that often letters were more appropriate for certain types of information, perhaps, than spoken words. He said that

> in the way in which some people prefer under circumstances involving unhurried communication the use of a letter to speech, because they can express the most delicate and also the worst better with a pen than with their mouth, the letter just may be more efficient for business transactions, because it must be based upon a firm prior decision, and it does document the conclusions which it initiated.[44]

Thus, the time element became an important aspect in the transmission of business information, because promptness and reliability of a transportation system were crucial for the execution of business transactions. News, as opposed to other material goods, thrived under conditions which emphasized speed and time.

Knies looked upon the telegraph as a technological development that met the conditions of providing a means of fast and continuous service not only for those who operated newspapers but also for those whose information needs became a prerequisite for the successful conduct of business and the exchange of material goods. He described the achievement of the telegraph in terms of its capability for "simultaneous news communication from places various distances away from one place, as well as from that place to other places located at various distances. This has been made possible, and for the first time, only because the time needed to bridge these distances is = 0."[45] Knies came to the conclusion that the capability of the telegraph surpassed the potential of the nervous system in a human body. He argued that while the body operated with a nervous system that differentiated between physical and psychological reactions, the telegraph was used to fulfill all functions regardless of their content: "In comparison to our body we must say that the central organ in the network is an ambulatory one ... the telegraph must appear to us like the eye and the ear of areas and countries, with which they perceive what is going on in the world."[46] Knies added that as a result of the telegraph events are experienced simultaneously around the world, as if a single sensation raced through one body.

Thus, if combined with the realization that news affects the behavior of individuals, the importance of the telegraph as an instrument of news communication in modern society must become self-evident. For Knies, telegraphs had "an overpowering strength to unite a compounded social body."[47] Although not always noticeable in the day-to-day operation of the news communication system, such effectiveness existed, nevertheless, and had to be taken into account. In any case, Knies suggested that economists, historians, and politicians, in particular, had an obligation to consider the contributions of the telegraph and to bear in mind the effect it had on the lives of millions of people.

In summary, Knies developed his arguments about the significance of communication from the perspective of the continuing need to perfect man's ability to function as a social being. The maturation of the social organism coincides with the improvement of the social communication system. Thus, the history of communication culminates in the development of occupational roles and institutional activities solely dedicated to the collection and dissemination of information. Knies acknowledged the interdependence of economic and cultural spheres of society in his discussion of news communication as a means of satisfying old needs and creating new ones. Not only did he treat the rise of commercial messages as a financial or economic necessity of modern press systems, but he also realized the information function that advertisements fulfill, not unlike news and other information. The newspaper occupies a central position in the societal communication process, according to Knies, who argued for the highest standards of education and professional ethics among journalists. He, too, knew about the dilemma of the newspaper enterprise caught between the economic necessity of advertising support and the need of society for an agent of news communication. He had no specific solution but to fall back on the question of supply and demand and professional standards that would regulate the press. The invention of the telegraph as the latest technological advancement signals the introduction of fast and continuous service capable of uniting a social system almost instantaneously in sharing larger quantities of information than before. Thus, technological advancements must become aspects of a social or cultural history of society.

NOTES

1. As cited in William A. Scott, *The Development of Economics* (New York: Century, 1933), 227.

2. *Die Politische Oekonomie vom Geschichtlichen Standpunkte* (Braunschweig: C. A. Schwetschke, 1883), 141.

3. Ibid., 143.

4. Ibid., 495.

5. Ibid., 253.

6. Ibid.

7. Ibid., 453.

8. *Das Geld Darlegung der Grundlehren von dem Gelde, insbesondere der wirtschaflichen und der rechtsgiltigen Functionen des Geldes, mit einer Erörterung über das Kapital und die Ubertragung der Nutzungen* (Berlin: Weidmannsche Buchhandlung, 1885), 23.

9. Ibid., 94 .

10. *Der Telegraph als Verkehrsmittel. Mit Erörterungen uber den Nachrichtenverkehr überhaupt* (Tübingen: Verlag der Laupp' schen Buchhandlung, 1857), 1.

11. Ibid., 4.

12. Ibid.

13. Ibid., 6.

14. Ibid., 8.

15. Ibid., 13.

16. Ibid., 14.

17. Ibid., 18.

18. Ibid., 44.

19. Ibid., 45.

20. Ibid., 47.

21. Ibid., 48.
22. Ibid., 55.
23. Ibid., 59.
24. Ibid., 103.
25. Ibid., 49.
26. Ibid., 50.
27. Ibid., 51.
28. Ibid., 52.
29. Ibid.
30. Ibid., 53.
31. Ibid., 60.
32. Ibid., 61.
33. Ibid.
34. Ibid.
35. Ibid., 62.
36. Ibid., 62-63.
37. Ibid., 63.
38. Ibid., 64.
39. Ibid., 66.
40. Ibid.
41. Ibid., 66-67.
42. Ibid., 67.
43. Ibid., 68.
44. Ibid., 72.
45. Ibid., 243.
46. Ibid., 244.
47. Ibid.

4

The Linkage of Society

Karl Bücher on Business and Journalism

BÜCHER: A BIOGRAPHICAL NOTE

The contribution of Karl Bücher (1847-1930) to the discussion of communication and the role and function of journalism in society occurred in the context of his economic theory of development, his emphasis upon exchange as a modern criterion for defining economic phenomena, and his analytical approach to the investigations of social and political institutions.

He was born in Kirberg near Wiesbaden, Germany, and attended the universities of Bonn and Göttingen, where he majored in history, political science, and classical philology. As a teacher and private lecturer, he gained his early professional experience in Göttingen (1869-1872), Dortmund (1872-1873), and Frankfurt (1873-1878) before he joined the editorial staff of Leopold Sonnemann's famous *Frankfurter Zeitung* as an expert on economic and social policy questions. At that time he had published widely already on historical topics ranging from medieval labor conditions to the position of women in the Middle Ages and medieval tax ordinances, and he had started his major work on the organization of guilds in the high Middle Ages.

Bücher resigned from the *Frankfurter Zeitung* after only two years, in a dispute over questions involving the position of the publisher vis-à-vis outside business interests. Unable to secure a similar position elsewhere, he turned to an academic career with the intellectual and financial support of Albert Schäffle. Bücher continued his studies at Munich and subsequently held university appointments as professor of statistics at Dorpat, Russia (1882), as professor of political economy and finance at Basel, Switzerland (1883-1890), at Karlsruhe (1890-1893), and at Leipzig, from where he retired in 1917 after succeeding with the establishment of a university-level institute for the study of the press and for the education of journalists.

In his economic theory of stages Bücher described the advancement of Western society in terms of the role and function of exchange. He identified three major stages of economic development from antiquity through the Middle Ages to modern times, at which the idea of exchange became more pronounced, ending with the observation of contemporary society as dependent upon an exchange economy. He also argued that human progress could be defined by the way in which production and consumption as basic social activities developed into separate functions over time, identified with distinct groups or organizations in society. Transportation and communication became increasingly important in an economic system that was based upon the exchange of goods and services to the point where state and private enterprise helped develop and maintain communication systems to maximize their efficiency and effectiveness. Thus, newspapers and journalism played major roles as carriers of information and as objects for study and research by economists and those in other disciplines interested in the workings of modern society.

Also, Bücher contributed to the literature of sociology with his treatise on work and rhythm.[1] In it he traced the relationship between work, play, and the underlying principle of rhythm. He criticized previous studies that had differentiated among play, sports, body movements, and work as separate types of activity and went on to describe rhythm as a basic human phenomenon across a wide range of civilizations and stages of human development.

Although Bücher had refused to compromise his position on newspaper ethics, as a scholar he became increasingly interested in the workings of the press and in its participation in the social

and political environment. He was also concerned about the
education of journalists. Consequently, he offered a course
dealing with the history, organization, and statistics of the press
system at the University of Basel. He argued that it was extremely
important for those students who planned to enter a public career
to have an opportunity for the study of the press as part of their
university curriculum. At the same time, it was the duty of universities to acknowledge the importance of the press in society by
offering appropriate courses. He restated his thoughts later on
at the University of Leipzig when he proposed that it was the
duty of the state to provide for the education of editors with
public funds, because editors held positions similar to those of
civil servants; he felt that newspapers could be defined as judges
who must make difficult and important decisions every day.

Bücher's idea of the press in society echoed Schäffle's theoretical discussions; he stressed the transportation function of the
press and its role as a link among various segments of society,
and he saw journalists as moderators and participants in the
communication process who served other leading elements in
society. Nevertheless, Bücher felt that the press and its journalists
must become the focal point for university-level research and
training.

In the plan of study for the education of journalists, published
in 1916 at the University of Leipzig,[2] Bücher's institute (*Institut
für Zeitungskunde*) was identified as a center which would
coordinate the education of journalists in various academic
disciplines with unique offerings of a newspaper-oriented plan
of study and research. The brochure mentioned specializations in
political, business, and literary journalism and described the
existence of a number of historical, statistical, and comtemporary
press sources. It ended with the statement that with the creation
of the institute the University of Leipzig expressed its belief that
the profession of newspaper journalists has to be ranked with
those of theologians, lawyers, teachers, and doctors.

Earlier Bücher had asked members of the International Statistical Institute to consider the compilation of a statistical work on
political newspapers in individual countries. His recommenda-

tions were accepted during the eleventh meeting of the organization in Copenhagen in 1907 with a plan to collect information about the national and local density of newspaper units, circulation, regularity of publication, subscription, and advertising rates.[3] Bücher had completed similar statistical accounts for Germany at Leipzig together with his students, among them Hjalmar Schacht, who completed a statistical analysis of the German press.[4]

In addition, the events of World War I provided new incentives to study the press and its propaganda function, in particular, and the effects of such communication.

Bücher considered the study of newspapers in the context of a historical treatment of the growth and development of cultural and social institutions in civilization. He did not want to establish a separate "discipline" of journalism but tried to point out the necessities for learning more about the press. Not only cultural historians but also economists should learn more about the role and function of advertising, and statistical compilations on press systems would contribute to a better and more widely accepted understanding of the importance of the press in society. Bücher said that

> the lecture courses that I gave at Basel and here at Leipzig on this subject I wanted to be seen as transmitting useful knowledge, not as the beginnings of a special science. It is possible that the sociological study of newspaper journalism, which hardly started, may furnish the building blocks for such a science; today we are still a long distance away from that point.[5]

In many respects Bücher supplemented Schäffle's work with his own systematic historical study of newspapers as social institutions; he applied his knowledge of statistics to the treatment of the press as a vehicle for societal communication, and he maintained the perspective of the professional economist and economic historian in his analyses of newspaper activities.

THE DEVELOPMENT OF MODERN JOURNALISM

Bücher addressed the problems of journalism in modern industrial societies rather early in his career. A collection of essays published in 1893 under the title *Die Entstehung der Volkswirtschaft* contained a hitherto unpublished paper on the "Genesis of Journalism," in which the author traced the development of journalism and its contribution to contemporary society.[6]

Commenting on the lack of scholarly attention paid to the study of the press, Bücher suggested that journalism could be studied "from the standpoint of political history, of literary history, of bibliography, of law, of philology even, as writings on the slovenliness of journalistic style give proof."[7] But he added that the political economist, in fact, should find the study of journalism most directly related to his concerns. Newspapers, according to Bücher, were commercial entities that had important functions to maintain in society which were identified with economic activities. Thus, newspapers ranked with postal services, railroads, and the telegraph among the technological means of society which connected and drew its members closer together. He said,

> In fact, the newspaper forms a link in the chain of modern commercial machinery; it is one of those contrivances by which in society the exchange of intellectual and material goods is facilitated. Yet it is not an instrument of commercial intercourse in the sense of the post or the railway, both of which have to do with the transport of persons, goods, and news, but rather in the sense of the letter and circular. These make the news capable of transport, only because they are enabled by the help of writing and printing to cut it adrift, as it were, from its originator, and give it corporeal independence.[8]

Bücher distinguished between letters and newspapers as means of private and public communication. But he added that the publication of newspapers presupposed some common interest in information about public affairs or commercial and trade activities, which, in turn, were based upon a political organization of the people, or what he described as a "certain community of life-interest."[9] Drawing upon the experiences of ancient times, he said that newspapers were unnecessary during that period because information needs could be satisfied by oral communication or by inscriptions:

> Only when Roman supremacy had embraced or subjected to its influence
> all the countries of the Mediterranean was there need of some means by
> which those members of the ruling class who had gone to the provinces as
> officials, tax-farmers and in other occupations, might receive the current
> news of the capital. It is significant that Caesar, the creator of the military
> monarchy and of the administrative centralization of Rome, is regarded as
> the founder of the first contrivance resembling a newspaper.[10]

Bücher traced the development of news communication
through the ages, from the beginnings of organized services in the
twelfth and thirteenth centuries to publications with limited
circles of readers throughout the next 400 to 500 years, to the age
of technology with the introduction of rapid transmission and
wide circulation of news and information. In this process, the
organization and handling of the collection and transmission
of information was similar to the system of commercial exchanges
and trade centers. Bücher pointed out that newspaper writing as
well as the collection of news was often practiced by large traders
in Germany, for instance, and in Italy. He said,

> The relations between wholesale trade and newspapers was somewhat
> clearer. Like the Nuremberg merchants mentioned above, some large
> trading houses in other localities had also organized an independent news
> service. Especially prominent were the Welsers and Fuggers. . . . The news-
> papers of the Fuggers regularly contain news from all parts of Europe and
> the East, and also from places still further removed: Persia, China and
> Japan, America. Besides the political correspondence, we have frequent
> reports of harvests and memoranda of prices, now and then even com-
> munications in the nature of advertisements, and a long list of Vienna
> firms—how and where all things could now be procured in Vienna.[11]

Discussing the relationship between written news sheets and
printing technology, Bücher suggested that the production of
written news sheets as a business could not be traced beyond
the period of the invention of the printing press; and he insisted
that the widespread use of written news sheets was not a result of
any particular censorship pressures, but rather an answer to the
economic question of finding a "sufficiently large circle of readers
to guarantee the sale necessary to meet the cost of printing."[12]

With the end of the sixteenth century, the development of the press underwent radical changes. According to Bücher, it rested

> on the separation of news collection from news dispatch (post), and on the commercial organization of the former into correspondence bureaux and telegraph agencies. To the telegraph agencies have fallen the duties of the earlier postmasters and news-scribes, but with this difference, that they no longer labour directly for the newspaper readers, but supply the publishing house with half-finished wares, making use in such work of the perfected commercial machinery of modern times.[13]

These changes were accompanied by a change in the role and function of the publisher, whose duties went beyond supervising the production and sale of particular products, because news, unlike books or pamphlets, did not form one single theme or subject matter. Bücher explained, "The news-items were brought together, taken from different sources, were of varying reliability. They needed to be used judicially and critically: in this a political or religious bias could find ready expression."[14]

The process continued and was intensified with the rise of political consciousness, the establishment of political parties, and the beginnings of a party press in Europe. Newspapers became instruments that supported or shaped public opinion, and Bücher saw the rise of the editorship as a result of these influences, while newspaper publishers now became dealers "in public opinion as well."[15] Throughout these periods of change, however, readers maintained their positions as powerful determinants of newspaper content. Bücher suggested that the wishes of readers remained "in the final analysis, the determining factors for the contents of the newspapers."[16]

The introduction of advertisements complicated the public-service features of newspapers. For Bücher this meant that private interests and private trade provided the press with opportunities to sell their readers to those who paid for advertising space. He said,

> In the same paper, often on the same page, where the highest interests of mankind are, or at least should be, represented, buyers and sellers ply their vocations in ignoble greed of gain. For the uninitiated it is often difficult

to distinguish where the interests of the public cease and private interests begin.[17]

Looking at the modern newspaper as it presented itself to society, Bücher called it a "capitalistic enterprise, a sort of news-factory in which a great number of people . . . are employed on wage, under a single administration, at very specialized work."[18] He emphasized the complexity of the modern press and the problems of mass circulation and competition in the marketplace when he said,

> This paper produces wares for an unknown circle of readers, from whom it is, furthermore, frequently separated by intermediaries, such as delivery agencies and postal institutions. The simple needs of the reader or of the circle of patrons no longer determine the quality of these wares; it is now the very complicated conditions of competition in the publication market. In this market, however, as generally in wholesale markets, the consumers of the goods, the newspaper readers, take no direct part; the determining factors are the wholesale dealers and the speculators in news: the governments, the telegraph bureaux dependent upon their special correspondents, the political parties, artistic and scientific cliques, men on "change," and last but not least, the advertising agencies and large individual advertisers.
>
> Each number of a great journal which appears to-day is a marvel of economic division of labour, capitalistic organization, and mechanical technique; it is an instrument of intellectual and economic intercourse, in which the potencies of all other instruments of commerce—the railway, the post, the telegraph, and the telephone—are united as in a focus. But our eyes can linger with satisfaction on no spot where capitalism comes into contact with intellectual life; and so we can take but half-hearted pleasure in this acquisition of modern civilization. It would indeed be difficult for us to believe that the newspaper in its present development is destined to constitute the highest and final medium for the supplying of news.[19]

A few years later Bücher attempted to define newspapers again when he addressed the role and function of the press in modern society.[20] He summarized the historical developments and suggested that newspapers as cultural phenomena arose from political needs to unite segments of society distributed over large areas, from commonly shared interests in events outside nationally or socially defined boundaries, and from the need to maintain and establish new social and economic relationships. Despite the establishment of different types of newspapers, such as mass-circulation or party newspapers, their organizations shared a common characteristic. They were enterprises "which produced advertising space as a commodity that could only be sold because of an existing editorial section."[21] With this definition Bücher emphasized the overriding economic interests that had changed newspapers into business-oriented, commercial organizations.

One of the noticeable trends in newspapers during the nineteenth century was the expansion of their coverage and the increase in editorial attention given to all spheres of social life. Thus, the output of news items created more interest among readers: *Wer vieles bringt, wird manchem etwas bringen* became the motto of the press.[22] This practice resulted in more subscribers and therefore more advertisers. Commenting upon the rise of independent mass-circulation newspapers, Bücher warned that they constituted also a national danger. He said, "The far-reaching influence makes them profitable objects of political, literary and speculative-financial corruption, and favorite hiding places for open or veiled advertising.[23] He criticized the developments in other European countries and suggested that the developments in Germany were neither unique nor more alarming than those abroad. The rise of newspaper monopolies and the domination of major news agencies by a few industrial interests were the results of modern technology. But Bücher added, "The modern means of communication, especially the telephone, wire services and correspondence bureaus, support this development which, without doubt, works to the advantage of maintaining depth and diversity of the national culture while it also prevents the rise of an all too powerful press oligarchy."[24]

Despite the growth of the press and the expansion of its coverage, Bücher felt that its effects as a cultural messenger were limited and of rather secondary importance. He followed Schäffle's ideas on this point and suggested that the press was a conduit, a transmission belt between the intellectual currents of the people and their leaders. The differences were that during earlier times newspapers provided these services for the administration; later they performed a similar task to satisfy intellectual demands, and most recently the press as a political propaganda organ exerted political and social influences. He said,

> The active, leading elements from whom those currents flow are found above, not inside the press. Editors and contributors do not fit into an independent, creative and leading role. They are organs of adaptation. . . . Their work is primarily one of moulding. They forge the metal which is discovered by the creative, intellectual work in politics, science, art and technology into small coins so that it may be circulated. They disperse the intellectual impulses, which emanate from political and cultural centers, among the masses and collect their reactions to return them to the centers of the intellectual movement.[25]

THE PRESS AND PUBLIC OPINION

In describing these processes and the role and functions of journalists, Bücher implicitly presented his ideas concerning public opinion. He saw the press as an organ of public opinion, involved in collecting and formulating ideas that originated with the people. At the same time, however, he acknowledged the possibility of newspaper influences upon public opinion. According to Bücher, the press could be used, for instance, to publicize judgments or ideas of individuals or groups as those reflecting the sentiments of the masses. He commented, "A well known trick of demagogy consists of presenting subjective ideas and special interests as ideas and interests of the people."[26]

It would be incorrect, however, to assume that the press created public opinion. Bücher differentiated between the existence of general sentiments and ideas which always existed in society, and dispositions that were based upon particular events. In the latter cases, the opinions of the people became "public" with their appearance in newspapers. He added that newspaper coverage often amplified those opinions, because journalists succeeded well in formulating and expressing these opinions most effectively. The ability to detect and describe the moods and opinions of the people, then, marked the success of the press.

Bücher stressed the importance of mass appeals in modern society and the necessity for capturing the masses in ways that would assure the stability of the economic, social, and political system. Although he recognized the importance—and effectiveness—of face-to-face communication, he was convinced that the press with its built-in capability of reaching the masses regularly and repeatedly with the same messages containing the same ideas and suggestions was more effective, and that its effects would be longer lasting. The results of massive, regular coverage of public events, and of editorial opinions and critical judgments were such that readers would begin to see newspaper stories as reflections of their own impressions of the world around them. Furthermore, the emphasis upon timeliness and competition for supplying news and opinion among daily newspapers prevented most readers from drawing their own conclusions. He explained that the reader

> has no time, to form his own judgment and to compare it to an independent judgment and to correct his own. Everything is pre-digested for him; news is mixed with judgments, opinions and feelings in each column, each small item in the newspaper. . . . Finally, a view presented by one or a few members of the press turns into a common view, a moral opinion into mass morality.[27]

Bücher felt that despite increasing education and the spread of knowledge the masses would remain incapable of making critical judgments concerning daily press coverage; on the contrary, the masses would follow newspaper leadership blindly, thus expressing their confidence in the press. Under these circumstances the press had to realize that the dangers of misleading the masses were great. Bücher added that the organization of the modern newspaper as a business enterprise with substantial financial investments provided an opportunity for profit-oriented publishers, for instance, to sell out to special interests or parties. In addition, he felt that the press might find it impossible anyway to resist financial and business interests which typically worked through the business pages of newspapers and through advertising.

On the other hand, Bücher described the positive aspects of the press in terms of its enormous amount of cultural and social information which could help bring nations closer together through mediated participation in aspects of societal life. Ideas and events became shared experiences and thus contributed to creating a common spirit. He added, "The fact that the newspapers attract everything that lends itself to arousing public interest, maintains and stimulates culture."[28] But again, he recognized dangers in the effectiveness and efficiency of the press as an interpreter of foreign customs and ideas. Bücher warned that the press could easily be used to aid special interest groups with hostile propaganda and defamation of national character. In an article written at the outset of World War I, he described these dangers more closely when he attacked the power of news agencies, in particular. Referring to the damage caused by the publication of one-sided materials over longer periods of time, Bücher called these attacks more vicious and serious than any attack on the battlefield. The large news agencies with their connections reaching around the world had access to many newspapers; their news dispatches were printed without criticism by most newspapers and thus contributed to the spread of public opinion through the activities of the wire services. He said, "The men who sit at the controls of the far-reaching press apparatus know only too well how critical the first impression of telegraphic news transmission is. They don't have to report falseties; in the manner in which they suppress disagreeable events and report what is favorable to them one finds a continuing influence upon public opinion in favor of their employers and against us."[29] Consequently, Bücher argued that international news agencies had prepared the way for the dissemination of lies and distortions that contributed to the general atmosphere of distrust; and he criticized the press systems everywhere for having neglected their duties to serve the truth and to fight attempts to manipulate news coverage in the press through censorship or monopoly ownership.

Since the press would always be forced to reduce contents of ideas and feelings to a level of common understanding for its readers, since superficiality was a by-product of the modern press and contemporary life, these dangers would always increase. Bücher observed that a generation grew up "which tastes everything but enjoys nothing in a leisurely manner, a general intellectual lethargy prevails that cannot be forced into alertness by even the most powerful typographical means" (for instance, sensational headlines).[30] He concluded that it came as no surprise when newspaper reading finally became a business; and he referred to clipping services that politicians and others had used as early as 1870 in England, and later in France and Germany. The steady demand for such services led to the establishment of an industry with branches all over Europe.

As a scholar and historian, Bücher recognized the importance of newspapers as sources of information. He argued that the press would constitute perhaps the most important source for future historians. They would be able to extract a sense of the cultural currents of the times quite accurately and minutely from copies of old newspapers if they would act with care and understanding. Newspaper archives and collections had been established in several countries, according to Bücher, who demanded that each country should designate one location where complete sets of newspapers would be collected and stored for future use. In this connection, Bücher commented upon the press as a means of continuing education and training throughout life. Although time consuming, competing against books, and overflowing with information, newspapers constituted the only reading material for many individuals. He observed,

> there is a large segment of the population which would have no opportunity to read without a newspaper, those subscribers of local newspapers, who will be enabled to participate, in a modest way to be sure, in the cultural exchange, and who are lifted above the drab routines of work and their narrow existence by the newspaper which guides them to see the events around them and which expands their vision.[31]

Again, there were disadvantages for others in such a system. The more educated members of society, for instance, would be prevented from reading other materials, notably books and magazines, because of the amount of daily information that was communicated by the press. Thus, many magazines tried to compete with the press for current information by publishing more frequently, monthly instead of quarterly editions, then weekly editions with more information, more articles competing for the same amount of space. Bücher mentioned that scholarly publications, too, had been affected by these developments and that monographs were becoming a mode of publication, replacing the book-length manuscript. He concluded, "Finally, the book as a form of publication will be preserved only in the compendium, the textbook, the encyclopedia and similar aids for scholarly education and professional work."[32] Bücher noted a similar trend among books of fiction. Here, too, magazines and newspapers replaced the book. Newspapers often acted as midwives for publishers who even waived prepublication rights for the press to run chapters or sections of books before they were available in print. Together with publicity pieces composed by the publishing houses they constituted the basis for much of what readers would ever know about these books. Bücher observed that book reviewers acted as agents for publishing houses to perform tasks that complemented the work of clipping services: "Contributors assume the professional task of reading books for the public and of furnishing extracts—the shorter the better."[33] Underlying most of these ideas was Bücher's main interest, the economic conditions of society and the way in which the press contributed to the welfare of society and to the maintenance of the economic system.

COMMERCIALISM AND PRESS REFORM

As a conduit, newspapers organized the stream of information into intelligible parts that provided the basis for the decision-making process and that contributed to an up-to-date knowledge about the world. Bücher was convinced that all kinds of information, not only purely economic or business-related news, helped create the necessary understanding for the reality of day-to-day activities. Science, technology, and politics were equally important sources for news coverage, along with stock market trends or industrial growth. Finally, Bücher recognized the necessity for advertising in newspapers. He called advertising a "child of the capitalistic age,"[34] which supported the diversity and amount of social communication through the press. Advertising revenues enabled publishers to improve their products and to reduce their prices. Although he recognized the dangers of subversion by economic interests, historical developments produced conditions which merged the demands for news and information with the demands for access to potential customers through advertising columns. Bücher added,

> One can always admit that the fantastic organization of political and economic news services could not have been accomplished without the rich resources of the advertising section, and that our newspapers would be less abundant, less educational, not as cheap and therefore less widely circulated without it. . . . The historical reality of combined public and private communication can hardly be changed, it does have the advantage of economic expediency.[35]

A few years later Bücher confronted the question of press reforms again in a number of publications. He maintained a position that editorial and advertising matters warranted separate considerations because of their different functions. Thus, newspapers served public interests in their news coverage, but private interests in there advertising columns. Bücher repeated his suggestion that editorial matter served to make space more attractive to the advertisers, and he came to the conclusion that "the editorial section is an annoying, expensive element of the organization, and it is carried only because without it there would be no subscribers leading to no advertisers. 'Public interests' are cared for by newspapers only in so far as they do not obstruct the profit motives of publishers."[36]

The dilemma of the press had been the subject of discussion and reform movements before. Karl Marx once proclaimed that the first freedom of the press is not to be a business, and others, including Schäffle, recognized the shortcomings of an emerging mass-circulation press without effective controls to protect the interest of the people in a free and open flow of communication. In an article about the future of the press in Germany, Bücher had mentioned the possibility of treating the press not unlike the railroads, another important transportation link in society, with the goal of nationalizing newspapers to achieve a separation from business interests. Later he developed a plan for the creation of advertising sheets under community control. These newspapers would be distributed free to households and would contain entertainment, some news, and other features. Bücher basically supported Ferdinand Lasalle, who had called for a separation of information and advertising functions of newspapers. In the context of his political commitments Lasalle had advocated that advertising be located in federal or communal registers or gazettes, since the corruption of the liberal press resulted from their involvement with advertisers. He explained,

> What has to be done simply is to separate two things that have nothing in common with each other anyway. As far as the press represents intellectual interests it can be compared to a public speaker or preacher . . . as far as it carries advertising it is a public announcer. . . . In a social-democratic state there must be a law which prohibits the publication of any advertisement by a newspaper, and which assigns advertisements to official gazettes published by the state or by communities.[37]

Along similar lines, Bücher developed his argument that capitalism had successfully organized intellectual energies to produce newspapers that could be exploited for commercial gains with effects also upon social and cultural aspects of life. Therefore, a system of communal advertising gazettes would help solve the problem. Bücher used the analogy of transportation in society to explain that

> advertising is a creation of transportation, like postal service, telephone and railroads and cannot be left in the hands of private concerns. The transfer of advertising to come under public administration follows considerations similar to those of the last generation in connection with

the nationalization of the railroads: it intends to protect the general
interest which is tied to transportation.[38]

Although none of these plans succeeded and questions of "socialization" or nationalization of the press were dropped, Bücher
had hoped that his proposals would help create a more responsible press and one that would be economically healthy.

Specifically, Bücher had drafted a bill for consideration and
possible adoption by the Bavarian legislature that would have
set up and maintained an official community press. He based his
proposal on the observation that the German press was basically
a local press and that the regulation of local advertising and
official announcements would provide a solid economic foundation for a community-oriented press system. He explained that
he had intended to create an advertising monopoly for the
benefit of counties instead of the state government. Such a plan
would have been consistent with the observation that most of
the advertising in the German press had a local character; thus,
local newspapers would be the logical choice for placing these
advertisements. At the same time, regional and national advertising could be continued in special publications; in no case would
the political press be allowed to carry advertising, however.
The size of the circulation as well as the frequency of publication
were to be determined by the size of the county. Bücher envisioned the free distribution of these newspapers. Since he realized
that the readership of a paper that carried only advertising and
official announcements would be low, he added an editorial
section, whose content would be divided between news agency
news and feature materials designed to educate and to entertain
readers. In order to reduce the production costs, all editorial
sections would be produced centrally and delivered to newspapers
in the form of readymade plates. These newspapers could reprint
announcements from other newspapers only after payment of set
fees, whereas announcements originating in their own counties
would be carried free of charge.

Bücher was aware of the consequences for the privately owned
press. He suggested that such newspapers would compete with

official newspapers for local information and feature materials, but that these newspapers could, in addition, carry more news and add their political component to the presentation of information. The privately owned newspapers would be significantly more expensive than they were before such a reorganization of the press; however, Bücher felt that the few who would want to continue reading such newspapers would be able to afford the higher price.

According to Bücher, transportation and transmission of information were forms created by society, and his proposal was designed to maximize these forms of communication for the benefit of the general public. He expressed less concern for private enterprise and profit motives of newspaper publishers than for the establishment of an independent forum that would serve the best interests of local communities. He said,

> The county would gain control over an area which belongs to it like public streets and water systems. The state would have the opportunity to achieve the best for the information and instruction of the population, who would breathe a sigh of relief if it could be freed from the pressure of a sensational and business-oriented press. What is new in the world would be communicated to the poorest household day after day; in addition, there would be advertisements to acquaint it with what could become economically useful, and its curiosity concerning local events would not remain unsatisfied. . . . It is obvious that whatever remains of the contemporary newspaper press would gain a new basis. Freed from the pressure of the business interests of the publisher, editorial staffs would represent their own convictions and have no other goal but to serve the common good.[39]

THE ROLE OF JOURNALISTS

Another and longer-lasting approach to the question of press reforms consisted of discussions about the role and function of journalists. Bücher commented upon the tremendous impact of the war on the press; and he saw the newspapers as central agents in the development of a modern, postwar society. he said, "The great upheaval of social values as a result of this war cannot go unnoticed, especially not by the daily press. With the tremendous influence it gained upon the intellectual life of peoples, it becomes a measure of their culture and a criterion for the development of future goals."[40] Journalists, then, had a major part in the shaping of the press, and although Bücher had often talked about their work in terms of providing messenger services between the leaders and the people, he did not underestimate the importance of this role. He added,

> One cannot think highly enough of the work of the genuine journalist. What an abundance of judgments, available knowledge, experience and political tact, presence of mind and humor, creative talent and word usage that are utilized each day by the press of a country; its amount is difficult to measure.[41]

At the same time, he realized that journalists often gave up careers as authors and writers and that their talents were wasted in exchange for the privilege of remaining in constant communication with large numbers of readers. He talked about power and influence that were connected with the position and the dangers of abuse that were ever-present.

According to Bücher, journalists occupied a profession that could be located between the functions of civil servants and businessmen. With the former the journalist "shares the necessity for a comprehensive education without the respect for the position with its built-in influence, title and social status. He is connected with the business world by his incorporation into a capitalistic enterprise without participating directly in its profit and in its success."[42]

Bücher also differentiated in his views of journalists as professionals between those employed by large newspaper operations and others, whose work was mainly confined to the small-town press. And he pointed out that between intellectually and morally qualified editors and those who occupied editorial positions on smaller papers were many individuals who depended upon the interests of their publishers. These interests, by the way, were often dealt with less awkwardly by journalists who did not have to represent them in signed articles. He added that

The qualification for the responsible profession of a journalist needs no legal proof, and there will be no one who would want to change this. But one must not overlook the dangers caused by this condition. This means, then, to close both eyes, when one talks of the profession of journalists and of obtaining special rights for it which are useless for the good ones, because they don't need them, anyway, and which can't be granted to the others, because there could be a danger of misusing them.[43]

Bücher attacked sharply the widely used anonymity which had a negative effect upon the moral and intellectual climate in newspapers, but which also made journalists dependent upon publishers. He argued for more signed articles, which would help identify good journalists who would build up their own circles of readers and move into positions that would make them more independent and critical of their newspapers. Bücher realized that journalism as a profession with a free access must have its drawbacks. Indeed, there were no laws or regulations that protected the individual journalist except his own ability to resist internal and external influences, and his own moral code. This was not a calling for weak or undetermined individuals. He said that this was not a course of action for just anyone, "especially not for those with weak characters, for individuals who can maintain their internal balance only in a secure, professional situation."[44] The continued pressures of daily routines destroyed many journalists, and Bücher added that it must surprise the observer to find that "despite all of it this class embraces a very large number of valuable and unique individuals, which outsiders would not guess easily."[45]

He did not support demands for regulating entry into the profession, however. Bücher felt that the German press situation was such that any attempt to develop a system of qualifications would fail in light of the diversity of types and economic conditions of newspapers. However, he strongly believed in a sound education for journalists, a topic that he discussed frequently. He told of suggestions from former colleagues, whose university education did not prepare them for newspaper careers, who argued that reporting and editing, for instance, could be learned to some degree in classroom situations; furthermore, courses dealing with the history, organization and problems of the press would help focus the attention of those students who intended to join editorial staffs of newspapers or magazines after graduation.

JOURNALISM EDUCATION

Initially, however, Bücher displayed a less passionate interest in the creation of a university-level program of journalistic studies than could be expected. He seemed to agree with some of the arguments, but he had observed the developments in Switzerland and the United States, and he did not like some of the results. For one, he was sure that an attempt to introduce journalism as a science would be met with skepticism if not hostility in the academic community. In his judgment, journalism was not a science; and the education of journalists could be accomplished only in connection with any of the established university disciplines and courses of study. He explained,

> Indeed, there is no such science. One may treat the history of newspapers as part of a general history of culture. One could organize facts about the organization and technology of the contemporary press. The political economist must try and understand the position of advertising in modern-day economics, and newspaper statistics cannot be ignored by cultural statisticians. But to form a special science of journalism out of these elements which satisfy the demands for the unity of such a system, is unnecessary and impossible.[46]

Still, he developed a curriculum for the education of journalists at the University of Leipzig, where an institute became the center for his program. His plan for such an experiment was based upon the idea that the university already provided a thorough education for social or natural scientists within the respective disciplines, and that a combination of disciplines together with a course of studies in journalism (*Zeitungskunde*) would be sufficient for the preparation of future journalists.

From available lectures and seminars, Bücher developed a catalogue of courses for students who wanted to specialize in political, business, or literary journalism. In addition, he instituted a foundation course and several specialized courses which would introduce students to the details of newspaper work. Specifically, the foundation course was designed to acquaint students with relevant source materials, the workings of the press system and a scientific treatment of the modern press. The specialized courses were conducted by practitioners. Bücher argued that "with the quick changes in newspaper technology only persons who benefit from immediate daily experience can teach useful aspects, while my own, older observations together with my scientific studies might be sufficient to organize the major course."[47]

The plan of studies issued by the University of Leipzig in 1916, for instance, stated that students of journalism needed a three-year university-level education the details of which were determined by the specialization of the individual students. The extensive curriculum reflected Bücher's own interest and education in history and political economy. Thus, the requirements for political journalists read like a comprehensive course of social science studies. Students had to enroll in a variety of courses as specified in the catalogue:

1. History (ancient, medieval, modern with special consideration given to contemporary events, cultural, social constitutional, economic history).

2. Political economy (general and special as well as economic policy), finance, history of political economy, social legislation, particularly labor questions, colonialism.

3. Statistics (history, technique and organization, population statistics, demographics, economic, moral and cultural statistics).

4. Geography (especially political and economic geography).

5. Administration.

6. Politics and government.

7. Jurisprudence (international law, constitutional administrative, press law).

In addition other courses in philosophy, literature and anthropology may be added depending upon special interests.[48]

Requirements for the other sequences were equally comprehensive and demanding. Students were encouraged to complete their studies with a Ph.D. degree in one of the disciplines of the philosophical faculty. There were no particular exit examinations at the institute. Courses to be directed by practitioners were decribed as:

A. introduction to the work of political editors
B. about style and technique of the *feuilleton*
C. about business journalism
D. about local and provincial editorial bureaus
E. about production and accounting
F. about press law, copyright, business law as it relates to publishing houses.[49]

Bücher concluded the description of the journalism program with a statement about the role and function of journalists in society. According to the plan of study, the University of Leipzig had demonstrated with this curriculum that the education of journalists was as important as that for other professionals, among them theologians, lawyers, and doctors. It stressed the fact that it provided solid guidelines for students who were to avoid prolonged studies, loss of time, and insecurity in the selection of appropriate coursework. According to Bücher, the University of Leipzig intended to provide "the means for the education of professional journalists, who will be able to stand up to the important tasks of the contemporary daily press in terms of scientific, technical and moral preparation."[50] In another context Bücher referred to the need for educated journalists who could help bring about peace and understanding among nations. He envisioned international cooperation among the press during the years following the war. In particular, he mentioned the dangers of monopoly holdings of press services like Reuters and Havas, which he considered official and thus biased sources of information and which were partly responsible for the war propaganda activities. Bücher thought that an international cooperative fashioned after the Associated Press organization in the United States would prevent the dissemination of government information. He also criticized British ownership of transatlantic cables and suggested international regulation which would neutralize this means of transmission. And finally, he thought that the education of journalists would lead to their recognition as serious and independent judges. He said, "The daily press must act as an incorruptible judge opposite individual parties as well as nations; otherwise it will lose its right to exist."[51] Bücher was convinced that the appropriate eduction within a university setting necessitated special courses and a curriculum that would recognize the importance of the profession. Despite the involvement of practitioners in the teaching of some courses, however, he was not willing to follow the example of U.S. schools of journalism with their practical approaches. He was afraid that some of those practices would support trends towards sensationalism, for instance, which he found undesirable for the German press. In this context he mentioned the work in editing courses in which students learned the art of writing headlines and said, "One can easily imagine how often truth and honesty are the losers."[52] Bücher hoped, on the other hand, that the establishment of university courses would aid students in finding their way to journalism as a career early enough while discouraging those "unsuited elements" who could recognize their mistake of selecting a course of studies for which they were not talented enough.[53] His concerns about the future of Germany's press system were expressed in his statements about the social role and function of the journalist as well as in his attempts to structure the education of journalists.

ANONYMITY AND PROFESSIONAL ETHICS

A factor that played a major role in discussions related to the position of journalists in society was the question of anonymity. Specifically, questions of professional integrity and freedom of the press were often related to the issues of identification and publicness of writers and their statements. Bücher, as was pointed out earlier, participated in these debates surrounding anonymity.

In a historical review of the principles of anonymous journalism, he wrote that, undoubtedly, "the principle of anonymity advanced across the continent from England, and that it gained ground with the spreading of representative government everywhere."[54] He explained that the acceptance of this principle was based upon the argument that the press represented an anonymous public opinion and, therefore, had to communicate ideas in just that manner. Thus, questions of freedom of the press and anonymity were seen not as contradictory elements but as necessary and related issues. The opposite would be true under a system which suggested an individual right of free expression that would carry with it a duty to publicly stand behind the statements.[55] Bücher argued that the trend towards anonymity in the communication process supported tendencies to be inaccurate, careless, and perhaps irresponsible in the writing process. He thought that anonymity could easily breed a kind of journalism that would not be respected by readers. Thus, in these cases "anonymity must lead necessarily to a superficial, uncritical treatment, which will attempt to hide the lack of expertise behind the use of slogans, which invites frivolous demagoguery, ignorant criticism after the fact, flippant, personally offensive polemics."[56] He observed the increasing amount of impersonal news communication, and he warned against the dangers of sinking to a level of mediocrity that would not be in the best interest of all concerned. In his *Memoirs* Bücher summarized his ideas about the ethics of journalism when he concluded, "There must never be a lack of awareness of speaking to a large circle of readers and of being responsible for their thought and desire in public matters."[57]

This statement suggested that Bücher believed in professional freedom and intellectual integrity of journalists as basic conditions for the exercise of their duties. Of course, there were constant threats to the development of professional responsibilities. Bücher had warned previously about the dangers of press concentrations. He was afraid that the results of economic pressures would convert newspapers to mass production enterprises that compiled information packages for the public. Journalists, therefore, who entered such organizations faced the possibility of becoming just minor functionaries in a larger system. He said,

> Joining an editorial staff is like entering a lion's den: many tracks lead into it, none of them leads out of it. The talent and competence of an editor is known to the publisher, and his professional fate continues to depend on him. He has no opportunity to distinguish himself: day after day his intellectual work disappears in the anonymous pulp of the news content. He slaves with his pen like the cottager with his hoe or sickle for the powerful squire. There is no advancement for him; and when he loses his position, he is lucky if he is allowed to start again someplace else.[58]

Bücher was convinced of the negative aspects that accompanied the use of anonymous articles in the press; at one point he thought that material which contained any names of persons should always be signed by the journalist. At the same time, however, he also agreed that there could be exceptional circumstances that warranted an anonymous approach to news writing. He explained,

> News and explanations, whose source or mediator have justified reasons to remain hidden, need not be excluded entirely. They would be able to continue appearing under the responsibility of the managing editor (and not of a strawman), but they should be limited to exceptional cases, in which the existence of a higher public interest in the publication should be demonstrated together with the fact that it could not be done in any other way.[59]

JOURNALISM AND POLITICAL ECONOMY

Despite Bücher's success as an organizer and defender of professional education of journalists within a university setting and as an investigator of press behavior, his major contributions were to be found in the context of political economy. Thus, the discussions of journalists and the press must be seen as part of his much broader attempt to explain the development of economic systems. He concluded that the rise of national economy with its growth of production and the creation of physical and political conditions that improved the communication among people also resulted in the establishment of the press.[60] From a historical perspective he noted that commercial communication had been highly developed already in the economic systems of primitive people, and could be identified with the beginning of any economic history. He added that this type of communication had "enjoyed the fullest development which we would naturally associate only with the highest culture, namely, the *communication of news*. It forms indeed the . . . kind of trade for which primitive peoples have created permanent organizations. We refer to the courier service and the contrivances for sending verbal messages."[61] Bücher then went on to describe the elaborate system creating symbolic signs and means for the transmission of intelligence in a number of primitive societies.

Another, related concept that was central to the study of human evolution was imbedded in the idea of mobility. Bücher thought that migration provided a key to the explanation of social, economic, and cultural history. He said,

> Each fresh advance in culture commences, so to speak, with a new period of wandering. The most primitive agriculture is nomadic, with a yearly abandonment of the cultivated area; the earliest trade is migratory trade; the first industries that free themselves from the household husbandry and become the special occupations of separate individuals are carried on itinerantly. The great founders of religion, the earliest poets and philosophers, the musicians and actors of past epochs are all great wanderers. Even to-day, do not the inventor, the preacher of a new doctrine, and the virtuosi travel from place to place in search of adherents and admirers—notwithstanding the immense recent development in the means of communicating information?[62]

With the continued advancement of society, producers of goods became stationary, however, and Bücher added that "the Thespian carts and the resident theatre mark the starting and the terminal points of this evolution."[63] As a result, the amount of fixed capital grew and affected the conditions for economic development. In recognizing "capital as the creative influence in modern national economy,"[64] Bücher suggested the importance of the entrepreneur in modern society. He added,

> To-day the entrepreneur determines what we shall eat and drink, read
> in the papers and see at the theatre, how we shall lodge and dress. That
> means everything. For a great part of the goods we consume the right
> of self-determining is taken away. And since uniform production on a
> large scale is most advantageous to the manufacturer, there is operative
> in the sphere of *consumption* an increasingly active *uniforming pro-
> cess.*[65]

In this connection, finally, the question of advertising occupied
a central position in Bücher's discussion of the role and function
of the press and the contributions of journalists to what he
basically considered a business enterprise. Bücher noted in
passing that the social sciences so far had neglected advertising
as a modern phenomenon, and he reported about the efforts of
the German Foreign Office to collect samples of advertising
messages from many countries to be published in collections
that could yield valuable raw data for the researcher.

Bücher defined advertising as a tool of a general, social selection process through which individuals seek to obtain success,
while camouflaging their intentions with suggestions that their
efforts will benefit the general public. Bücher stated quite em-
phatically that deception was part of the definition. He described,
in particular, the attempts to present advertising messages in
the form of news stories which easily convey the impression of
being editorial matter and thus trustworthy. He exluded display
advertising and other matters clearly identified as advertisements.
Bücher described also the similarities between advertising and
propaganda, but suggested that the goals were different ones:
"Propaganda wants to recruit followers for an idea or institution,
but it precludes efforts to obtain material gains. Advertising,
on the other hand, always serves to obtain customers and through
them an increase in profits."[66] He traced advertising from the
economic conditions of the Middle Ages, where it rested in the
personal relationship between producers and consumers of
goods, to modern times. The early period was characterized by
Bücher as an era that emphasized the "production" of customers
and that continued until the liberation of trade and commerce.
With it began the era of the production of goods which separated

customers from producers and demanded a new form of communication through which both parties could meet to satisfy their needs. Later, and throughout the current age of mass production, producers were separated from consumers by distributors and individual sales outlets. As a result, personal ties no longer existed and the moral responsibility which had also characterized the relationship between production and consumption disappeared from the marketplace.

Advertising became fully recognized as a means of communication when other means of distribution of goods were insufficient. Bücher offered a system of studying advertising that was based on five categories: retail sales, outdoor, indoor, newspaper, and demonstration. Under each of these headings he considered, in succession, the custom of marking prices on sales items in stores, outdoor advertising in all its forms, advertising in closed spaces, newspaper advertisements in all kinds of print publications, and live demonstrations of goods and descriptions of articles and their usefulness.

He maintained that the press had come to depend on advertising to a point where the periodical press would not be able to exist, because production costs would be too high to guarantee a reasonable price and a profit for the publisher. Advertising provided the necessary subsidy and thus ensured the continuation of the press. Bücher added that publishers sell to advertisers not only white space and a percentage of the printing costs, but also the power inherent in a printed and published periodical.

We may like it or not, according to Bücher; advertising is here to stay: "It is a necessary component of the capitalistic system of economy and who can say whether it will not survive that system?"[67] Thus, it must be pointed out that consumers benefit from the disclosure of information in advertisements that emerge from the free enterprise system and that let them participate in all aspects of economic progress. On the other hand, he recognized that advertising helped raise the amount of capital necessary to enter and remain in business and that it seemed to have promoted the rise of big business. Nevertheless, Bücher saw advertising as a historical necessity; its development was unavoidable, and he suggested that "it is unproductive to get excited about it."[68]

Bücher provided by far the most extensive discussion of the press in modern times. Obviously influenced by Schäffle, he began to formulate the practical consequences of such theoretical views, and he offered possible solutions to the dilemma of contemporary newspapers, including the education and training of journalists. The press as a cultural phenomenon created by the social and political needs of society was, at the same time, also an economic enterprise that sold space as a commodity and identified with the business community. Bücher addressed himself to the resulting effects upon editors and journalists that tested their personal integrity and raised questions about professional responsibility. He clearly recognized the dangers of abuse by economic and political powers, and he supported ideas suggesting a separation of advertising and news functions of newspapers. As an economist, he was never in doubt about the historical necessity of advertising and commercial messages as an outcome of general economic developments; at the same time, however, he argued that only a press that featured an independent and undiminished news function could contribute to the well-being of the people and to the advancement of society. Bücher realized the need for a continued study of the press as one of the most important institutions in modern society, but he refused to argue for the establishment of a separate, scientific discipline. Although he brought an economic perspective to his work about the press, with his interest in social communication he established a broad framework for the study of the press as a determinant of social, economic, and cultural movements.

NOTES

1. *Arbeit und Rhythmus* (Leipzig: B. G. Teubner, 1909).

2. Reprinted in Karl Jaeger, *Von der Zeitungskunde zur publizistischen Wissenschaft* (Jena: Verlag von Gustav Fischer, 1926), 103-106.

3. Karl Bücher, "Zeitungsstatistik für das Deutsche Reich im Jahre 1885 und 1906," *Bulletin d l'Institut International de Statistique* 17 (1908).

4. Gerhard Muser, *Statistische Untersuchung über die Zeitungen Deutschlands 1885-1914* (Leipzig: Emmanuel Reinicke, 1918). This was the first volume of a series edited by Karl Bücher under the title *Abhandlungen an dem Institut für Zeitungskunde an der Universität Leipzig.*

5. *Unsere Sache und die Tagespresse* (Tübingen: J.C.B. Mohr, Paul Siebeck, 1915), 67.

6. Karl Bücher, *Industrial Evolution* (New York: Henry Holt, 1901). The translation by Morley S. Wickett is based upon Bücher's third edition of *Die Entstehung der Volkswirtschaft* (Tübingen: Laupp'sche Buchhandlung, 1898).

7. "The Genesis of Journalism," *Industrial Evolution*, 215.

8. Ibid., 216.

9. Ibid., 217.

10. Ibid., 218.

11. Ibid., 230.

12. Ibid., 238.

13. Ibid., 239.

14. Ibid.

15. Ibid., 240.

16. Ibid.

17. Ibid., 241.

18. Ibid., 242.

19. Ibid., 242-243.

20. "Ursprung und Begriff der Zeitung," *Gesammelte Aufsätze zur Zeitungskunde* (Tübingen: Laupp'sche Buchhandlung, 1926).

21. Ibid., 21.

22. Ibid.

23. Ibid., 52.

24. Ibid.

25. Ibid., 53.

26. Ibid.

27. Ibid., 55.

28. Ibid., 57.

29. *Unsere Sache,* 13.

30. "Ursprung," 57.

31. Ibid., 59

32. Ibid., 60.

33. Ibid., 61.

34. Ibid.

35. "Das Zeitungswesen," in Paul Hinneberg, ed., *Die Kultur der Gegenwart, ihre Entwicklung und ihre Ziele* (Berlin: B. G. Teubner, 1912), 530.

36. *Zur Frage der Pressreform* (Tübingen: J.C.B. Mohr, Paul Siebeck, 1922), 12.

37. Excerpt from *Die Feste, die Presse und der Frankfurter Abgeordnetentag,* quoted in Otto Groth, *Die Zeitung* (Mannheim: J. Bensheimer, 1930), III, 335.

38. Quoted in Otto Groth, *Die Geschichte der deutschen Zeitungswissenschaft, Probleme und Methoden,* (München: Buchverlag Dr. Konrad Weinmayer, 1948), 291-292.

39. Bücher, *Gesammelte Aufsätze*, 426-427. The bill, as drafted by Bücher, and as reprinted in Bücher's *Gesammelte Aufsätze*, 416-418, read as follows:

§1. In each county with a population of 2,500 the county government must issue a county newspaper, which will be disseminated without delay, free of charge to all households.

§2. The county newspaper appears in counties with populations between 2,500 and 5,000 at least twice weekly, between 5,000 and 10,000 at least four times a week, over 10,000 daily.

§3. The county newspaper has the exclusive right to publish state and communal announcements as well as all private advertising. Newspapers which are published privately are forbidden to engage in the printing of any kind of advertisement.

§4. The rate for advertisements is to be determined by local customs, and it must not exceed the linage rate of newspapers published previously in the town.

§5. Besides advertisements each county newspaper contains an editorial part which must be confined to the reproduction of the latest news and to instructional and entertaining articles. Any contributions aimed at spreading political influence are categorically excluded. It is permitted, however, to accept local news.

The content of the editorial part as well as the state announcements are delivered to the counties in time for the printing of the newspaper and in the form of boiler plates and readyprint materials.

Contributions regarding county affairs must be accepted any time and, in as much as they do not contain punishable material, be printed in the next edition.

§6. Advertisements of local significance are offers and demands for goods and labor as well as family advertisements, announcements of all kinds of presentations and meetings in town.

§7. All official newspapers published by private persons cease publication on. . . .

§8. Persons who are not county residents may receive the county newspaper through the mail and after payment of a subscription fee which must reflect the production costs. Also, several small communities may combine for the publication of a community newspaper with the permission of the regional government.

§9. The reprinting of official announcements and news that appear in the county newspaper by other newspapers is allowed only with the permission of the county governments and after payment of a reasonable fee.

§10. Those who act against the regulations of this law, will be fined up to . . . marks and in the case of a repeated violation will face a jail sentence of not less than one month.

40. *Die deutsche Tagespresse und die Kritik* (Tübingen: J.C.B. Mohr, Paul Siebeck, 1915), 106.

41. "Ursprung," 62.

42. Bücher, "Die Anonymität in den Zeitungen," *Gesammelte Aufsätze*, 147.

43. Ibid., 143.

44. As quoted in Groth, *Die Zeitung*, I, 157.

45. Ibid.
46. *Unsere Sache*, 66-67
47. Ibid., 68.
48. As reprinted in Jaeger, *Von der Zeitungskunde*, 103.
49. Ibid., 106.
50. Ibid.
51. *Unsere Sache*, 63.
52. Ibid., 49.
53. Ibid., 70.
54. "Die Anonymität in den Zeitungen," 110.
55. Groth, *Die Zeitung*, IV, 185.
56. Ibid., 190 (citing Bücher).
57. *Lebenserinnerungen* (Tübingen: Laupp'sche Buchhandlung, 1919), 231.
58. "Die Anonymität in den Zeitungen," 146.
59. Ibid., 159.
60. "Volkswirtschaftliche Entwicklungsstufen," in Karl Bücher, E. Heimann, E. von Philippovich, J. Schumpeter, *Grundriss der Sozialökonomik*, I. Abteilung, 1. Teil (Tübingen: J.C.B. Mohr, Paul Siebeck, 1924), 14.
61. *Industrial Evolution*, 77.
62. Ibid., 347.
63. Ibid., 348.
64. Ibid., 310.
65. Ibid.
66. Bücher, "Die Reklame," *Gesammelte Aufsätze*, 243.
67. Ibid., 256.
68. Ibid., 263.

5

The Mirror of Society

Ferdinand Tönnies on the Press
and Public Opinion

TÖNNIES: A BIOGRAPHICAL NOTE

Ferdinand Tönnies (1855-1936) showed a life-long interest in the study of social and political problems; he was equally committed to securing the place of sociology in the university setting. His major contribution, however, was his work in theoretical sociology which began with the publication of *Gemeinschaft und Gesellschaft* in 1887.

Tönnies was born in Schleswig-Holstein and studied at the universities of Jena, Leipzig, Bonn, Berlin, and Tübingen between 1871 and 1877. He acquired an extensive background in philosophy, history, ancient languages, and archeology before he concentrated his studies in the social sciences. His *Habilitationsschrift* in 1881 qualified him for a university-level teaching position; but he was not appointed until 1913 when he joined the faculty at the University of Kiel, Germany. At that time he had already published several works, including *Gemeinschaft und Gesellschaft* (1887) and *Die Sitte* (1909), and Hobbes' *Leben und Lehre* (1896). Tönnies resigned after three years to devote his time completely to his studies and to writing for scholarly and popular journals. His second major work, *Kritik der öffentlichen Meinung,* was published in 1922, one year after he had returned to a teaching position at Kiel. The completion of his third major work, *Einführung in die Soziologie,* fell into this period. It appeared in

1931, two years before he was forced to resign from his duties as a result of Hitler's rise to power. At that time he also relinquished his position as president of the *Deutsche Gesellschaft für Soziologie,* the German sociological association he had founded together with a number of colleagues, among them Georg Simmel, Max Weber, and Werner Sombart.

His philosophical studies had led Tönnies to the writings of Thomas Hobbes, Herbert Spencer, and August Comte. He had become interested in the organismic theories of both Spencer and Albert Schäffle, which had stimulated his curiosity about the biological sciences; he also took a great interest in philosophy of law, particularly as represented by Rudolph v. Jhring and Sir Henry Maine. Hobbes' writings on law and government and Karl Marx through *Das Kapital* became major influences upon his scholarly thought and writing. Accepting the secularized concept of natural law and recognizing the importance of economic aspects of social life, Tönnies formed his own approach to the study of society. He concluded from his study of the meaning of natural law that "what is social emanates from human willing, from the intention to relate to each other, a together-willing *(Zusammenwollen),* as it were; and I set myself the task of penetrating to the essence of this willing."[1] At the same time, Tönnies accepted the basic ideas of historical materialism. But he proposed a sociological rather than an economic explanation of society, because economics, in his way of thinking, could not be identified with the well-being of individuals or of community, that is to say, with essential will.

According to Tönnies, sociology must be divided into general and special sociology; the former describes the study of human relationships and coexistence with approaches through social biology or social psychology, whereas the latter is divided into pure sociology, applied sociology, and empirical sociology.

Pure sociology, in turn, deals with the basic concepts of *Gemeinschaft* and *Gesellschaft,* the theory of social entities, the theory of social norms, the theory of social values, and the theory of social structures of institutions. Tönnies based the subdivisions of pure sociology on social entity as the underlying concept of the system. He explained that social entity is "that which is not directly experienced; it must be seen and comprehended through the medium of the common thought and will of those individuals who are part of such an entity and who designate it."[2]

Tönnies insisted that *Gemeinschaft* and *Gesellschaft* are fundamental concepts which help define types of human existence. He said,

> The meaning of these concepts is that all relations among people as well as the derived relations of social corporations with individuals and with each other, even the relations between men and their gods, which like social entities are products of their imagination—all these complexes of positive relations which constitute a bond among men—(*vinculum*) have a twofold origin: either man's essential will or his arbitrary will.[3]

Tönnies understood *Gemeinschaft* as based upon essential will with its roots in feelings, habits, and beliefs, and *Gesellschaft* as built upon arbitrary will as an artificial, deliberate, or conscious act. With this description, he not only tried to depict the full range of human existence, but also attempted to offer a new way of understanding the origin and growth of Western society.

The reasons for the division of sociology, as explained by Tönnies, are to be found in methodological differences; for him "pure sociology is constructive, applied sociology is deductive, and empirical sociology is inductive."[4] In addition, he saw differences between pure and applied sociology also in the fact that the former "restricts itself to the study and description of a social entity as static, that is, in the state of rest, [whereas] the applied sociology is throughout concerned with the dynamics, or the state of motion, of social entities."[5]

Differences between applied and empirical sociology hinge upon the question of method; in the latter there is the suggestion of an integration of an inductive empirical social research method into the need for concept formation and theory building. Tönnies saw that the first task of empirical sociology was to describe and analyze specific rather than general social phenomena. Thus, he advocated a study of facts and their relationships based upon true insights and knowledge of the subject matter. He proposed, for instance, that "for empirical sociological studies, our own country in which we were born and reared will always present itself intellectually as the nearest and most easily penetrable subject, not considering emotional attachment."[6]

In this quest for understanding the social environment, Tönnies felt that empirical sociology must, indeed, utilize a variety of analytical methods. He said that "a science cannot emerge from mere application of a particular method. If the description of social reality is the object of such a science, then every available means of analysis ought to be utilized."[7] Thus, Tönnies advocated the use of quantitative as well as qualitative methods in empirical sociology.

His studies of contemporary problems (e.g., crime, suicide, strikes) serve as an example of how empirical sociology can be used in understanding social conditions and in providing a basis for critical judgment and correction of social ills. Also, this work reflects the continuing interest of Tönnies in his social and political environment and his engagement as a concerned social scientist who hoped to bring new insights to the task of improving social conditions in Germany. Given this commitment, Tönnies joined the Social Democratic Party in the wake of Hitler's rise to power as a demonstration of his own position, his political ideas, and, perhaps, as an example for others to step forward and be recognized as an opponent of the regime. His political activities which he had avoided previously to protect his scholarly work now surfaced on many occasions. The following excerpt from an open letter published in a Kiel newspaper describes his position and reveals the intensity of his reaction to the rise of Nazism in Germany.

> I am speaking to you, my dear compatriotes, as an old man. An old man is an experienced man and experience means a great deal in politics. . . .
> This NSDAP is a party that does not want to be a party, yet necessarily must be one. It is a party whose leader is a foreigner who does not know anything about our problems. He is a man distinguished by unclear enthusiastic thinking, based on *ignorance of reality,* a man who in his feeble mind imagines that he can solve problems some of which the best minds of the nation have worked on for centuries, on

many of them certainly during the last hundred years; it is a party whose final goal could be nothing but *an irreparable disruption of all social conditions.* . . .

Adolf Hitler talks foolishly as one who does not know a thing about the nature and causes of this catastrophe of the capitalist economic system. In his ignorance he dares putting the blame on the German working class and on the party which represents the rights and interests of the German workers.

The NSDAP is a party that *promises everything to everybody* in such a way that what has been promised to one makes impossible promises given to others; it is party which substitutes *deliberate disregard of truth,* massive errors and blind emotions for rational thought.

In brief, it is a party to which a thinking person, particularly a politically thinking person, cannot commit himself.[8]

In the course of his life Tönnies commented repeatedly and extensively on the role and function of the press in society. The following section relies most heavily, however, on his remarks in connection with his work which appeared in *Gemeinschaft und Gesellschaft* and in *Kritik der öffentlichen Meinung,* a book that became an important contribution to the literature on the press and public opinion as it developed through the activities of a number of university institutes which devoted their work to the science of the press (*Zeitungswissenschaft*).

SOCIAL SIGNS, LANGUAGE, AND COMMUNICATION

Tönnies based his contributions to a theory of communication and public opinion, in particular, on the notion that social phenomena are products of human thought and will. Thus, knowledge, whether scientific or common, is based upon experience and recall facilitated by language, which is a "fixation in memory." He confronted the issues of communication, for instance, with his description of ideal and spiritual values, in which common language, together with "native customs and habits," becomes a particular social value; and with his emphasis on social signs, he distinguished among signs standing for social values, purposive signs, and symbols, and stressed that meaning and validity of signs are their most valuable property.

Specifically, to the signs standing for social values "belongs language as a system of signs for the ideal value of mutual understanding and the capability to communicate; further, writing, including printing, as a sign of signs. Finally, all the so-called value symbols are included here, the most important of which is money."[9] Included in the category of purposive signs are those signs "for the will that something should be or should be done. They are differentiated according to the norms which indicate what ought to be. Consequently, we have signs of valid order, valid law, valid morality."[10] Finally, symbols, according to Tönnies, are "signs expressed in words, actions, or objects, denoting in a more specific sense relations, situations, or norms which are understood either as existing, that is, having validity, or as desirable, that is, signs which ought to have validity.[11] He added that those signs could be determined or conditioned by essential or arbitrary will.

Tönnies returned to the discussion of signs and symbols in his *Einführung in die Soziologie,* in which he gave an elaborate and rather precise formulation of these concepts, conveying the idea, also, of the importance and significance of social signs as a type of social value. He stressed differences between individual signs, sense perceptions and memories, and social signs.

A sign, according to Tönnies, "is what is effective as a sign. One concludes from signs that something exists, or used to exist, or is going to exist."[12] Whether natural or artificial, signs must remain individual signs as long as they are not commonly shared. They can become social signs only "by serving several individuals, on the basis of a quality which is commonly known and serviceable to these several individuals, in such a way that it has the same effect on all participants, that it is understood and consequently correctly interpreted by all."[13] And he added that only "a social will creates social signs."[14] Given this approach to the study of signs, language became the most important system of social signs used for mutual understanding and developed from individual signs "through imperceptible changes and through gradual growth."[15] Language as a way of participating in the community rested upon shared experience and interpretation. The use of language also led to the question of social norms. He stated that "comparable to individual orders or commandments, social regulations may be made known not only through the general system of language but also by means of special signs, the meaning of which is mutually familiar."[16]

Signs can be defined as signals, documents, and symbols. Tönnies described artificial signs as examples of signals which are easily perceived accoustically or optically while remaining clear and distinct at the same time. He referred to international code books, for instance, which contain signals that are universally understood among seafarers, but he also included examples of communication in ciphers or coded dispatches to safeguard information.

The assertion of authority and proof of its validity are connected with the use of distinct signs, or certain forms, "and these forms in spoken or written words which have become formulae are the signs for the validity of such decisions."[17] Tönnies pointed out that documents, for instance, "are testimonials, and testimonials, written or oral, serve as proof of facts, especially of such facts that are chiefly facts of validity and therefore not provable by means of visible or other sensual evidence."[18] Again, he raised the question of communication in the context of social norms when he talked about signs of domination and signs of servitude, the promise of an oath, and the consequences of these acts. Commandments and prohibitions, for instance, involve communication, that is, the use of language for the purposes of prescribing what shall or shall not happen. They may be seen as attempts of restricting human freedom "to move or to induce someone to do or not to do something by means of words, spoken, written, or expressed in some other way. Words may be supported by actions, their influences strengthened, under certain circumstances even substituted, by means of gestures."[19] Since social norms are based upon forms of will, public opinion as a societal form of will plays a major role in the definition of individual and common goals. Tönnies proposed that public opinion is, in fact, "a common will which exercises critical judgment for the sake of a common interest and thereby affects 'private' forms of conduct and action in either a restraining or furthering manner."[20] Thus, the connections between language, signs as documents, and forms of will are important for the understanding of social norms.

Finally, he addressed the symbol as a social sign. He said, "These are visible signs represented by certain objects whose significance is to be understood in such a way that they indicate something that cannot be designated or expressed directly, especially if it must not be mentioned in words."[21] He suggested that symbols claim enhanced value, in particular, when communication with invisible or unreal beings is involved. Thus, "religious symbols cause a pious shudder in the heart."[22] Tracing the Greek origins of the word *symbol*, he concluded that in the origin of the word itself "is an element of something that secretly binds persons; hence it gained its significance that made it develop its particular religious connotation."[23] Tönnies mentioned other examples of symbols, without religious significance, that are used for "decoration," often by an authority or the state to encourage individuals or commend them for various activities. He observed that these social signs "always retain their significance in a centralized order, therefore chiefly in the army and similarly regulated large administrative bodies where order is definitely based on superordination and subordination, hierarchically descending from the chief to the private."[24]

Since these social signs are important, he warned of the danger for a democratic system that deemphasizes or abolishes these "decorations," because such decisions may increase the possibility of losing cooperation and control over individuals and groups in society.

Tönnies suggested the important nature of public opinion as well as the close relationship between press and public opinion as early as in his discussion of forms of "Concerted Will, Commonwealth, and States" in his *Community and Society*. Specifically, he indicated the importance of communication as a process through which public opinion will confront the individual. He said, "Such encounter is mainly brought about through that kind of communication wherein all human relationship, faith and trust between speaker and teacher on one side and listener and disciple on the other, is, or at least can be, effaced: the literary communication."[25]

As a matter of fact, a substantial amount of his writings concerning communication, however, was devoted to the question of the role and function of public opinion, its evolution and interpretation as an expression of the collective will.

THE CONCEPT OF PUBLIC OPINION

In his *Kritik der öffentlichen Meinung* Tönnies examined and explained the concept of public opinion; he explored the historical-political dimensions of the term, and he described different states of public opinion throughout the development of civilization. In his treatment of the concept he suggested that public opinion be separated from analyses of popular feelings and beliefs and discussed as a form of the social will. Tönnies specifically mentioned the close relationship between religion and public opinion, which he regarded as sources of strength that could unite society internally and that exemplified a will binding on members of society and often expressed as moral indignation and intolerance towards those with different ideas.[26] Finally, he provided some applications of his theoretical work on public opinion which he had actually begun much earlier.

Tönnies agreed with the general notion that public opinion was a hard-to-define concept, and he added that "it is more convenient to determine what it appears to be, to find what it is believed to be rather than what it *is*."[27] He described it as an apparent power in societal life; the belief that public opinion is "strong and forceful," however, also suggested the possibility that this "belief has become part of public opinion itself."[28] Commenting upon the lack of theoretical considerations by those who make judgments about public opinion, Tönnies observed that decisions were made on the basis "that there are certain signs by which public opinion can be recognized."[29] Specifically, such recognition occurred by what was heard, seen, and read, according to a general belief. Tönnies argued against such a simplified and overconfident approach to the description of public opinion. He warned that what can be heard, seen, and read was frequently misleading and that it often resulted in wrong judgments.

In his discussion of the concept and theory of public opinion, Tönnies traced the idea of public opinion from individual to collective expressions, differentiating, finally, among six forms of collective will under the aspects of community and society and noting varying degrees of complexity. He summarized the major points of his approach under the following categories:[30]

A. (Community)	B. (Society)
(a) understanding, (b) tradition, (c) faith	(d) contract, (e) norm, (f) doctrine
(aa) concord, (bb) custom, (cc) religion	(dd) convention, (ee) legislation, (ff) public opinion

Tönnies stressed the interdependence and relationships of these forms of collective and social wills; and he presented their existence as a description of the historical process: namely, the change from community to society when forms of the collective will also change. Thus, convention took the place of concord, customs were replaced by legislation, and public opinion replaced religion. He indicated that this was the process that marked the change from culture to civilization.[31]

Tönnies made a further distinction in his discussion of public opinion when he introduced three major states of aggregation which characterize individual as well as social opinions. Following the example of the natural sciences, he recognized the existence of solid, fluid, and gaseous states of public opinion.[32] He drew on the social-economic, political-legal, and intellectual-moral realms of society—often in a comparative way—to demonstrate the differences among these states of public opinion.

As a result, *solid* public opinion must be understood as a steadfast conviction of a public which represents a people or even a larger circle of civilized men. Thus, the ideas of personal and economic freedom, forms of government, and rationality *(Vernünftigkeit)* served as examples of solidity that typified aspects of modern European society. They also described the foundation of the social, political, and economic order that prevailed at that time.

The state of *fluid* public opinion, according to Tönnies, could also be understood as short-lived public opinion, made for the day, and therefore less stable since it was also formed without the support of solid public opinion. Instead, this type of public opinion was to be seen as consisting of partial opinions, formed, joined, and generalized often in opposition to the solid public opinion. Examples in this category could be described as contemporary issues: questions about attitudes toward work and women in the labor force, ideas concerning the rise of a constitutional monarchy, juvenile delinquency, and problems of a lax morality regarding positions taken vis-à-vis prostitution or fraudulent politicians.

The *gaseous (ephemere)* public opinion has several characteristics. According to Tönnies, it is highly unstable; it appears and disappears because it frequently changes the objects of its attention. It could be observed in cities like Paris, an example of an urban society where public attention was easily distracted and shifted from one subject to be focused on something else. This type of public opinion is also fast moving and hastily established. In addition, rapid and regular transportation and communication changed countries into urban societies where news could be circulated in a very short time. Consequently, this kind of public opinion was superficial, since it had to rely on speed; it also lacked the thoroughness that comes with proper study and evaluation. Thus, news must appear incorrect and unreliable, if not completely false to readers. This type of public opinion must be seen as credulous and uncritical, filled with prejudices, often persistent, and always affected by the events of the day. But still, not unlike public opinion in solid or fluid states, it would emerge as acting in support of the generally accepted social and moral framework.[33]

Tönnies argued that the degree of solidity of public opinion determined the degree of its unanimity.[34] His discussion of the various states of public opinion provided a way of distinguishing between highly influential (solid) and minimally effective (gaseous) public opinions and the possibility of change from one state to another; it allowed for a categorization of a wide variety of social, political, and economic activities which were commonly grouped indiscriminately under the label of public opinion, although they may have differed in strength and endurance.

Religion as a system of dogmas and cultural forms was an essential component of Tönnies' theory of public opinion. The idea of public opinion as a phenomenon which changed through states of aggregation from gaseous through fluid to solid forms approached ideally, at least, the concept of religion when it appeared firmly settled and as a widely accepted *Weltanschauung*. Both religion and public opinion are expressions of the social will, binding upon those who come under their influence, and equally determined in their rejection of opposing ideas. Also, both could be described in terms of their states of aggregation because religion, too, embraces a number of conditions, describing various degrees of depth or firmness of the religious belief.[35] Religion, rooted in the tradition of a people, in common experiences, and based upon the belief in an absolute truth, represented an earlier stage of human development, according to Tönnies, whereas public opinion rose from an era of criticism and rational thought and a belief in the age of science[36] which diminished and even negated the influence of theological or religious opinions. The Church and its priests were replaced as spiritual leaders when public opinion emerged under the leadership of scientists as teachers and as the "natural and real leaders of public opinion, directly, and even more so indirectly, insofar as their thoughts, research, and teaching covered or were related to questions of general significance."[37]

The future of religion, according to Tönnies, is tied to the future of public opinion, which he saw as developing into a universal *Weltanschauung* that stressed a belief in mankind. Incorporating the ideals of religiosity, public opinion could move a step closer to a world religion. Tönnies cited the recognized need for improved economic conditions, for instance, as a way of lifting the spirit of the people *(Volksgeist).* Social reform was a necessary condition; and Tönnies observed in this connection that "public opinion does not yet risk to accept 'socialism,' but it does no longer dare rejecting it."[38]

In his examination of public opinion Tönnies elaborated on a variety of essential elements in the communication process. He recognized the importance not only of signs but also of audience characteristics, message construction, communicator functions, and roles of the mass media, e.g., books and newspapers.

Specifically, Tönnies distinguished between mute and audible signs, which express intellectual and emotional states and are capable of communicating thoughts and feelings to others. Audiences were defined as consisting of a number of people sharing a particular space and, although different in many ways, acting united in their specific interests in the event. Large audiences *(grosses Publikum),* on the other hand, were described as people who think and judge alike, but who do not gather in a given place, although they may be heard. Tönnies thought of the world of educated individuals and political publics which are united by their knowledge and by information disseminated through the mass media. Messages, which were described by Tönnies as pictoral, oral, or written, form specific audiences which respond as a unit.

THE PRESS, NEWS, AND PUBLIC OPINION

Tönnies depicted writers and thinkers as communicators whose opinions create different kinds of followers; while creative writers and poets expressed ideas that often had an enduring quality regardless of the circumstances of their creation, philosophical and scientific works could be short-lived and characterized as expressions of particular places and times. But in all cases, books and newspapers served as vehicles for these ideas and could become weapons in the hands of political forces. Tönnies specifically pointed to the power of the press in social and political affairs, and he suggested that the "tremendous power [of the press] may become fully transparent in this [*the twentieth*] century."[39]

In a section entitled "News and the Public" Tönnies continued his discussion of communication as a social phenomenon, using a dichotomous approach to explain communication differences in community and society. He suggested that opinions, dogmas, and beliefs were transmitted in community settings by those interested in the continuation of certain traditions which were considered necessary for the survival of the group. There existed a spirit of cooperation and of common ideals which not only embraced contemporaries but also united generations within a community. Thus, community could be defined in terms of a hierarchical communication structure through which information was passed to those "inferior," e.g., younger or less experienced in the ways of life. In a modern societal context, on the other hand, the communication structure was manipulated by the conditions of equality, e.g., equal rights and equal status. As a result, information, opinion, and knowledge now were passed on by everyone. Tönnies suggested that authority was replaced by the ideas of exchange and social intercourse as primary forces of advancing and preserving society. Consequently, books and newspapers were addressed to a large, anonymous public. Differences could be detected, however, in the "intent" of specific media; books, for instance, might have a tendency to address readers from a higher, perhaps more elitist position, whereas newspapers made it a point to remain on one level with their readers. They offered a service and they needed acceptance. Newspapers, according to Tönnies, want to communicate from "stranger to stranger," regardless of the personal status of authors or writers, but under the cloak of anonymity which tends to help underscore the idea of factual and objective presentation of information.[40]

Since news is of particular importance in the context of societal communication, Tönnies discussed two major forms, political and business news. Political news consisted of the reporting of foreign and domestic affairs, and business news was news about "the position of markets, and also about the prospects for business"[41] Tönnies recognized the interdependence of both types of news in the interplay between economic and financial powers and political leadership in its internal and external policy-making roles. Since both merchant and statesman need a variety of information, they obtain their news through a number of channels.

Newspapers may supplement privately obtained official or business news; their major function is the distribution of those kinds of news, however, which are intended for the public or which have escaped from being kept secret. He described the newspaper as a "printed marketplace."[42] The importance of information and dissemination of news for the maintenance of society raised questions about the press as a carrier of true and false news items, its participation in cases of intentional or unintentional falsification of events, and manipulation of news. Tönnies illustrated his ideas with examples from wartime reporting when propaganda efforts colored the news and from the business world whose activities may be affected by the general news coverage. He stressed this point, because news as it was used and distorted remained a crucial element in the shaping of opinions. More blatant, however, must be the effects of the editorial or news analysis, which lend substance to a set of facts and which provide "color." Their use established the press as a forum from which ideas were adopted to help shape opinions in a more credible way than outright falsification of news events.

Newspapers, in particular, are the center of constant observation; they are indispensable as a medium for the expression of opinions by any individual or group in society. At the same time, they are held accountable by their particular economic and political sources. Since the press as a capitalist enterprise is organized to make a profit for its owners, newspaper journalists must take into account the real interests of the newspaper: the likes or dislikes of (a) readers, (b) subscribers, and (c) advertisers.[43] Tönnies knew that the newspaper as a business relied more heavily on advertisers than on subscribers; therefore, the managers of the press had to respect business interests, and they might have to yield to their pressures. The results of such activities may be confusing and misleading to readers. Tönnies cited the widespread practice (not limited to the German press) of advertising disguised in editorial sections of newspapers and not confined to the business pages.[44] He added that general corruption, as a sign of modern life, had also affected the press. Tönnies suggested the paradoxical situation that immediate transactions of the press are made for the power of capital in the press, and through the press for public opinion, which is not the most effective power.[45]

Tönnies devoted considerable attention to the role and function of the press as a propaganda device, and also as a considerable social force, since the power of public opinion often seemed to be equated with that of the press.

The press, then, played a crucial role in the propaganda of public opinion which involves the activities of political parties and their backers. As a result, public opinion is often made. Tönnies said,

> It has been said more than once that a particular public opinion has been manufactured, as one manufactures any manner of merchandise. One produces merchandise in order to sell, and one sells in order to make a profit. One produces opinion because one expects an advantage from it if it should come to be shared by many, and this advantage differs little from the profit which the merchant and entrepreneur are seeking. The powers of capital are intent not only to bring about a favorable opinion concerning their products, an unfavorable one concerning those of their competitors, but also to promote a generalized public opinion which is designed to serve their business interests, for instance, regarding a policy of protective tariffs or of free trade, favoring a political movement or party, supporting or opposing an existing government.[46]

He stated, in effect, that governments in their attempts to influence public opinion seek to convert their own opinions into public opinion. Similar activities can be attributed to other, spiritual-moral powers in society. Religion, for instance, and the sciences also have a stake in the shaping of public opinion not only regarding their own affairs but also with respect to political matters. Tönnies even suggested that "public opinion is easily accessible to these influences because it is itself a spiritual force."[47]

The use of the word, the printed word through the press, in particular, becomes their most effective instrument.

In his attempt to identify sources and participants in the public opinion process, Tönnies explained,

> Very generally, one can say that public opinion is the opinion of the educated classes as against the great mass of the people. However, the more the masses move upward and the more they participate in the advance of education and political consciousness, the more will they make their voices count in the formation of public opinion. Always public opinion remains the judgment of an elite, that is, a minority, frequently, to be sure, a representative minority, at times, however, a minority that is entirely out of contact with the mass of the people.[48]

CAPITALISM AND THE PRESS

Looking at the question of power, he agreed tha the power of the press "is more obvious than the power of public opinion."[49] He described the political, economic, and intellectual forces, constituting another kind of elite that often stands behind the press in modern times. Since "industrial capital" had become a major influence, even more powerful than landed estate, Tönnies argued that it also regulated the power of the press. He said,

> Capital enjoys a natural advantage over landed estate with regard to power of the press for the following reasons: (1) commerce, communication, banking, industry are more intimately connected than is landed estate with the spirit of modernity and thereby with the press; (2) commerce, and capital generally, is closely related to the world of information and communication, which is served by the press, and thereby to the doings in national and international politics; (3) the newspaper itself is, and becomes more and more, a capitalist enterprise; the main business of a newspaper is advertising, which is a tool of commercial and industrial capital; (4) the press is in line with the great body of literature inasmuch as it is carried along by the progress of scientific thinking and stands in the service of a predominantly liberal and religiously as well as politically progressive consciousness; consequently the press *ab initio* has been an effective weapon of the cities, especially the large

commercially oriented cities, against the feudal forces that are
rooted in dominion over the soil; the press addresses itself primarily
and preferentially to an urban, especially a metropolitan, public
because this is the public that is most eager to read, most accustomed
to and capable of reading, and therefore most inclined to do battle
by means of script and speech.[50]

He suggested also that in the competition of capitalistic ideas a
capitalistic press was, theoretically at least, in the position of re-
fusing access to other capitalistic powers, until those forces had
managed to gain control of the press. Tönnies cited examples of
corruption in a capitalistic press system through monopoly
ownership and corporation control, and he interpreted these
developments as more general expressions of the corruption of
public life in the United States. Although he acknowledged the
work of press critics, he predicted that their independent voices
would eventually disappear, or yield to the dictates of conglomer-
ates and monopolies instead of reflecting public opinions.
Tönnies listed a number of American sources to support his arguments. Among them were E. A. Ross, who had stated in 1920 that
the sellout of newspapers to business interests had never been as
widespread as at that time, and Lester Ward, who had declared in
Pure Sociology that newspapers were organs of deception: "Every
prominent newspaper is the defender of some interest and everything it says is directly or indirectly (and most effective when
indirect) in support of that interest. There is no such thing at the
present time as a newspaper that defends a principle."[51]

His description of the use of modern communication media by
special interest groups, governments, and others, as well as their
mode of operation, focused on business practices; it fore-
shadowed mass media activities. He observed,

In this form of communication, judgments and opinion are wrapped
up like grocers' goods and offered for consumption in their objective
reality. It is prepared and offered to our generation in the most
perfect manner by the newspapers, which make possible the
quickest production, multiplication, and distribution of facts and
thoughts, just as the hotel kitchen provides food and drink in
every conceivable form and quantity. Thus the press is the real instru-

ment ["organ"] of public opinion, weapon and tool in the hands
of those who know how to use it and have to use it; it possesses
universal power as the dreaded critic of events and changes in social
conditions. It is comparable and, in some respects, superior to the
material power which the states possess through their armies,
their treasuries, and their bureaucratic civil service.[52]

Tönnies recognized the potential power of a modern press
system—and he did not confine it to a particular country; on the
contrary, he envisioned a worldwide influence, a force capable of
uniting others and establishing a world power. He explained that
the press,

in its tendencies and potentialities, is definitely international, thus
comparable to the power of a permanent or temporary alliance of
states. It can, therefore, be conceived as its ultimate aim to
abolish the multiplicity of states and substitute for it a single world
market, which would be ruled by thinkers, scholars, and writers
and could dispense with means of coercion other than those of a
psychological nature. Such tendencies and intentions will perhaps
never find a clear expression, let alone realization, but their
recognition serves to assist in the understanding of many phenomena
of the real world and to the realization of the fact that the existence
of natural states is but a temporary limitation of the boundary-
less Gesellschaft.[53]

And again he cited the United States as an example of a modern
society which "can or will least of all claim a truly national
character."[54]

Tönnies concluded that the press must be understood as an
instrument of liberal thought, a force used to exert influence
upon more conservative elements in society; this assessment
implied an allegiance with ideas of less "church-oriented religiosity" and "an agnostic world view connected with the natural
sciences."[55] Consequently, he argued that

if and inasfar as public opinion is subject to the same influences
and developmental causations as the press, public opinion will
be reflected in the press, so that the power of the press expresses
the power of public opinion to the extent that the identification of the
press and public opinion becomes understandable and within
certain limits justified.[56]

Tönnies discussed the overriding effects of liberalism, making it a "constitutive part of public opinion everywhere, except in areas of cultural transition."[57] He concluded that given the development of the modern age the press had become a protection and defense of liberal ideas. In this regard "the power of a unanimous press reflects the power of a unanimous public opinion, and if both follow the same direction they are irresistible. The press, then, is *the* organ of *the* public opinion. It is the power of the 'spirit of the age.'"[58]

Tönnies distinguished between public opinion, however, that is the sum total of all of the voices reflected in the press, as one kind of power, and *the* public opinion which consists of a "unified harmony of many thoughts and opinions" making up a "generalized opinion of a people or a public as a whole."[59] In his definition of public opinion, Tönnies separated "unarticulated" from "articulated" public opinion. Although both forms rely on aspects of public communication and deal with public matters, the former definition refers to general participation in public expression of ideas and opinions (public opinion), whereas the latter suggests, essentially at least, a politically united entity which operates on the basis of common opinions or judgments (Public Opinion).[60] It was his intention throughout the *Kritik der öffentlichen Meinung* to differentiate between those terms, one describing "a conglomerate of diverse and contradictory views, desires and intentions" and the other standing for "a unitary force, the expression of a common will."[61] Tönnies used an analogy to describe these differences; an assembly, for instance, displays the features of public opinion *(öffentliche Meinung)* under conditions of deliberation, when it is divided and torn apart by argument; it resembles *the* public opinion *(öffentliche Meinung)* under conditions of making decisions or rendering verdicts, when it stands behind these decisions or verdicts as "a unified whole or a moral person."[62] He described the latter also in terms of a "unified public opinion" and as an "expression of social volition" which claimed binding powers and strove for general acceptance. Tönnies added that "public opinion may be compared to a dominant faith and, like faith, it is all the more intolerant the more sovereign its rule."[63] He felt that public opinion, not unlike religion, is part of the "spiritual-moral sphere of social life; they compete within this sphere to the point of conflict."[64] And he added,

> Religion as well as public opinion strive to be morally supreme, so that all varieties of religious faith have a powerful tendency to become *the* religion, and all particular expressions of public opinion have the tendency to become *the* public opinion. Both are engaged in propaganda. Public opinion propaganda, especially political propaganda, is modelled on religious propaganda. As religious propaganda propagates faith, so political propaganda propagates opinion.[65]

The future of public opinion, its rise, perhaps, to a world religion, and its role as the social conscience of mankind must be accompanied, however, by improvements of the communication system. Since the press would continue to play an important part in the dissemination of ideas, Tönnies envisioned the establishment of an independent press. His suggestions were based upon the writings of an American journalist[66] who had advocated the creation of a completely independent press system with newspapers that could rely on an independent news service and that were financially free, supported by large circulation rather than by advertising. He also mentioned Karl Bücher's attempts to contribute some ideas to a reform of the German press,[67] as another example of the possible direction for newspaper development.

THE SCIENTIFIC STUDY OF THE PRESS

Tönnies regarded the press as a central force in a society in which public opinion had become the guiding spirit. His publications on matters regarding the press as well as his role in the German Sociological Association brought him in contact with members of the institutes for the study of the press (*Zeitungswissenschaft*), who had jealously protected their claims over investigations of the role and function of the press. Tönnies, however, refused to believe in a separation of these concerns, and his views were expressed publicly a number of times.

The 1930 convention of the German Sociological Association included a debate concerning the press and public opinion. Tönnies presided at the meeting, and he contributed to the debates by raising a number of issues at the end of the formal discussion.

He expressed his disappointment over the fact that none of the speakers had attempted a systematic treatment of the press as a capitalistic enterprise which has developed into a powerful social force with the production of news. He commented upon the dangers of interference in the process of communication by advertisers, and upon the threats to freedom of expression of journalists. But he also wondered about the generation of opinions and value judgments. Specifically, he asked how free these opinions really were, how they were related to other opinions, and how close they came to other "verified" opinions present in other areas of social life. He specifically referred to opinions of educated individuals whose contributions to social policy and reform were needed, but whose ideas were either reflected in a distorted manner or rarely published. Tönnies mentioned national economists, among them Brentano, Schmoller, Wagner, and Knapp, whose opinions, because they were close enough to be identified with socialistic ideas, were suspect in the eyes of the bourgeois and, in particular, the Catholic press. Tönnies concluded, almost despairingly, that "when men and women of this calibre are dead, they may get rather beautiful necrologies; as long as they live, they find themselves pushed to the wall and rarely listened to; that is an experience, which I want to emphasize on the basis of my long life."[68]

He rejected the accusation that he did not like *Zeitungswissenschaft* as a field of special inquiry. In a response to Professor Emil Dovifat he stated that it was really unnecessary to establish a new science for every new area of scholarly investigation, but he thought that the advocates of *Zeitungswissenschaft* could make highly valuable contributions to a *critical* history of the press, especially under philosophical and sociological points of view. He expressed the hope—and he included those who represented *Zeitungswissenschaft* with his reference to a lack of a critical approach to press studies—that the convention might contribute toward a liberation from the press, in general, and from party affiliations and dependence upon respective newspapers.[69]

Tönnies elaborated his position vis-à-vis *Zeitungswissenschaft* again in a letter published early in 1931. In it he denied the charge that he wanted to define the study of the press as an exclusive part of sociology. But he felt that the investigation of the press constituted an important area of sociography, that is to say, empirical sociology. He suggested that the treatment of the literature of society must be part of defining its significance for the social life of a people; newspapers were part of this literature. He also blamed the failure of an intense sociological study of press systems on the newness of sociology as a discipline in Germany.[70]

In summary, Tönnies provided an extensive discussion of communication phenomena, public opinion, and the press, as part of his effort to develop a broad sociological framework beginning with *Gemeinschaft und Gesellschaft*. In this context, he contributed a detailed historical analysis of the concept of public opinion and he offered a definition that took into account the dynamic nature of his own conceptual scheme of societal development. Tönnies seemed particularly concerned with the rise of public opinion and the power of communication media. He demonstrated the shifting relationship between religion and public opinion, and he commented upon the dangers inherent in the capitalistic nature of the press in modern society.

His ideas concerning the rise of public opinion to a universal social conscience vis-à-vis religion and the role and function of the press in this evolutionary schema suggest a novel approach to popular culture phenomena. His demands for a systematic treatment of the influence of capitalistic enterprises upon the press—and therefore upon public opinion—could be considered a challenge for mass communication research that is critical and responsive to contemporary social problems and the need for solutions.

NOTES

1. "Mein Verhältnis zur Soziologie," *Soziologie von Heute,* edited by Richard Thurnwald (Leipzig: C. L. Hirschfeld, 1932), 103-122; as translated in Werner Cahnman and Rudolf Heberle, eds., *Ferdinand Tönnies, On Sociology: Pure, Applied, and Empirical* (Chicago: University of Chicago Press, 1971), 4.

2. "Einteilung der Soziologie," *Zeitschrift für die gesamte Staatswissenschaft* 79: 1 (1925); as translated in Cahnman and Heberle, 131.

3. Ibid., 132.

4. Ibid., 131.

5. *Einführung in die Soziologie* (Stuttgart: Ferdinand Enke, 1931); as reported by E. G. Jacoby, "Three Aspects of the Sociology of Tönnies," in Werner Cahnman, ed., *Ferdinand Tönnies: A New Evaluation* (Leiden: E. J. Brill, 1973), 92.

6. "Statistik und Soziographie," *Allgemeines Statistisches Archiv* 18 (1929), 546-558; in Cahnman and Heberle, 237.

7. Ibid., 238.

8. Translated and reprinted in Cahnman, 286-287. The newspaper was the *Schleswig-Holsteinische Volkszeitung,* Kiel, 29 Juli 1932.

9. Tönnies, "Einteilung," in Cahnman and Heberle, 139.

10. Ibid.

11. Ibid., 140.

12. Einführung, in Cahnman, 177.

13. Ibid., 178.

14. Ibid.

15. Ibid., 179.

16. Ibid., 180.

17. Ibid., 181.

18. Ibid.

19. Ibid., 187.

20. Tönnies, "Einteilung," in Cahnman and Heberle, 137.

21. Tönnies, *Einführung,* in Cahnman, 182.

22. Ibid.

23. Ibid., 183.

24. Ibid., 185.

25. *Community & Society (Gemeinschaft und Gesellschaft),* translated and edited by Charles P. Loomis (New York: Harper Torchbooks, 1963), 221.

26. *Kritik der öffentlichen Meinung* (Berlin: Verlag von Julius Springer, 1922), vii. A discussion of the major points is available in an essay by Gillian Lindt Gollin and Albert E. Gollin, "Tönnies on Public Opinion," in Cahnman, 181-206.

27. Cahnman and Heberle, 251.

28. Ibid.

29. Ibid., 252.

30. *Kritik,* 219.

31. Ibid., 80.

32. Ibid., 257.

33. Ibid., 245-250.

34. Ibid., 137.

35. Ibid., 232.

36. Ibid., 207.

37. Ibid.

38. Ibid., 572.

39. Ibid., 91.

40. Ibid., 94.

41. Ibid., 95.

42. Ibid., 97.

43. Ibid., 180.

44. Ibid., 181-182.

45. Ibid., 183.

46. "Macht und Wert der (Oeffentlichen Meinung," *Die Dioskuren, Jahrbuch für Geisteswissenschaften* 2 (1923), 72-99; cited in Cahnman and Heberle, 262.

47. Ibid.

48. Ibid., 264.

49. Ibid., 254.

50. Ibid., 255-256.

51. Tönnies, *Kritik* 184-186. He referred to an article by E. A. Ross in the *International Ethical Review* in 1920, and he quoted from Lester Ward, *Pure Sociology. A Treatise on the Origin and Spontaneous Development of Society* (New York: Macmillan 1919), 487.

52. Tönnies, *Community,* 221.

53. Ibid.

54. Ibid.

55. Tönnies, "Macht und Wert," in Cahnman and Heberle, 256.

56. Ibid.

57. Ibid., 257.

58. Ibid.

59. Ibid., 258.

60. Tönnies, *Kritik,* 131-132.

61. Ibid., vi.

62. "Macht und Wert," in Cahnman and Heberle, 258.

63. Ibid., 260.

64. Ibid., 261.

65. Ibid.

66. Tönnies, *Kritik,* 574. Tönnies reported the activities of Ferdinand Hansen, who had requested that the American people establish a $1 billion fund for the operation of independent newspapers, among other projects.

67. Ibid., 575.

68. Verhandlungen des Siebenten Deutchen Soziologentages, 28 September bis 1. Oktober 1930 in Berlin (Tübingen: J.C.B. Mohr, Paul Siebeck, 1931), 74.

69. Ibid., 72-74.

70. "Offene Antwort," *Zeitungswissenschaft* 6:1 (1931), 1-2. The letter was written in response to a letter by Hans A. Münster, Berlin, a member of the Deutschen Institut für Zeitungskunde, who had raised the issue of the study of newspapers as a science.

6

The Conscience of Society

Max Weber on Journalism
and Responsibility

WEBER: A BIOGRAPHICAL NOTE

The scholarship of Max Weber (1864-1920) crossed a number of boundaries, ranging from economics and history to law, religion, and sociology. Much of his work seemed to reflect a central theme: his lifelong interest in the problems of leadership in society. Numerous books in recent years have focused on Weber's contribution to the social sciences;[1] the following discussion concentrates on his interests in journalism, and the press, as a vehicle for the dissemination of social and political thought.

Specifically, Weber's concern with the press from the points of view of the publicist and the social scientist may be an indication of the importance he attached to questions of the role and function of journalists as disseminators of ideas and of the press as the source of information about social and political issues of the day. Furthermore, if, as Parsons once suggested, conditions of successful control provide an appropriate focus of sociology for Weber,[2] then the study of the press and its agents as components of a social and political institution in modern society becomes a major task of sociological research. And finally, a study of Weber's own position as a scholar-publicist may contribute to an understanding of his theory of political leadership in light of his position vis-à-vis the phenomenon of political journalism in early twentieth-century Germany.

Weber's social and political writings represent a substantial effort for a publicist; they reflect not only his intimate knowledge of political problems but also his continued participation in public life through journalistic activities. They also reveal his fascination with the idea of leadership; as a political journalist, he wrote with charismatic authority, but as social theorist, he recognized the dangers of charismatic leadership to individual freedom and liberty.

Underlying much of Weber's analysis of Germany's political and economic problems during the latter part of the nineteenth century was his awareness of social change, specifically, the rise of labor, the failure of the bourgeoisie to provide responsible leadership, and the advances of big business and industry toward a new brand of feudalism. In his early effort to seek solutions to the country's internal problems, Weber was attracted to Martin Rade's *Chronik der Christlichen Welt*[3] with its interest in labor-related issues and in the development of a social policy. He joined the publication in 1890 as a contributor. One year later he assumed editorial duties for *Evangelisch-soziale Zeitfragen,* a publication founded by his cousin Otto Baumgarten,[4] whose activities in the Christian-Social movement also brought Weber into contact with a number of liberal theologians. Among them was Friedrich Naumann, who represented the left-wing interests of the organization. Naumann succeeded in 1894 with the publication of *Die Hilfe,*[5] and he asked Weber to become a contributor. When the journal embarked upon a major editorial campaign in support of a social democratic movement and against the powerful industrial interests that attempted to suppress liberal sentiments, it became recognized and established ifself firmly among journals that appealed to liberal intellectuals, although at the expense of the original idea which had envisioned broad support from workers and artisans.[6] At the same time, Weber published an attack upon Germany's industrialists in the *Neue Preussische (Kreuz-)Zeitung.*[7] Basically interested in the collaboration among all groups in German society for the purpose of retaining the status of a power state, Weber joined others in the condemnation of political attitudes that had surfaced as intolerance against Social Democrats and other liberal groups and individuals. The article appeared only after considerable editorial changes, however.[8]

In the meantime, Weber's friendship with Naumann led to a more intense participation in the political life of the 1890s which culminated in the establishment of the *Nationalsozialer Verein* in 1896. Although Weber was critical of Naumann's programme, he joined him in the effort to launch a daily newspaper as a necessary platform for the new party. The result was the founding of *Die Zeit,* a daily newspaper which survived for about a year.[9] A lack of popular support for the party and lack of funds for the continuation of the newspaper contributed to the early demise of the enterprise.[10]

A few years later, however, Weber found his own public forum; he began to write for the *Frankfurter Zeitung,* which was at that time one of Germany's leading newspapers. He was a prolific writer, and the topics of his articles ranged from the democratization of Germany to problems of academic freedom.[11] Not unlike the readers of *Die Hilfe,* the readers of the *Frankfurter Zeitung* belonged to the social and intellectual elite of the country, and Weber could expect an unusually high degree of knowledge and understanding of the subject matter from them. As Lachmann points out, "He was even entitled to expect (and doubtless did) from the educated and well-to-do readers of the *Frankfurter Zeitung* to whom as a rule he addressed himself in the first place, a degree of sophistication which would permit them to discount some of the rhetorical excrescenses of his polemic style, and nevertheless realize the very serious nature of the issues at stake."[12]

On one occasion, after a series of articles on the past and future of parliamentary rule in Germany in which Weber attacked the Kaiser as a political dilletante, the *Frankfurter Zeitung* experienced official pressure when military censors confiscated one issue and stepped up their censorship of the paper. The confrontation with censorship became a political issue and led to a question about the nature of preventive censorship before the *Reichstag.*[13] Furthermore, and as an example of his intense feelings with which he wrote about the political issues, Weber insisted during a subsequent meeting with acquaintances that he would continue to attack Wilhelm II after the war to bring about a confrontation in court. He hoped to see men like Bülow, Tirpitz, Bethmann, Jagow, Falkenhayn, Hindenburg and Ludendorf reveal under oath the sins committed against the German people. Theodor Heuss, who recalled the episode, suggests that Weber saw himself in the role of a direct opponent of Wilhelm II.[14]

Although destined to play a major part in the political development of postwar Germany, Weber decided to continue his work as a scholar. Nevertheless, he returned to the editorial duties of a contributor to the *Frankfurter Zeitung* and participated in the discussions of events leading to the establishment of the Weimar Republic. Again, his views (about the revolution, for instance) were not always entirely shared by other journalists; reporting about his experiences with the editorial staff, he said, "I am writing one article after another . . . but it is impossible to influence the editorial staff, it cannot be done by an outsider, they rebel internally."[15]

There were other outlets for his journalistic writings as well; he contributed to the *Berliner Tageblatt*, another of Germany's major liberal newspapers, and to the *Berliner Börsenzeitung*. In addition, he wrote for the *Münchner Neueste Nachrichten*, a major newspaper in Southern Germany which at that time operated in the tradition of the liberal press.[16]

Many of Weber's major political contributions to the press are collected in his *Gesammelte Politische Schriften*.[17] Taken as a whole, they show Weber's intimate knowledge of political events before and during World War I; they also reveal an almost missionary zeal with which he put to work his sharp analytical mind to direct and report the social and political conditions of the day. Dronberger summarizes Weber's merits as a journalist by pointing out that he succeeded in merging events "leading up to and during World War I with a profoundly exhaustive analysis of German political institutions of his time—all by the means of an account of historical events and the roles played by the Kaiser, the chancellor, other influential public figures, the military, the bureaucracy, groups with vested interests, and political parties."[18]

His work as a political journalist, or publicist, reflected his concern with the problems of power and the responsibilities of political leaders. He, too, had assumed leadership among journalists of his day whose political *Weltanschauungen* were widely disseminated by influential newspapers. After all, it was his activity as a journalist—and as a public speaker, and not his academic position—which contributed to the rise of his popularity and which made him a potential candidate for a political career.

However, Weber also liked his involvement with the press for personal reasons; he appreciated being around decent and intelligent journalists who knew their business. Heuss suggests that the *Frankfurter Zeitung* provided not only a platform for his political views, but also the opportunity for close contacts with professional journalists for whom he gained much respect over the years.[19] At one time, during the last year of his life, he shared his feelings about being a journalist in a letter to his wife in which he wrote about earning enough money. He remarked, "I have nothing against joining a newspaper or a publishing company instead of playing professor."[20] The attractions of journalism as a professional career and also as a medium for Weber's own intellectual activities are described by Heuss, who says that Weber was extremely taken by the role of educated and responsible journalists, that he appreciated their participation in the formulation of public opinion, and that he sought and needed the exchange of ideas with journalists.[21] To be sure, he also must have valued the freedom he experienced as a publicist in the choice of his material and the manner of its presentation in the *Frankfurter Zeitung*. It must also be noted in this connection that the editorial staff of the *Frankfurter Zeitung* consisted of carefully selected and well-educated individuals who—as a group—decided editorial matters of content or direction. Weber's association with these journalists represented a unique experience—at least for German conditions—and could not be compared with the encounter with other editorial staffs during those years in Germany.

THE ROLE OF THE JOURNALIST

Weber's most extensive statement regarding the role of political journalists is found in his lecture on "Politics as a Vocation,"[22] in which he discussed the ethical consequences of a career in public life. Characterizing the political journalist as the most important representative of the "demogogic species," Weber described the position of journalists as sharing the fate of lacking a "fixed social classification with lawyers and artists." He proposed that the journalist belongs to "a sort of pariah caste, which is always estimated by 'society' in terms of its ethically lowest representative."[23] Coming to the defense of the responsible journalist, Weber continued,

> Hence, the strangest notions about journalists and their work are abroad. Not everybody realizes that a really good journalistic accomplishment requires at least as much "genius" [*Geist*] as any scholarly accomplishment, especially because of the necessity of producing at once and "on order," and because of the necessity of being effective, to be sure, under quite different conditions of production. It is almost never acknowledged that the responsibility of every honorable journalist is, on the average, not a bit lower than that of the scholar, but rather, as the war has shown, higher. This is because, in the very nature of the case, irresponsible journalistic accomplishments and their often terrible effects are remembered.[24]

Weber spoke with the experiences of a veteran journalist and highly respected scholar; he knew about the agony of journalistic decision making and the consequences of scholarly discoveries. He said,

> Nobody believes that the discretion of any able journalist ranks above the average of other people, and yet that is the case. The quite incomparably graver temptations, and the other conditions that accompany journalistic work at the present time, produce those results which have conditioned the public to regard the press with a mixture of disdain and pitiful cowardice. Today we cannot discuss what is to be done. Here we are interested in the

question of the occupational destiny of the political journalist and of his chance to attain a position of political leadership.[25]

The involvement in political writing for mass consumption, however, was more than an ordinary editorial assignment. It provided the foundation for a political career. Journalism, in this sense, became the training ground, the vocational school, for political activists. The press, then, created not only an appropriate medium for political communication; it was also by its very nature a potential leader of the masses. The political journalist was in a position of power; he could, at least theoretically, control the dissemination of information and opinion, and rise, simultaneously, to a position of political prominence.

In reality, there was little evidence of this development, and Weber pondered the failure of political journalists to suceed in political careers. He noted,

> Thus far, the journalist has had favorable chances only in the Social Democratic party. Within the party, editorial positions have been predominantly in the nature of official positions, but editorial positions have not been the basis for positions of leadership.
>
> In the bourgeois parties, on the whole, the chances for ascent to political power along this avenue have rather become worse, as compared with those of the previous generation. Naturally every politician of consequence has needed influence over the press and hence has needed relations with the press. But that party leaders would emerge from the ranks of the press has been an absolute exception and one should not have expected it. The reason for this lies in the strongly increased "indispensability" of the journalist, above all, of the propertyless and hence professionally bound journalist, an indispensability which is determined by the tremendously increased intensity and tempo of journalistic operations. The necessity of gaining one's livelihood by the writing of daily or at least weekly articles is like lead on the feet of the politicians. I know of cases in which natural leaders have been permanently paralyzed in their ascent to power, externally and above all internally, by this compulsion. The relations of the press to the ruling powers in the state and the parties, under the old regime [of the Kaiser], were as detrimental as they could be to the level of journalism; but that is a chapter in itself. These conditions were different in the countries of our opponents [the Allies]. But there also, and for all modern states, apparently the journalist worker gains less and less as the capitalist lord of the press, of the sort of "Lord" Northcliffe, for instance, gains more and more political influence.[26]

He blamed the larger, capitalist newspaper organizations for the breeding of political indifference, and advertising for its potential as an economic determinant of political influence. Weber concluded,

> Thus far, however, our great capitalist newspaper concerns, which attained control, especially over the "chain newspapers," with "want ads," have been regularly and typically the breeders of political indifference. For no profits could be made in an independent policy; especially no profitable benevolence of the politically dominant powers could be obtained. The advertising business is also the avenue along which, during the war, the attempt was made to influence the press politically in a grand style—an attempt which apparently it is regarded as desirable to continue now. Although one may expect the great papers to escape this pressure, the situation of the small ones will be far more difficult. In any case, for the time being, the journalist career is not among us, a normal avenue for the ascent of political leaders, whatever attraction journalism may otherwise have and whatever measure of influence, range of activity, and especially political responsibility it may yield. One has to wait and see. Perhaps journalism does not have this function any longer, or perhaps journalism does not yet have it.[27]

He addressed the controversial question of anonymity in journalistic practice as it might relate to the development of responsible journalism but felt that dropping the principle of anonymity may not increase the awareness of responsibility. He said,

> Some of the papers were, without regard to party, precisely the notoriously worst boulevard sheets; by dropping anonymity they strove for and attained greater sales. The publishers as well as the journalists of sensationalism have gained fortunes but certainly not honor. Nothing is here being said against the principle of promoting sales; the question is indeed an intricate one, and the phenomenon of irresponsible sensationalism does not hold in general. But thus far, sensationalism has not been the road to genuine leadership or to the responsible management of politics. How conditions will further develop remains to be seen.[28]

Nevertheless, he regarded the activities of a responsible political journalist as an avenue to political careers, at least for those individuals who were strong enough to endure the gamble. He suggested,

It is not a road for everybody, least of all for weak characters, especially for people who can maintain their inner balance only with a secure status position. If the life of a young scholar is a gamble, still he is walled in by firm status conventions, which prevent him from slipping. But the journalist's life is an absolute gamble in every respect and under conditions that test one's inner security in a way that scarcely occurs in any other situation. The often bitter experiences in occupational life are perhaps not even the worst. The inner demands that are directed precisely at the successful journalist are especially difficult. It is, indeed, no small matter to frequent the salons of the powerful on this earth on a seemingly equal footing and often to be flattered by all because one is feared, yet knowing all the time that having hardly closed the door the host has perhaps to justify before his guests his association with the "scavengers from the press." Moreover, it is no small matter that one must express oneself promptly and convincingly about this and that, on all conceivable problems of life—whatever the "market" happens to demand—and this without becoming absolutely shallow and above all without losing one's dignity by baring oneself, a thing which has merciless results. It is not astonishing that there are many journalists who have become human failures and worthless men. Rather, it is astonishing that, despite all this, this very stratum includes such a great number of valuable and quite genuine men, a fact that outsiders would not so easily guess.[29]

Weber continued to develop his idea of ethically oriented conduct, which he suggested be guided by one of two maxims: described as an ethic of ultimate ends or an ethic of responsibility. Although he did not specifically refer to journalists and their activities, he proposed that a calling for politics necessitates a union of both maxims in the conduct of a man. He said,

> it is immensely moving when a *mature* man—no matter whether old or young in years—is aware of a responsibility for the consequences of his conduct and really feels such responsibility with heart and soul. He then acts by following an ethic of responsibility and somewhere he reaches the point where he says: "Here I stand; I can do no other." That is something genuinely human and moving. And every one of us who is not spiritually dead must realize the possibility of finding himself at some time in that position. In so far as this is true, an ethic of ultimate ends and an ethic of responsibility are not absolute contrasts but rather supplements, which only in unison constitute a genuine man—a man who *can* have the "calling for politics."[30]

Weber's view of political journalists and their role in modern society can be discussed also in the framework of a legitimation of charismatic domination by the journalist as a type of political leader. He acknowledged the power of the press, and he granted the political journalist the freedom to use his abilities for a political cause. Again, Weber spoke as an insider whose acquaintance with journalists added to his own experiences as a publicist. In fact, Weber would have liked to exercise political power; as Aron points out, "He . . . dreamed of being a statesman rather than a party leader—the head of state being, at least in the imagination of outsiders, a man who accedes to the nobility of politics without accepting its servitude. Max Weber was neither a politician nor a statesman, but an advisor to the prince—unheeded, as is so often the case with advisors to the prince."[31] Having chosen an academic career, however, his desire for political engagement found an outlet in his journalistic writings; thus, he was able to combine the life of what he had described as a responsible journalist with his interests in the social sciences. He reached a compromise, it seems, between *Gefühl* and *Verstand,* that is, between an emphasis upon action as an expression of political power and upon knowledge as a goal of scientific inquiry. As a result, he participated in both worlds, respected as a diagnostician of society and as a leader among social theorists. Groth, who had followed Weber's suggestions concerning empirical studies of the press, suggests that journalists are not unlike apostles; and he refers to them as missionaries, using Weber's terminology.[22] It is also a fitting description of Weber as a publicist working for the cause of a strong German state.

THE PRESS AS INSTRUMENT OF CHANGE

Indeed, Weber regarded the press as an important instrument for social and political changes in a democratic society and a necessary tool for the success of political actions. He stated, "Naturally every politician of consequence has needed influence over the press and hence has needed relations with the press."[33] At the same time, he warned that the creation of new parties along with their press organizations requires financial burdens which often make it quite impractical to consider a political move when coming up against an already established press empire.[34] Nevertheless, the press in the machinery of political propaganda was the primary tool of persuasive mass communication and, therefore, indispensable in the political arena. Weber's idea of the utility of newspapers as sources of information and opinions was based on the fact that he was convinced of the effectiveness of the press as a mass medium. In the context of a discussion regarding national unity and cultural heritage, he remarked that "newspapers which certainly do not collect the most sublime examples of literary culture, however, cement the masses together quite effectively."[35]

The importance of a well-functioning press organization to support political campaigns was expressed in Weber's observation that the "need for party correspondences and ready print services for the party press as well as for advertisements of all kinds, grows constantly. . . . Bismarck's press undoubtedly reigned supreme in the unscrupulous use of its means and its tenor. The experiments to create a local press that depends completely on the ruling bureaucracy have not ceased."[36]

Implicit in these concerns about the availability of a press system that serves the particular needs of a political movement is the struggle for authority. It is a struggle in which the masses participate according to the wishes of political leaders. Weber observed that "so-called 'public opinion' under the conditions of mass-democracy is a communal activity born of irrational 'feelings' and normally stage-directed by party leaders and press."[37] He thus placed the press in the hands of the few, who on the basis of their position as members of a political elite are responsible for the manipulation of the masses. Under these circumstances politics turned into a vocation and the idea of democracy, including the notion of freedom of the press, served as a vehicle for charismatic leadership. In this context, Weber's statement regarding the position of the political journalist takes on the character of an imperative: With the rise of a plebiscitary democracy, journalists must reach for the realm of politics; their ethics of responsibility dictate a devotion to action.

Given Weber's wide range of interests, it was no suprise that his personal involvement in journalism and his political concerns regarding the press in society also stimulated his thoughts with respect to the development of a systematic, scientific treatment of the press. As a social scientist, Weber's commitment to the pursuit of knowledge pushed his interests in the workings of the press system beyond the curiosity of a political observer into the realm of scientific investigation. Although a difficult task, the study of the press, if completed successfully, could yield valuable insights into the relationship between the practice of newspapers and the conduct of society.

Specifically, Weber had participated in the founding of the German Association for Sociology in 1909, an outgrowth of his interest in theoretical aspects of the social sciences and in empirical sociological research. In his address to the first Sociological Congress held in 1910 in Frankfurt, Weber, among other suggestions, introduced an outline for some empirical research. Among the three projects was a study of the press.

Again, his assessment of the importance of the press as a mass medium had surfaced much earlier as part of a question in a survey of farm workers in 1892. Under the heading of ethical and social conditions, Weber had asked about the need for reading materials among workers, the selection of materials, and the newspapers which were most often read by them.[38] As a matter of fact, the proposed press study was Weber's sixth and final empirical effort.[39] His acknowledgement of the press as an important social institution and as a useful source for sociological inquiry, however, helped reinforce already existing ideas in Germany that the press as an influential mass medium should receive appropriate attention in the framework of the university-level studies.[40]

THE PRESS AS OBJECT OF SCIENTIFIC STUDY

Weber's address to his colleagues during the 1910 meeting of German sociologists was, in effect, the second attempt to provide an empirical base for the interpretation of the press as a societal institution.[41] Weber envisioned a project that would involve the cooperation of practicing journalists as well as theorists, like Emil Löbl, whose *Kultur und Presse*, published in 1903, was an attempt to develop a scientific system of the periodical press. It was a pioneering effort to conceive of *Zeitungswissenschaft* systematically.[42]

Based upon the premise that quantification of relevant data is the first step toward the formulation of qualitative statements about the role and fucntion of the press, Weber described the framework for the investigation in broad terms. "We must examine the press to this end: What does it contribute to the making of modern man? Secondly, how are the objective, supra-individual cultural values influenced, what shifts occur, what is destroyed and newly created of the beliefs and hopes of the masses: of the *Lebensgefühle*—as they say today—, what is forever destroyed and newly created of the potential point of view?"[43]

Weber's remarks to the Congress were based upon an earlier undated, six-page plan for a press survey entitled "Preliminary Report of a Suggested Survey of the Sociology of Newspapers."[44] Weber attempted in this report to outline the project and to touch upon a number of issues which he felt should be dealt with in the survey. Stating the general goals of such a press survey, Weber remarked, "In the last analysis a survey of the newspaper system must be aimed at the significant cultural problems of the present: I. The way in which that device to influence minds is organized and with which modern society continuously endeavors to adapt and conform the individual: the press as one of the means of forging the subjective character of modern man. II. The conditions created by public opinion, whose most important determinant today is the newspaper, for the formation, maintenance, destruction, change of artistic, scientific, ethical, religious, political, social, economic aspects of culture: the press as a component of the objective character of modern culture."[45]

The investigation of the press was to be conducted in two major parts, categorized as "newspaper business" and "newspaper opinion"; the former contained a number of preliminary questions concerning the quantitative measures of formal, business aspects of the newspapers; the latter concentrated on questions dealing with qualitative tendencies of newspapers.

Weber intended to deal with the business aspects of the press in a number of ways. He proposed to look at the questions of (1) ownership, (2) need and turnover of capital, (3) running costs of production, (4) procurement of material; under this heading Weber envisioned inquiries into news services of telegraphic agencies, production of feature and special sections, party and political news, official and semiofficial materials, as well as origin, costs, and special nature of business news. He said, "The influence upon the objective content of the newspaper through business conditions could be grouped into sub-problems which are connected with the aforementioned: internal service and ways of distributing materials."[46] Weber included in this category also the role of editorials, multiple daily editions of large newspapers, "Americanism" in the press, and ways of distributing material among personnel. Also connected with it were advertising and advertising sales; (5) income, (6) competition and monopoly, (7) newspaper and journalism, and (8) other newspaper employees.

The problems of newspaper opinions were to be dealt with in three major categories: (1) production of opinion, (2) external influences on newspaper opinions and (3) production of public opinion. Specifically, in his notes that dealt with the production of opinion, Weber said,

> Collectivism and individualism in the creation of the content of the newspaper. The anonymity of the newspaper; its reasons: business (for example, difference between subscription and single sales press), political (for example, greater or smaller degree of elasticity of the party organization as an underlying condition), social (for example, the effort to maintain the tradition and the prestige of the newspaper

as such and the preservation of the balance of power between newspaper capital and journalism), cultural (for example, more or less authority of the printed, particularly the anonymously printed word, which appears as a collective product before the reader according to his kind of political education, etc.). Its effects: upon the journalist—upon advancing or blocking the education of public opinion—upon the political and cultural significance of the newspaper as such.[47]

Under the next heading Weber discussed the external influence upon the views of a newspaper. He concentrated upon the binding force of tradition and mentioned owners, stockholders, readers, as well as official influences, as means of affecting the position of the press.

Under the last heading Weber wanted to investigate the production of public opinion by the press. He paid considerable attention to the effects of reading, and particularly the reading of newspapers on thought and expression of individuals; and he wondered what the role of the press was in the creation of celebrities and what demands readers make on press content. He also asked about the relationship between the necessary condition of publicity and public morality. He realized the difficult task ahead, admitting that these were questions about which it was relatively easy to compose an essay, but incredibly difficult to offer a scientific explanation.[48]

These remarks, together with his explanations which make up part of his speech to the first Sociological Congress, reflect not only Weber's understanding of the relationship between press and society, but they also describe the path of mass communication research in the next 65 years. Weber had succeeded in defining the crucial areas for scientific inquiry; his own background in a number of academic disciplines enabled him to incorporate problems that dealt with the economic and political components of the press, as well as with psychological and sociological issues that treated the impact of the press on man and society.

An example of Weber's insights into the economic problems of the press may be provided by his question about "Americanization" raised in the preliminary paper.[49] He referred to the tendency of monopoly ownership of newspapers and its effect upon the independent press as well as on the party press in Germany. It was an issue hotly debated in the country and summarized by Walter Hammer, who predicted that in the "Americanized press anything would be up for sale, from the editorial to the local news item."[50] Weber was also concerned about the psychological effects of the press. He cited the mounting literature on the effects of newspapers on individuals. In his presentation to the Congress he referred to the contradictory nature of many findings. He suggested that while the exposure to newspapers, and other reading materials, may have an effect on individuals, so may other influences and that, in any case, it may be difficult to define the problem precisely.[51]

SPEECH TO GERMAN SOCIOLOGICAL ASSOCIATION

In his remarks to the first meeting of German sociologists in 1910, Weber outlined two basic areas for sociological study, the press and formal organizations in German society. The following section provides a full account of his plan for a systematic study of German newspapers and the beginnings of a sociology of the press.[52]

> Gentlemen, the first subject deemed suitable by the Society for a purely scientific treatment is a sociology of the press. Admittedly, this is an enormously comprehensive subject, which not only demands an extremely large amount of material support for the preliminary work, but which also—regarding the objectivity of this matter— requires the trust and goodwill of the leading circles of those interested in the press. Should we encounter the suspicion among representatives of newspaper publishers or on the part of journalists that the Society pursues for whatever purposes a course of moral criticism of the existing conditions, it will be impossible to reach our goal—I say this, because we cannot reach it, if we cannot be supplied more than adequately with material by just that side. A committee will be formed which soon will try to gain the cooperation of press experts, the numerous theoreticians of the press—as you know, we have already some brilliant theoretical publications in

this field (let me remind you of Löbl's book[53] because it deserves
to be known better than it is)—and the practitioners of the press. There
is some hope after the preliminary talks that when we will, as
expected, turn to the large press organizations and to the newspaper
publishers' and editors' associations we will be met with understanding.
If this should not happen,the Society would rather refrain from a
publication than arrange for one which probably would not amount
to anything.

Gentlemen, it is useless to speak here of the magnitude
of the overall importance of the press. I would immediately be
suspected of flattering the representatives of the press, the more
since what has been said about it by respected sources cannot be
surpassed. When the press was compared to commanding generals—
this has been said of the foreign press only—nevertheless, everyone
knows: there exists nothing worthier on earth, and it would be
necessary to reach for the regions of the supernatural to find any
comparisons. I simply remind you: erase the press from your memory
and think what modern life would be without the kind of publicity
created by the press. Life in antiquity, gentlemen, also had
its publicity. With horror did Jakob Burckhardt[54] face the publicness
of Hellenistic life which included the existence of the Athenian citizen
in the most intimate details. This kind of publicity does not exist
today, and it is interesting, indeed, to ask: what does contemporary
publicity look like, and what will it look like in the future, what
is publicized by the newspaper and what is not? When the British
Parliament 150 years ago forced journalists to apologize on their
knees before them for breach of privilege after they reported about
its sessions, and today when the press with a mere threat not to
print the speeches of representatives forces Parliament to its knees,
then apparently the idea of parliamentarianism, as well as the position
of the press has changed. At the same time, there must be local
differences, when, for instance, American stock market exchanges
until recently used frosted glass windows to prevent the communication of market fluctuations to the outside, and when we can also
see, on the other side, that almost all relevant characteristics of
putting a newspaper together are at least partly influenced by the
necessity to take stock market announcements into account. We do
not ask what should be made public. Opinions differ widely, as
everyone knows. It is, of course, interesting to find out the opinions
that exist about it today, and those that existed earlier, and who
held them. This, too, is part of our task, but it does not go beyond
this factual observation. Everyone knows, for instance, that on
this issue opinions in England differ from ours, and that when an
English lord marries an American woman one can see in the

American press a detailed account of the physical and psychological attributes of the American woman, and of her dowry, of course, while according to our prevailing ideas at least a newspaper with self-respect would reject this approach in Germany. Where does this difference originate? When we must say that in the case of Germany today, serious representatives of the newspaper business seriously attempt to exclude from newspaper publicity purely private affairs—for what reasons and with what results?—then we must also observe the opinion of a socialist publicist like Anton Menger:[55] that in a future society the press would have the task to serve as a forum for events that cannot be placed under the authority of a court of law, to assume the role of the ancient censor. It is worthwhile to note: which ultimate *Weltanschauungen* are the basis of one or the other tendency. Only this, without an expression of opinion, would be our task.

It will be our task to examine the balance of power which is created by specific newspaper publicity. It is different and of decisively lesser importance for scientific accomplishments, for instance, than for those that are short-lived, like the accomplishments of a performer or conductor, and it is especially important for everything reviewed in the feature section: in certain respects the theatrical and also the literary critic is the individual on the newspaper who can most easily create and destroy careers. For every part of the newspaper, beginning with the political section, however, the balance of power varies most significantly. The relations of the newspaper to political parties here and elsewhere, its relations to the business world, to the numerous groups and interests who influence and who are influenced by the public; this is an enormous area of sociological work, currently in an early state of construction.—But let us return to the real starting point of the examination.

A sociological treatment of the press requires an understanding that the press today is necessarily a capitalistic, private enterprise, but that the press also occupies a completely unique position in contrast to any other business, in that it has two totally different types of "customers": the one consists of newspaper buyers who in turn are either overwhelmingly subscribers or single-copy buyers—a difference which results in decisively different characteristics of the press in advanced societies—the others are advertisers, and between these groups of customers exist the most peculiar interrelationships. For instance, for a newspaper to have many advertisers, it is certainly important that it have many subscribers, and, to some extent, vice versa. But not only is the role the advertiser plays in the press budget much more important than that of the subscriber, as we know, it actually can be stated: a newspaper can never have too many advertisers, however—and this is in contrast to any other seller of goods—it can have too many buyers, namely, when it is unable to raise advertising rates to cover the costs of the constantly expanding circulation. This is quite a serious problem for some types of newspapers and generally means that starting with a certain circulation figure the expansionary interests of newspapers cease—at least this could happen under those conditions when an increase in advertising rates meets with difficulties. This is a characteristic of the press alone and is of a purely commercial nature, but it has numerous consequences. Admittedly, the international comparison of size and type of relationships between the press, which wants to educate and objectively inform the public about politics and other subject matters, and the business community, whose needs for publicity are reflected in advertising, is extremely different, if one uses France as an example. Why? With what general consequences?—these are the questions, although frequently addressed, that we will have to raise again, because only a partial consensus of opinions exists.

But let us continue: a current characteristic, in particular, is the growth of the capital needs of press enterprises. The question is, and this question has not yet been decided, because the best-informed experts disagree about it: to what extent does the increasing need for capital mean an increasing monopoly of already-existing enterprises. This could perhaps vary depending upon the circumstances. Because regardless of the effect of increasing capital needs, the strength of the monopoly position of already-existing newspapers differs, depending on whether the press relies regularly on subscriptions or on single sales, like abroad, where the individual has the choice each day of buying a different paper than he bought the day before, which—so it seems at first glance—perhaps facilitates the founding of new papers. Perhaps this phenomenon should be examined and combined with the effect of increasing capital needs to answer the question: does the increase of the investment also mean increasing power to mold public opinion according to one's own judgment? Or vice-versa—as it has been stated but without clear proof—does it mean an increasing sensitivity of individual enterprises to fluctuations in public opinion? It has been said that the obvious opinion change of certain French papers—one usually recalls the *Figaro* at the time of the Dreyfuss affair—can simply be explained by the fact that the large, fixed capital investment of the modern newspaper enterprise becomes increasingly sensitive to and, therefore, dependent on the public at times of public dissatisfaction, which results in

cancellations, that it finds economically unfeasible—this takes
into account the prevalent single-copy sales in France which
accommodate the ease of the change. This would mean, therefore, that
increasing dependence on current opinions is a consequence
of a growing need for capital. Is this true? That is a question we must
raise. It has been supported by press experts—I am not such an
expert—others have denied it.

   Furthermore, are we facing as a result of the increase of capital
investments among newspapers perhaps, as is often the case with
increasing capital needs, a move towards newspaper trusts?
What are the possibilities of such a trend? Gentlemen, this has been
denied most vigorously by renowned press experts, theoreticians as well
as practitioners. Of course, their major spokesman, Lord Northcliffe,[56]
could know more than he is saying, perhaps, since he is
one of the most important magnates of the press. What would be the
consequences for the character of newspapers if this would
happen? That newspapers of the large, already-existing companies
often display characteristics different from other papers is obvious.
Enough—I only used these examples to show how much the
business side of press enterprises must be taken into account—we
must ask ourselves: what is the meaning of the capitalist
development within the press enterprise for the sociological position of
the press in general, and for its role in the process of public
opinion formation?

   Another problem: the "institutional" character of the modern press
in Germany finds a specific expression in the anonymity of
what appears in the press. An infinite amount has been said "for" and
"against" the anonymity of the press. We do not take sides
but ask: how is it that this phenomenon can be found in Germany,
for instance, while abroad different conditions prevail, in France, for
example, while England is more closely related to us. Actually,
there is only one newspaper in France that operates strictly
on the basis of anonymity: the *Temps*. In England, on the other hand,
newspapers like the *Times* have most rigorously adhered to
anonymity. This may have been for quite different reasons. It
could be—as it seems to be the case with the *Times*—that
personalities from whom the newspaper receives its information are
frequently so important that it would be impossible for them
to release information under their own names. In other cases
anonymity may be used for exactly the opposite reason.
It depends: how does this question look in the light of conflicts of
interest which exist undeniably between the interest of the
individual journalist to become well known and the interest of the
newspaper not to become too dependent upon the cooperation

of this individual journalist. Again, there are differences depending
on commercial interests and on whether single sales dominate or not.
And above all, the political nature of society plays a role;
for instance, depending on whether a nation, and Germany
is an example, tends to be impressed more by the institutional powers
of a newspaper that acts like a "supra-individual" being
than by the opinion of an individual,—or whether it is free from this
type of metaphysics?—These are questions that already lead
into the area of part time journalism which looks different in Germany
than in England and in France, for instance, where the
part time journalist is a common phenomenon. And this invites the
question: who writes for the newspaper from outside the field,
and what? And who doesn't and what isn't written? And why not? This
leads now to the general question: how does the press
obtain the material that it offers to the public? And what does it really
have to offer, all in all? Is the steady increase in the importance
of purely factual accounts here a general phenomenon?
This is certainly the case in England, America, and Germany, but not
entirely so in France:—the Frenchman wants primarily an
opinion sheet. But why? For the American, for instance, wants nothing
but facts from his paper. Whatever opinions are published in
the press about these facts he regards as not worth reading; as a
democrat he is convinced that, in principle, he can interpret
as well as the newspaper writer, perhaps even better. But
the Frenchman, too, wants to be a democrat. Where does the difference
come in? In any event: in both cases the social function of
the press is an entirely different one.

Since there is the news service which despite these differences not
only burdens the budget of the press increasingly in all
countries of the world, but which as such is coming to the fore
more prominently,—this raises the next question: what are ultimately the
sources of this news:—the problem of the position of large news
agencies and their international relations among themselves.
Important studies must be conducted about this, the
beginnings of some are already available. The statements
advanced about the conditions of this area of study have been partly
contradictory, and the question remains whether objectively
it would be possible to secure more material than can currently be
obtained.

However, as long as the content of the newspaper consists neither of
news nor of boiler plate material—as is well known, there is a
mass production of press contents, from sports and puzzle
corner to the novel, a variety of items, by large, independent
enterprises—I say, as far as neither such syndicated material nor

straight news fill the pages of the press, there remains the
production of what is being offered today as a journalistic
accomplishment in the press, which is of fundamental
importance to the evaluation of the individual newspaper, at least in
Germany as opposed to non-German states. We cannot be
satisfied with the examination of the product at hand, but we must
respect its producer and ask about the fate and the situation
of journalism as a profession. The situation of the German
journalist, for instance, is quite heterogeneous with respect to conditions
abroad. In England, under certain circumstances, journalists
and publishers have entered the House of Lords. Men who were
known for no other accomplishments than that as businessmen
they created for their party an excellent paper which undercut—may one
say in this case: do not surpass—everything else. Journalists
became ministers in France, and in large numbers. In Germany,
however, this would be a great exception. And—even
disregarding this obvious superficiality—we must ask: how have
the conditions of professional journalists changed in individual
countries in the recent past.

What is the origin, the education, and what are the
professional demands upon the modern journalist?—And what is the
professional destiny of the German as compared to the foreign
journalist?—And finally what are his chances in life—possible outside
his profession—here and abroad? The general situation of
journalists is, apart from other aspects, rather variable, depending on
parties, type of newspaper, etc., as everyone knows. The
socialist press, for instance, is a special phenomenon which must be
treated separately, as must be the position of socialist editors;
and even more so the Catholic press and its editors.

Finally: what are the effects of this product, which presents the
complete newspaper, as it is to be examined by us in this way?
There is an enormous amount of literature, which is highly
valuable in parts, but which also contains extreme contradictions
even though experts have contributed to it. Gentlemen, as we
know, there has been an attempt to examine the effects
of the press on the human brain, the question about the consequences
of the fact that before he leaves for his daily work modern
man has become used to absorbing a journalistic hotch-potch which
forces him on a hurried trip through all areas of cultural
life, from politics to the theatre, and many other subjects. That this
makes a difference is obvious. It is quite possible and easy
to make some general remarks about it, in terms of how
this development merges with certain other influences to which

modern man is exposed. But the problem cannot be moved easily beyond the most elementary stages.

One will have to start with the question: what is the effect of newspapers on the kind of reading habits of modern man? On this all kinds of theories have been constructed. There was also the argument that the book is being replaced by the newspaper. It is possible; although German book production quantitatively "blossoms" in unbelievable ways as in no other country in the world; nowhere are there as many books thrown onto the market as here. The sales figures for the same books, however, show an inverse ratio. Russia, and this happened before the introduction of press freedom, had printings of 20,000 and 30,000 copies for such incredible books—with all respect to Anton Menger—as his *Neue Sittenlehre.*[57] There existed widely-read magazines which without fail experimented with a "final" philosophical base for their individuality. This would be impossible in Germany, and it will become impossible in Russia under the influence of at least relative press freedom; the beginnings are already visible. The press is involved in making what are, without doubt, tremendous changes in reading habits, and immense changes of the character and of the manner in which modern man absorbs the external world. The constant change and the acknowledgement of the widespread changes of public opinion among the universal and inexhaustible possibilities of points of views and interests, rest with an enormous weight upon the uniqueness of modern man. But how? This we must examine. I cannot go into details and close with the following remark:

We must examine the press first to this end: What does it contribute to the making of modern man? Secondly: how are the objective, supra-individual cultural values influenced, what shifts occur, what is destroyed and newly created of the beliefs and hopes of the masses; of the *Lebensgefühle*—as they say today— what is destroyed forever and newly created of the potential point of view? These are the last questions which we must raise, and you see immediately, honored members of the audience, the road to the answers to such questions is extremely long.

You will ask now: where is the material to begin such studies? This material consists of the newspapers themselves, and we will now, to be specific, start quite narrowly with scissors and compasses to measure the quantitative changes of newspaper contents during the last generation, especially in the advertising section, in the *feuilleton,* between *feuilleton* and editorial, between editorial and news, between what is generally carried as news and what is not presented. Because conditions have changed

significantly. The first steps of such investigations which try to
substantiate this exist, but only beginnings. From these
quantitative analyses we will proceed to qualitative ones. We will
have to pursue the kind of stylistic approach of the newspaper,
the way in which the same problems are discussed in newspapers
and outside of them, the apparent repression of the emotional
in the newspaper which at the same time has formed the
basis for its own capability to exist, and similar topics, and
finally we may approach the point where we may hope to slowly
close in on the wide-ranging question, it is our goal to answer it.

Weber knew that a project of this magnitude needed the cooperation not only of newspaper practitioners, including publishers, but also of his colleagues, and particularly those with an
interest in the study of the press. His proposal was highly am-
bitious and the goals clearly marked; it was, in a sense, typical
of Weber's approach to a problem area. What he needed was
evidence to construct a theory of the press. Not less. It has been
remarked that Weber's press study reflects more than any other
research proposal his plan to establish social science research
permanently in Germany.[58]

Unfortunately, the press survey did not succeed; Weber was
involved in a law suit against a newspaper that had printed an
anonymous article attacking his wife for her role in the women's
emancipation movement. He felt that he should resign from his
position as the chief investigator, but there was little interest
among the members of the sociological society to relieve him of
these duties. Weber gave an account of the developments during
the first day of the 1912 session of the German Sociological
Society. He expressed some confidence that the study would be
able to progress in the near future and that he had tried to support
some of the work currently under way. In particular, he mentioned studies of the meaning of classified advertising in the
German press, the press in Württemberg, the local press of West
Prussia, and the development of the newspaper feature. He
promised that he would be available for consultation concerning
the study, if the Society so desired. Marianne Weber described
these attempts to save the study:

> It became especially evident that none of the "great ones" were
> willing to lead the collective investigations. The organization

of the newspaper survey remained stuck on Weber. For months
he makes a great effort to get the work going but he is left
to seek help among real beginners. A few valuable investigations are
finally produced, but because of the difficult nature of
the subject matter, only on partial aspects of the problem. . . . After a
year and a half of efforts Weber realizes that he is merely
wasting his energies.[59]

The beginning of World War I may have added to the decision
to permanently delay the work. His ideas, however, continued in
a number of dissertations which tried to answer some of the
questions posed by Weber in his original plan. Among those who
followed up on Weber's suggestions was Groth, who examined
the press of Württemberg utilizing a quantitative content analysis to describe the coverage of ten newspapers of various types
over a one-year period.[60]

Finally, Weber's understanding of journalism and the press
must be viewed in the context of the political situation in Germany to which he responded. His intellectual involvement in
politics and science merged in his role as a political journalist.
Weber's professional attachment to the academic world and to
scholarship equipped him with the conceptual framework necessary to ask penetrating questions about his political and social
environment, but as a social theorist he also benefited from his
practical experiences as a journalist. Although Weber acknowledged the separation of politics and science, his journalism and
his theorizing about the role and function of the press in society
provide the best example of his pragmatic approach to life, in
which he drew freely upon all of his experiences while understanding, at the same time, that each profession has its own rules
and its own way of defining responsibility. It seems arbitrary
to consider Weber only in the context of one or the other professional environment; any assessment of his contribution must
take into account the whole person. His *engagement* as a political journalist is a case in point.

Weber's assessment of the role and function of the modern
press was also based upon his observation of an increasing
bureaucratization of society. Newspapers played a major part as

instruments of social and political change and as shapers of man. Thus, journalists occupied key positions in the struggle for authority to determine all facets of public opinion and to organize political, social, and economic aspects of culture. Weber, not unlike Tönnies, recognized the influence of economic pressures upon the press, and he suggested, for the first time, that a detailed, scientific study of newspapers would serve as a basis for a more precise definition of the function of the press in modern times. His ideas, as outlined in his notes and speeches, form a comprehensive agenda for press and mass communication research; they anticipated many developments in the research patterns as they developed particularly in the United States some decades later.

NOTES

1. Among the books are Reinhard Bendix, *Max Weber: An Intellectual Portrait* (New York: Doubleday Anchor, 1962); Ilse Dronberger, *The Political Thought of Max Weber: In Quest of Statesmanship* (New York: Appleton-Century-Crofts, 1971); Paul Honigsheim, *On Max Weber* (New York: Free Press, 1968); Arthur Mitzman, *The Iron Cage: An Historical Interpretation of Max Weber* (New York: Alfred A. Knopf, 1970); Walter G. Runciman, *A Critique of Max Weber's Philosophy of Social Science* (Cambridge: Cambridge University Press, 1972).

2. Talcott Parsons, "Max Weber 1864-1964," *American Sociological Review* 30:2 (1965), 174.

3. *Chronik der Christlichen Welt,* a weekly publication, appeared in newspaper format beginning in 1891. Details can be found in Joachim Kirchner, *Das Deutsche Zeitschriftenwesen: seine Geschichte und seine Probleme* (Wiesbaden: Otto Harrassowitz, 1962), vol. II, 276.

4. Wolfgang J. Mommsen, *Max Weber und die Deutsche Politik 1890-1920* (Tübingen: J.C.B. Mohr, Paul Siebeck, 1974), 21.

5. *Die Hilfe* was founded for the dissemination of Christian ideas concerning human welfare and social justice. Weber was among the financial guarantors of the publication, which reached a circulation of about 12,000 after one year. See Kirchner, 288.

6. Rolf Taubert, "Die Hilfe (1894-1943)," in Heinz-Dietrich Fischer (Hrsg.), *Deutsche Zeitschriften des 17. bis 20. Jahrhunderts* (Pullach: Verlag Dokumentation, 1973), 260.

7. *Neue Preussische (Kreuz-) Zeitung,* a conservative newspaper, was published in Berlin beginning in 1848. Details about the position of this newspaper in German politics are available in Kurt Koszyk, *Deutsche Presse im 19. Jahrhundert* (Berlin: Colloquium Verlag, 1966).

8. Reported in Eduard Baumgarten (Hrsg.), *Max Weber Werk und Person* (Tübingen: J.C.B. Mohr, Paul Siebeck, 1964), 692.

9. It was published in Berlin and edited by Heinrich Oberwinder and Hellmut von Gerlach beginning in October 1896; from 1897 until 1903 it was published as a weekly journal. See Koszyk, 139, 158-159.

10. Marianne Weber, *Max Weber, Ein Lebensbild* (Tübingen: J.C.B. Mohr, Paul Siebeck, 1926), 233, 235-236.

11. Among Germany's prestige newspapers with a liberal position, Frankfurter *Zeitung* was published beginning in 1856 by Leopold Sonnemann. For details, see Kurt Paupié, "Frankfurter Zeitung (1856-1943)," in Heinz-Dietrich Fischer (Hrsg.), *Deutsche Zeitschriften des 17. bis 20. Jahrhunderts.* Pullach: Verlag Dokumentation, 1973, 241-256.

12. Ludwig M. Lachmann, *The Legacy of Max Weber* (Berkeley: Glendessary Press, 1971), 95-96. Also, Baumgarten, 224.

13. Baumgarten, 710.

14. "Max Weber in seiner Gegenwart," in Johannes Winckelmann (Hrsg.), *Max Weber Gesammelte Politische Schriften* (Tübingen: J.C.B. Mohr, Paul Siebeck, 1958), xvi.

15. Baumgarten, 501. (my translation)

16. A chronological index to Weber's journalistic writings can be found in Marianne Weber's book, which lists 20 entries; another useful source is the collection of materials in Baumgarten's book, listed as part of the *Zeittafel.*

17. The items were collected and issued by Winckelmann and cover Weber's talks as well as his writings dealing with the political situation in Germany.

18. Dronberger, 6.

19. Heuss, xxiv.

20. Reported by Marianne Weber, 706. (my translation)

21. Heuss.

22. Originally given as a lecture at Munich in 1918; published as "Politik als Beruf," in Johannes Winckelmann (Hrsg.), *Max Weber Staatssoziologie* (Berlin: Duncker & Humbolt, 1966), 83. (my translation); an English-language version can be found in H. H. Gerth and C. Wright Mills, *From Max Weber: Essays in Sociology* (New York: Oxford University Press, 1946), 77-128.

23. Ibid., 96.

24. Ibid.

25. Ibid., 96-97.

26. Ibid., 97.

27. Ibid., 97-98.

28. Ibid., 98.

29. Ibid., 99.

30. Ibid., 127.

31. Raymond Aron, *Main Currents in Sociological Thought* (Garden City: Doubleday, 1967), vol. II, 282.

32. Otto Groth, *Die unerkannte Kulturmacht: Grundlegung der Zeitungswissenschaft* (Berlin: Walter de Gruyter, 1960), vol. V, 119. (my translation)

33. Gerth and Mills, 97.

34. Winckelmann, 389, 390.

35. Baumgarten, 422.

36. Winckelmann, 83.

37. Quoted by Ursula Jaehrisch, "Max Weber's Contribution to the Sociology of Culture," in Otto Stammer (ed.), *Max Weber and Sociology Today* (New York: Harper & Row, 1971), 235.

38. Baumgarten, 383.

39. As reported by Paul L. Lazarsfeld and Anthony R. Oberschall, "Max Weber and Empirical Research," *American Sociological Review* 30:2 (1965), 192.

40. See Hanno Hardt, "The Development of Mass Communication as a Field of Study in Germany: An Introduction," unpublished paper, School of Journalism, University of Iowa, February 1974.

41. Weber's original remarks are published in *Max Weber Gesammelte Aufsätze zur Soziologie und Sozialpolitik* (Tübingen: J.C.B. Mohr, Paul Siebeck, 1924), 433-441.

42. Emil Löbl (1861-1935) was an Austrian writer and journalist: he worked for the *Wiener Zeitung* and became managing editor of the *Neue Wiener Tageblatt* in 1917.

43. See below for full text of the address.

44. Reported in Karl Weber, "Zur Soziologie der Zeitung," in *Festgabe Fritz Fleiner zum siebzigsten Geburtstag* (Zürich: Polygraphischer Verlag, 1937), 421.

45. Ibid., 422. (my translation)

46. Ibid., 423.

47. Ibid.

48. Ibid., 424.

49. Ibid., 422.

50. As reported by Koszyk, 274.

51. See details below.

52. The essay is part of a speech delivered by Weber in 1910, at the first meeting of German sociologists in Frankfurt. In his talk he outlined two basic areas for sociological study: the press and formal organizations in German society. Source: Max Weber, *Gesammelte Aufsatze zur Soziologie und Sozialpolitik* (Tübingen: J.C.B. Mohr, Paul Siebeck, 1924), 434-441.

53. Weber refers here to Löbl's *Kultur und Presse* (Leipzig: Duncker & Humblot, 1903).

54. The mention of Jakob Burckhardt should be understood in the context of Burckhardt's work as a historian of ancient cultures. See his four-volume work, *Griechische Kulturgeschichte* (Berlin: W. Spemann, 1898).

55. Anton Menger (1841-1906), lawyer, professor. A social democrat, whose books reflected his political leanings.

56. Lord Northcliffe (1865-1922) was founder of England's first mass-circulation newspaper, the *Daily Mail*, 1896. He was, with his brother, Lord Rothermere, the owner of a number of other newspapers.

57. Weber refers here to Menger's *Neue Sittenlehre* (Jena: Gustav Fischer, 1905), in which the author describes the role of the press and public opinion as social powers.

58. Anthony Oberschall, *Empirical Social Research in Germany, 1848-1914* (The Hague: Mouton, 1965), 142.

59. *Max Weber, Ein Lebensbild*, 429.

60. Otto Groth, *Die Politische Presse Württembergs*. (Stuttgart: Scheufele, 1915).

7

The "American Science" of Society

Small, Ross, and Sumner
on Communication and the Press

SOCIOLOGICAL THOUGHT AND SOCIAL REFORM

The history of the social sciences in the United States is, at least in part, the story of individuals who participated in the transfer of cultural and social ideas from Germany. Most of the exposure to German scholarship occurred at such universities as Leipzig, Berlin, and Heidelberg, where thousands of American students engaged in graduate work throughout the latter part of the nineteenth century. Jurgen Herbst has described the experiences of those days and the influence of German thought on the development of American scholarship. Recognizing the complexity of tracing any direct effects or a "transfer of culture" in specific instances, Herbst came to the conclusion that

> the Americans who went to German universities to acquire the tools of scholarship brought home not only tools but ideas as well. When the ideas proved difficult to assimilate to American conditions, the scholars sought to modify or discard them, only to realize that their scholarly equipment, torn from its ideological setting, would no longer serve until a new context of ideas could be developed.[1]

This context was provided by a focus on society, by a recognition of process and change as elements in the definition of society, and by a perceived need for social reform. Thus, a tradition emerged that treated the social sciences as relevant and quite accessible for questions of societal needs and as a useful source for suggestions of change and improvement of social conditions. Although German scholars, among them Albert Schäffle, Karl Knies and Karl Bücher, were also engaged in the discussion of social reforms, this approach was a uniquely American way of combining scholarship with social action.

Specifically, it has been suggested that American sociology developed as a response to urbanization and industrialization through the work of a number of individuals and institutions that represented an intellectual commitment to improve social conditions and to work through university-level courses that stressed social problems and helped identify social issues. Hinkle and Hinkle commented in their historical account of American sociology that the discipline

> emerged in a social context in which the city and the factory were principal monuments of change. Few of the early sociologists would have seriously questioned the propriety of defining as progress the accumulating artifacts of living and the increasing mastery over nature wrought by the application of science to technology in the nascent urban-industrial society.[2]

Describing such potential problems areas as the differences between urban and rural interests, the power of economic and political control, and the effects of technology upon working conditions, the authors observed, "Among those who hoped to employ science in the amelioration of social evils were the sociologists."[3] The contributions of early American sociologists were based upon the theories of Comte and Spencer, in particular, and they showed the influence of other European scholars, notably Schäffle, but they also reflected the particular social, economic, and political conditions of the time. Thus, Albion Small found widespread agreement among his colleagues when he formulated four basic assumptions which according to this observation provided the framework for sociological thought in the United States. He described the reaction to these propositions by sociologists in 1906, writing that:

> (1) They accepted the task of searching for scientific laws of human behavior, which resemble invariant *natural laws* governing physical and

organic phenomena. (2) They identified social change as social evolution and interpreted it as *progress* toward a better society. (3) They regarded such upward human development as subject to acceleration by direct human *melioristic intervention,* using knowledge of sociological laws. (4) Finally, they conceived of social behavior and society as constituted of *individual behavior* and particularly emphasized the motivations of individuals in association.[4]

But Small was only one of several scholars who were regarded as the fathers of American sociology and whose works influenced the direction of the field for several generations.

Given this context of early American sociology, an attempt will be made to describe the thoughts of major American sociologists and to suggest the similarities of some of their ideas with those of their German teachers and colleagues. Specifically, the ideas of communication and mass communication in society as they were reflected in the works of Edward A. Ross, Albion Small, and William Sumner may help provide some understanding of their relationship with European, notably German, ideas as they appeared in the writings of Schäffle, Knies, Bücher, Max Weber, and Ferdinand Tönnies.

The group of American sociologists represented a generation of intellectuals who grew up during the latter part of the nineteenth century and who witnessed decisive economic and social changes in society. The rise of industrialization, coupled with the growth of American capitalism, particularly provided a major target for a criticism of the economic system. Among the many voices of protest and pleas for social reform were social scientists as well as journalists, many later identified as the muckrakers of their time, whose writings attacked corruption in the cities, the plight of the workers, and the power of big business. Among them were E. L. Godkin, founder of the *Nation*, with his attacks upon plutocracy in America, and Henry Demarest Lloyd, whose *Wealth Against Commonwealth* (1894), labeled as a "reporter's book of facts," anticipated the crusades of the muckrakers a few years later. With the aid of S. S. McClure a number of individuals launched their attacks upon the social and economic conditions of the United States to reach a fast-growing number of readers. In

January 1903, for instance, *McClure's* announced that it contained articles about

> capitalists, workingmen, politicians, citizens—all breaking the law, or letting it be broken. Who is left to uphold it? The lawyers? Some of the best lawyers in this country are hired, not to go into court to defend cases, but to advise corporations and business firms how they can get around the law without too great a risk of punishment. The judges? Too many of them so respect the laws that for some "error" or quibble they restore to office and liberty men convicted on evidence overwhelmingly convincing to common sense. The churches? We know of one, an ancient and wealthy establishment, which had to be compelled by a Tammany hold-over health officer to put its tenements in sanitary condition. The colleges? They do not understand.
> There is no one left; none but all of us.[5]

The problems of big business and the effects of technology and industrialization were reflected in the writings of individuals like Ida Tarbell, Ray Stannard Baker, Lincoln Steffens, who, together with Josiah Flint (*The World of Graft*) and James Howard Bridge (*The Inside History of the Carnegie Steel Company*), set the pace for others whose work was to appear in such magazines as Edward Bok's *Ladies' Home Journal*, as well as *Everybody's, Leslie's, Hampton's, Cosmopolitan and American Magazine*, which had been taken over by Steffens, Tarbell, Baker, Peter Finley Dunne, and William Allen White. These writers and editors, together with others, represented what has been described as

> a new moral, radical type of writing by men and women who yesterday had been entirely unknown or had written less disturbingly. These writers savagely exposed grafting politicians, criminal police, tenement eyesores. They openly attacked the Church. They defended labor in disputes which in no way concerned them personally, decried child exploitation, wrote pro-suffragist articles, and described great businesses as soulless and anti-social.[6]

But the press itself came under attack also, having moved through decades of rapid technological development to assume an important place among big business interests in this country. The managers and owners of the press moved to define inde-

pendence in terms of economic stability and realized that profit-
ability rested upon advertising revenue and their abilities to
attract large numbers of readers. Thriving upon its visibility,
the press was admired and condemned at the same time by those
who recognized its powers as a mover of society as well as the
abuse of its leadership role. Thus, there were admirers like Mable
Dodge, who called her time the "age of communication" and who
surrounded herself with those who represented power and influence, among them "heads of newspapers;"[7] and there were others,
whose indictment of the press left little doubt about their experiences with American journalism—like Upton Sinclair, whose
The Brass Check: A Study of American Journalism appeared in
1919.

The concern about the proper role of the press was reflected
also in scientific and literary journals. Articles appeared in the
American Journal of Sociology, for instance, that dealt with the
press and public opinion, journalism education, effects of newspaper coverage, and press ethics. They were sometimes accompanied by references to the fact that sociologists, in particular,
had an obligation to deal with the role and function of the press
in society and should address such problems in their work. Victor
S. Yarros pointed to the conflicts between the duty of a press to
inform the people and the desire to make money which resulted
in slanted news coverage. Sixteen years later in another article
he advocated the founding of privately endowed newspapers to
improve the service of the press, saying, "We have plenty of
syndicated trash, syndicated falsehood, syndicated malice, syndicated vulgarity and sensationalism. Why should not decency
and integrity, sobriety and common-sense use the resources of
cooperation and beneficence?"[8] George Vincent, who had col-
laborated with Albion Small, described a journalism course he
had taught for three years at the University of Chicago which
covered practical as well as theoretical aspects of the field,
devoting one section, for instance, to "The History and Organization of the American Press."[9] Frances Fenton investigated
the question of the effects of crime reporting upon criminal
activities in a two-part series asking, "Do people get the idea of,

or the impulse to committing criminal and other anti-social acts from the reading of such acts or similar acts in the newspapers?"[10] A year earlier, an "independent journalist" had published an article that raised the question of the possibility for an honest and sane press in the United States.[11] There were other outlets for critical essays dealing with the press, as well, which provided social scientists with an opportunity to participate in the general discussion. Thus, W. I. Thomas wrote on "The psychology of the Yellow Journal" in *American Magazine*,[12] and E. A. Ross reported about "The Suppression of Important News" in *Atlantic Monthly*.[13] Typical examples were such contributions as "Our Chromatic Journalism" by John A. Macy in *Bookman*[14] or Samuel W. Pennypacker's "Sensational Journalism and the Remedy" in the *North American Review*.[15]

In general, there developed a diverse and critical literature of press responsibilities and rights and obligations of journalists in the United States that reflected not only individual or scholarly concerns but also a perceived need for a regular and systematic treatment of the problems of mass communication in modern society. These writings, particularly by social scientists, remind contemporary readers of the universality of the problem and the number of issues still unresolved despite enormous efforts throughout the last thirty years to understand the workings of the communication process.

It was, then, in the context of such a widespread discussion of economic and social problems among literary, philosophical, and journalistic circles that social scientists added their ideas and provided yet another perspective to the social reform movement that characterized those times.

The group of early American sociologists whose contribution to communication and mass communication theories will be described in an exploratory manner to provide some idea of the cross-cultural nature of scholarly concerns in this area shared a number of experiences. They were widely educated: Ross began his career in economics; Sumner and Small added theology and history to their studies in economics. In addition, their academic careers were often preceded by practical experience. Although

Small and Ross had focused on academic careers, they often participated in the discussion of contemporary events. Sumner had worked on a religious newspaper besides his work as a clergyman. In terms of their writings as a reflection of political leanings, Sumner represented the conservative element in the group, with the belief in the Protestant ethic and the good of the individualistic enterprise. Small, on the other hand, through his work in Chicago and his European studies, reflected a broader interpretation of democratic ideals. Ross, finally, represented the democratic ideals of the Midwest, which championed political and economic equality and condemned plutocracy. They were also contemporaries of Thorstein Veblen, whose work as an evolutionary social philosopher reflected similar ideas or stimulated the later writings of a number of sociologists, notably Ross and Small.

SMALL AND HIS IDEA OF SOCIOLOGY

Albion Woodbury Small (1854-1926) was a keen observer of German sociology, and he was influenced by his contact with German scholarship early in his academic career when he encountered Albert Schäffle. In his review of American sociology Small discussed some of his own experiences, and he admitted, "For several years my lectures were an elaboration of Schaeffle, with one eye constantly on Spencer and Ward. This is a deliberate confession that during those years these writers about social phenomena got between me and the reality itself."[16] Small had reviewed Schäffle's *Bau und Leben des Sozialen Körpers* for the *American Journal of Sociology* in 1896/1897,[17] and he described his own approach to general sociology several times throughout his discussion of the "Scope of Sociology," which appeared in the same journal a few years later.[18] In his treatment of a functional approach to society Small stated,

> The most vital tendency in sociology since Comte has appeared in
> the attempts to analyze modern society functionally. This is the content

which gives to Schaeffle's work its permanent value despite the limitation which we have pointed out above. . . . Structural and functional analysis of activities within the state, or within society as a whole is prerequisite to classification of the associations that make up the state of society.

Briefly, this analysis of actual association in modern states was what Schaeffle attempted in his *Bau und Leben,* 1875. With merely the necessary minimum of attention to the other phases of the situation, he carried through a minute static analysis. He showed in great detail how different parts of the associational process interpenetrate each other and together maintain the entire individual and social life-process. He was far ahead of his time in prevision of the scientific and practical demand for this analysis. It has been the rule, ever since the first edition of his work appeared, to abuse and misrepresent it and its author in a fashion which indicates more plainly than anything else that people had not read the volume. They could not have originated or repeated such stupid judgments if they had made themselves familiar at first hand with the treatise itself. There are numerous and gratifying signs that the provincialism manifested in this treatment of Schaeffle is giving place to more critical and liberal appreciation. The respect with such a man as Schmoller, for instance, refers to Schaeffle shows that people who have less ability to make up sane opinions on the merits of evidence, but who are not above echoing secondhand judgments, will soon be obligated to acquire a new set of estimates of *Bau und Leben.*

At the same time it must be repeated that Schaeffle's analysis is, after all, only an incident in progress toward teleological analysis and classification of associations within states.[19]

A few years later in his elaboration of a general sociology, he came to the conclusion that Schäffle and Spencer must be given credit for a new interpretation of society. He said,

Almost at the same moment with the publication of Roscher's book, Schäffle was writing the preface of *Bau und Leben des socialen Körpers* (1875), and Spencer was delivering the first instalment of *Principles of Sociology* (1874-1877). "Society" had been rediscovered by a publicist whom Roscher himself had called "certainly one of the foremost economists of our time" . . . and by a cosmic philosopher who was doing more than any contemporary to advise the world of the significance of Charles Darwin's generalizations. Both of these writers were ridiculed and abused, but the opposition attacked non-essentials and was blind to that part of their work which marked an achievement in objective

apprehension of human reality. Both overworked biological analogies
as vehicles for exposition of the interconnections between human facts;
but all their crudities of method were outweighed by their service
in visualizing literal relations between different human activities.
Schäffle and Spencer had outgrown the obsessions which credited "state"
and "society" with "spheres" set off in mystical ways from persons.
They had advanced to the perception that human experience, from
earliest to latest, is a function of innumerable group relationships. . . .
We may characterize the Schäffle-Spencer stage of societary interpretation as assured of the continuity of human relationships, of interconnections of personal actions and reactions, from the minutest or
most casual human group out to the most comprehensive and permanent, as having made a creditable beginning of analyzing the social
groups and their interactions, from family to humanity, and (perhaps
most significant of all) as having in principle suspended all favoritism
toward particular types of groups. The clue which their analyses followed
was that society is a plexus of personal reactions mediated through
institutions or groups. One among these reaction-exchanges was the
state; but the state was no longer presumed to be in the last analysis
of a radically different origin, office or essence from any other group
in the system. It simply had to pass muster with the other groups, on
the merits or the demerits of its performance.[20]

Another indication of Small's identification with Schäffle's
approach to the study of society was his definition of sociology,
which moved from a direct adoption of Schaffle's formulation to
a more elaborate discussion of human associations that, many
years later, still showed signs of Schäffle's influence. For instance,
in his 1890 syllabus, *Introduction to the Science of Sociology,*
Small argued,

> Sociology is the science which has for its subject-matter the phenomena of
> human society, viz., the varieties of groups in which individuals are associated,
> with the organization, relations, functions and tendencies of these various associa-
> tions.
>   In other words, sociology is the science which combines and correlates all
> the special social sciences.[21]

In his elaboration on the essence of sociology Small summarized
his solution with a specific acknowledgment of Spencer, Schäffle,
and Ratzenhofer. In 1905, he said,

Human experience composes an associational process. The elements of that process are interests lodged in individuals. These interests may be reduced to least common denominators containing relatively simple essentials, but in the conditions of actual life, even at the most primitive stages, the interests express themselves in wants capable of infinite variation and combination. The individuals thus stimulated seek satisfactions of their wants, and efforts to this end bring them into contact with each other. At first these contacts are most evidently collisions; interest clashes with interest. The immediate result is formation of groups for offensive and defensive purposes. These groups in time vary more and more from the primitive animal type. As the variation increases, association becomes an accelerated process of differentiation or permutation of interests within the individuals, of contacts between individuals, of conflict and of co-operation among individuals and the groups into which they combine. Incidental to this pursuit of purposes, and to the process of adjustment between persons which results, individuals enter into certain more or less persistent structural relationships with each other, known in general as "institutions," and into certain more or less permanent directions of effort, which we may call the social functions. These social structures and functions are, in the first instance, results of the previous associational process; but they no sooner pass out of the fluid state, into a relatively stable condition, than they become in turn causes of subsequent stages of the associational process, or at least conditions affecting details of the process. There comes a time when some of the individuals in association begin to reflect upon the association itself in a fragmentary way. They think of their family, their clan, their tribe, their nation, as having interests of its own, instead of confining themselves to impulsive action stimulated merely by their individual interests. These men coin and utter thoughts and feelings and purposes which become current in their group. There are thenceforward more or less distinct group-programs, co-ordinating the instinctive endeavors of the individuals, and producing a certain mass-movement, in addition to the molecular motions, in the associational process. That is, the groups, as such, entertain purposes, and combine their efforts with some degree of reference to them. With this consumation the associational process is in full swing. All that follows is merely differentiated in detail. Interpretation of specific stages or areas of human experience is consequently a matter of qualitative and quantitative analysis of the experience in terms of these primary factors. History, or our own current experience, records its meaning in the degree in which it discloses the forms, the quality, the force, and the proportions with which these various powers of the different elements and conditions of association participate in the given action.[22]

COMMUNICATION AND SOCIETY

These lengthy statements reflect Small's commitment to a view of society as an organism; they also demonstrate his knowledge of the development of theoretical discussions in Europe and the controversies that surrounded the work of Schäffle, in particular. Given this theoretical orientation, Small would have to follow Schäffle's emphasis on communication as a necessary condition for the development of society and of language as a medium for the passing on of traditions. Thus, he explained in terms reminiscent of Schäffle's ideas,

> The development of society depends upon a free, rapid and accurate communication of physical impulses throughout the organism. The family group aids in this function in a way vaguely analogous to its distribution of material wealth. Ideas do not enter the family circle, however, through only one parent or both, but are introduced by every member and communicated to all who are mature enough to comprehend.[23]

These communication activities are possible because of the use of language which, according to Small, must be considered the "most flexible means of capitalizing human experience and of making it at the same time a circulating medium."[24] He characterized language further by pointing out,

> (a) Language stores up previous experience in forms available for present application. (b) Language makes past discoveries instantly available. (c) Language is a master-key to choice between processes that will and will not serve present purposes. (d) Language is a deposit of valuations which are like lighthouses for the sailor. They make navigation a matter of comparative safety and certainty, whereas without these guides it would be extra-hazardous.[25]

Small and Vincent in their 1894 *Introduction to the Study of Society* developed a communication model that appeared to be based upon the biological analogy of Schäffle's theory of communication as a nervous system of society. According to the authors, the communication system, as part of a regulatory system in society, penetrates the social organism and should be considered in a relationship "as the nerve fibers to the coordinating and controlling centers in the animal organism."[26] Communication in society is partly psychical and partly physical; it consists of a combination of psychical and physical changes which bring about the successful transmission of messages. Small and Vincent argued that "every social communication is effected between individuals, and every individual is a part of many different channels in the social nervous system."[27] This suggested that individuals are not only mediating but also "terminal cells" in the communication process. The authors described the individual in society as

> structurally a center from which radiate a greater or less number of psycho-physical channels. If we regard any two of these converging channels as continuous, the individual is a connecting cell. On the other hand, from the standpoint of the individual, he is a terminal cell, or end organ, of all the lines of communication which radiate from him into society.[28]

Individuals communicate ideas through a variety of symbols which preserve and render them transmissible, according to the authors, who listed among those symbols "oral, written, and printed language, vocal and instrumental music, gestures, drawings, photographs, paintings, statues, theatrical and operatic representations."[29] This listing of symbols followed Schäffle's elaboration on symbols and communication and rendered the basis for a discussion of dissemination and transmission of knowledge and information throughout society. The preservation of ideas through writing, printing, sculptures, or pictorial presentations as well as the coordination of communication efforts through postal services or telegraph companies suggested a structure through which the communication of ideas could be provided with technical devices to accommodate the presentation of symbols over space and time.

In their discussion of the arrangement and coordination of communication channels, Small and Vincent argued that social communication systems are based upon the existence of communication channels in social groups and upon their coordination with respect to a source of authority. They identified a general communication system in society as consisting of a number of clearly distinguishable parts: "(1) the press, (2) the commercial system, (3) public address, (4) the educational system, (5) the ecclesiastical system, (6) the governmental system."[30] At the same time they pointed out that these parts were, indeed, inseparably interwoven with other parts of the system; and they added that the press "is incorporated in nearly every division of the psycho-physical communicating apparatus, and is almost as general in its scope as the post office itself."[31] The authors proceeded to discuss the significance of these communication systems in society, among them: the communication process in the economic organization "by which production, transportation, and exchange of wealth are coordinated;" the public speaker as center of "as many different psycho-physical channels as he has hearers"; the functions of schools to increase and to communicate knowledge; the church which presents "pecular psychical impulses" from the religious standpoint; and organized government which is described as "the clearest and most complete example of a social communicating structure."[32]

Most significant, however, is the description of the press as "all the arrangements of communicating channels for the collection of ideas, the embodiment of them in printed symbols, and the distribution of the latter throughout social groups of greater or less magnitude."[33]

THE ORGANIZATION OF THE PRESS

Small and Vincent saw the organization of the press as "convergence of psycho-physical channels toward a center, where there are devices for making symbols, which are distributed by various means of transportation among larger or smaller numbers of individuals."[34] They commented upon the existence of general interest newspapers which cater to the needs of larger segments of society and of "group" papers which are designed to satisfy the interests of special groups or organizations rather than of society as a whole. In addition, the communication network also consists of news agencies on national and international levels, press syndicates, and plate makers which help disseminate identical messages throughout the societal system with the aid of agencies, such as wholesalers, retailers, and carriers, which are responsible for the transportation of printed materials. As an illustration of the communication of news items, Small and Vincent used the working conditions of a telegraph editor:

> The telegraph editor is the connecting link between the paper and the outside world. He reads the messages sent from the head office of the general press association, and selects such matter as he deems desirable. The general manager of this press service, sitting in his office in New York or Chicago, receives reports from his special correspondents in all parts of the country. These he sifts and then transmits to several central distributing points, whence they are telegraphed to the various papers in the association. Now and then, a cable message arrives from an international agency in London or Paris, where news from all over the world is being collected and distributed to meet the demands of different countries. Thus the report of an anarchist outrage in Seville finds a ready channel via Madrid, Paris, London, and New York or Chicago to any American city or large town.[35]

They emphasized the effects of social and economic developments upon the spread of knowledge; and they pointed out that with the division of labor, for instance, demands for information increased among individuals:

> Other important means of education in the form of books and newspapers now enter the community in considerably larger numbers, relatively to the population—an increase due both to greater regularity of transportation, and to the new demand which, as we have seen, is created by the modified conditions of village life.[36]

Further developments of larger population centers resulted in the rise of opinion leaders and the power of newspapers, as social institutions, to influence their environment. The authors concluded that "newspapers, and the expressed opinions of societies, parties, churches, and other aggregates and organs not only largely control their immediate constituencies, but often wield power in much wider circles."[37] Small and Vincent continued to describe the growing influence of those whose expertise in one field led to their acceptance as opinion leaders over a wide range of topic areas. The authors suggested that influence is wielded by authorities in the position to provide leadership and "to give direction to social knowledge, feeling, and volition."[38] Their views of the press in its relation to leaders and their publics recall Schäffle's discussion of newspaper activities in the context of the political and social advancements of society. The press becomes the most instrument for the communication of ideas between authority and followers, since personal contacts and public meetings present severe limitations of efforts to exert direct and constant influence. Small and Vincent concluded,

> The press, therefore, is the chief medium of communication between
> the greater authorities and their followers. Scholars present the results
> of their researches in books and journals; theological leaders have papers
> of their own, and also gain admission to the general press; statesmen
> and politicians often control personal newspapers; while parties, factions,
> syndicates, and other groups either manage their own organs or exert
> influence upon other journals. The authorities of fashion communicate
> impulses by means of special newspapers, as well as through the general
> press.[39]

The authors also remarked upon the influence of the press and came to the conclusion that the daily experiences with the press demonstrated the widespread use of newspapers by those who sought to impress and lead their fellow citizens in all matters of public interest. They suggested that advancing studies of society will yield more evidence to suggest the "immense influence of the press," and they added,

> In reality, the impulses communicated by this organ, regarded as a
> whole, give stimulus and direction to social activities of every kind.
> The fact that large numbers of individuals are not reached directly by
> the newspaper does not materially weaken this statement. The press
> influences all, at least, who are capable of exercising leadership, and
> through them makes itself felt to the very limits of the psychical organ-
> ism.[40]

They concluded their discussion of press influences with the observation that coercion of authority can be accomplished by a reversed process, that is, by the use of letters to the editor and that "personal communications to officials, mass meetings, etc., are among the means employed by the public to influence authority."[41]

PRESS CRITICISM

Small and Vincent also included a critical assessment of press performance in their discussion of newspapers as among the most pervasive communication systems in society. They seemed convinced of the influence of the press and advocated, therefore, that the service of press enterprises undergo a close examination to review the practices and to comment upon the duties and responsibilities of newspapers. According to the authors, the press did not provide adequate services in reporting facts, giving directions to public opinion, and regarding form and contents of their information. Despite its highly organized character, the press remained careless and inefficient in its news coverage; Small and Vincent felt that the "average newspaper as a reporter of reality is the old-time gossip in print."[42] They suggested that sensationalism combined with self-interest, and sometimes corruption, led to a distortion of facts which made it almost impossible to glean from newspapers a knowledge of social activities and a proper sense of the ethical attitudes of the people. Thus, they felt, "Suggestive picture and plays are a constant menace to society, as a source of psychical changes in individuals, which, finding outward expression in ill health and vice, affect the whole organism from the family to the state."[43] On the other hand, the authors urged to refrain from condemning the press as being solely responsible for activities that resulted in antisocial behavior. For them, the press was part of the social fabric, and its expressions had to be seen as reflecting societal developments. They observed that newspapers "exhibit all the phenomena of interdependence that characterize other organs."[44]

Small and Vincent acknowledged the economic dependence of the press, pointing to the importance of subscriptions and advertising as major economic forces that influenced the well-being of newspapers. One which did not succeed was looked upon as "an organ which fails to secure adequate sustenance, [and] must perish. Hence the first question with any newspaper is, in the nature of things, economic."[45] Secondly, newspapers had to submit to their readers in order to remain attractive enough to large numbers of individuals. Thus, the content of the press reflected the products of authorities in society as well as public reactions. Small and Vincent observed that the "newspaper may lead its public positively, but it must adapt itself, in a measure, to that public's opinions, tastes, and prejudices."[46] Consequently, Small and Vincent ended their discussion of the press as an authority in society with the remark that although the press may exhibit pathological phenomena "the responsibility must be distributed throughout the whole organism, not fixed upon the newspaper as the ultimate source of the evils."[47]

Small's work reflects a strong and lasting influence of European, notably Schäffle's, social theories. In his own writings about the development of society, he saw communication at the center of sociological inquiries. But Small not only recognized the importance of symbols and language as means of social communication, he also described the interdependence of various communication channels, emphasizing the systemic character of the communication process in society. The press, and with it the complete system of public communication, occupied a central position as collector and disseminator of information. He suggested that more advanced studies of the press would yield evidence to show the immense influence of the press. Specifically, he recognized the gatekeeping function of editors, and he described the two-step flow of communication in his discussion of the press and opinion leaders, anticipating major areas of research in years to come. His assessment of the press as a most powerful instrument of social communication also implied that any suggestion for the improvement of society must begin with a critical investigation of the existing press system. At the same time, however, he advocated that the responsibility for a sound and well-working system of public communication must be placed not solely on the press, but on society as a burden to be shared equally by all participants in the process of social communication.

ROSS AND HIS CONCEPT OF COMMUNICATION

Edward A. Ross (1866-1951) combined scholarship with an intense engagement in social issues of the day; this orientation toward action made him unique among early American sociologists, notably Ward, Cooley, Giddings, Small, and Sumner. He was a keen observer and reporter of his social and economic environment, and his travels abroad and wide range of interests at home were reflected in a large number of publications. Ross, it seems, could also be considered a journalist, his contributions to the discussion of social issues appearing in a variety of magazines, scholarly journals, and books.

Problems of communication and mass communication remained part of his theoretical and practical concerns in many of his writings. Theoretically, Ross considered communication as one of the most important examples of the social process, a phenomenon that played a central role in his earlier scholarly work; whereas public opinion and the processes of publicity were dealt with as external agencies of social control. Practically, he observed the growing commercialization of the press, the impact of radio, and effects of film on the minds of young individuals as consequences of improved communication.

Ross defined communication not only in terms of symbols but also included the means of dissemination. Thus, he wrote,

Communication embraces all symbols of experience together with the means by which they are swung across gulfs of space or time. It takes in facial expression, attitudes and gestures, tones of the voice, speech, writing, printing, the newspaper, telegraphs, telephones, radios, railways, automobiles, airplanes, and whatever else facilitates mental contacts.[48]

He discussed the developments of transportation and communication as ways of improving human interaction and as the rise of "congenial association" beyond the physical limitations of small towns or neighborhoods and the intellectual confines of small groups: "But with the aid of modern facilities for communication you may discover distant choice spirits who are more congenial and stimulating to you than your near relatives or next-door neighbors."[49] Earlier, Ross had pointed out that the patterns of economic life demanded changes in the system of communication. He said that the "growth of potential exchange, in consequence of the greater local surpluses to be disposed of and the greater local deficits to be supplied from outside sources, makes it worth while to create avenues of communication, and these, in turn, promote the territorial division of labor."[50] The advancements of communication technologies had a number of consequences for individuals; not only was it possible to travel farther and to exchange ideas, it was also quite possible to receive through a number of communication media a variety of social stimuli and to belong to a number of different publics. Ross suggested that although an individual can be a member of only one crowd at a time, "by taking a number of newspapers one can belong to several publics with, perhaps, different planes of vibration."[51] He defined the public as a "dispersed crowd, a body of heterogeneous persons, who, although separated, keep so closely in touch with one another that they not only respond to a given stimulus at almost the same moment, but are aware of each other's response."[52] Ross described the differences between face-to-face communication and communication mediated by newspapers, for instance, and he commented upon the effects of such communication under these conditions:

> The member of a public brought into touch by the daily press cannot learn how others respond to a certain stimulus until hours have elapsed. . . . We have seen that in presence the means of expressing feeling are much more copious and direct than the facilities for expressing thought. In a dispersed group feeling enjoys no such advantage. Both are confined to the same vehicle—the printed word—and so ideas and opinions run as rapidly through the public as emotions; perhaps more rapidly, for is it not easier for a writer to be clear than to be forceful?[53]

He also summarized the consequences of technological advancement in communication by pointing to the fact that reading was
replacing face-to-face communication as a source of ideas. He
said,

> Even if the wider reading of magazines and books should check
> the manufacture of public opinion in this wholesale way by irresponsi-
> ble newspaper owners, it would still be bad for the bulk of people never
> to get beyond so unstimulating a way of gaining ideas. Welcome, there-
> fore, be the newer pedagogy which encourages the pupil to self-activity
> and trains him to debate and the oral interchange of ideas! Even
> more promising is the spread of "social centers." where neighbors in
> their common hall consider community problems of which they have
> first-hand knowledge.[54]

A similar approach was taken by Ross in his discussion of
oral and print cultures in which he came to the conclusion that
modern communication media contain an antitraditional bias.
Accordingly, the print media tend to create contacts with the
present rather than with the past. He said,

> Oral tradition overlaps time, books both time and space. Most of
> what the illiterate receive orally—lays, ballads, legends, myths, and
> proverbs—is *handed down* and consequently cuts a channel between
> past and present, but not between people and people. Therefore dif-
> fusion of the ability to read makes, on the whole, for progress, though,
> to be sure, the staple of reading may come to be an ancient sacred
> literature. To-day, at least, the power to read opens a door to the news-
> paper, which is the natural enemy of tradition, because it is bound to
> emphasize the new and to exaggerate the momentousness of the pres-
> ent.[55]

This view was also echoed a few years later when he wrote,

> With its emphasis on the *present* the newspaper weakens the grasp
> of traditions which hold groups apart. Readers of the same newspaper
> are oriented in the same direction and find new and common interests.
> The American "yellow" newspaper, which by means of scare-heads,
> color pictures, comic strips, and gong effects gains the attention of
> foreign-born, has been a potent agent of Americanization.[56]

Newspapers were organs of public opinion, according to Ross;
however, their self-serving interests often destroyed their value

as a reflection of societal interests or demands. Ideally, organs of public opinion not only were expressions of existing views, but also represented a factor in molding judgments. Ross felt that although advocates were worthless as indices of public opinion, they could be valuable on related topics. Thus, "the utterances of the great anti-saloon organ may be significant and representative on everything save prohibition."[57]

THE POWER OF THE PRESS

In another context Ross explained the potential dangers of the press in the hands of individuals who were determined to manipulate the public and to create the kind of public opinion that would enhance their own cause. He admitted that the newspapers had a "great and growing power over the public mind owing to its fixing the perspective in which current events are seen by the reader." He continued,

> By controlling the distribution of emphasis in the telling of facts, by stressing day by day one sort of facts and keeping the opposite sort in the background, by giving the news which he wants noticed the front page and bold type, while giving the news he wants overlooked an inside page and nonpareil, the newspaper-owner manufactures the impressions that breed opinion and, if he controls a chain of important newspapers, he may virtually make public opinion without the public knowing it![58]

Ross traced these activities to the competitive nature of the newspaper business, which must rely on advertising and circulation to survive and prosper. Among the devices to enhance its economic condition was the exploitation of the unique and bizarre aspects of life. Ross referred to the growth of the sensational press, which had succeeded in "distorting the significance of the moment." He described the character of the yellow press and concluded that

> the constant flitting from topic to topic brings upon the confirmed newspaper reader what we may call *paragraphesis,* i.e., inability to hold the mind on a subject for any length of time. Reading so inimical to

poise, self-control, and mental concentration as the sensational newspaper should be cut down to a minimum.[59]

Ross was convinced that newspaper publishers operated their
enterprises not as individuals aware of the press and its potential
effect as an instrument of social reform, but as businessmen
concerned about investments and profit margins. He observed
that "in newspaper publishing the capital factor gains constantly
on the service factor; less and less is the editor-owner able to
hire the capital he needs, while more and more the owner is a
capitalist who hires the editors he needs."[60] He acknowledged
the fact that newspapers were peculiar in that they united "two
services altogether different—the purveyance of news and
opinions and the sale of publicity in the form of advertising.
The former is a responsible public service, the latter the marketing of a ware."[61] And he added that advertisers because of their
economic strength exert influences upon the press that can be
translated into censorship of editorial matter and news coverage.
Ross went so far as to declare that the domination of the commercial mind over everything else was due, in part, to the
behavior of the press. He said, "The clandestine prostitution of
the great bulk of the newspapers to advertisers is the secret of the
astounding domination the business class have gradually gained
over us, a domination which arrests the attention of every
philosophic foreigner on his first visit to the United States."[62]
Ross warned that complete control by business interests over the
American mind could be resisted by teachers and some members
of the clergy only as long as attacks upon them did not succeed
in undermining their spirits. He commented upon the rise of the
press as a major weapon in the hands of the business world and its
insistence upon a special status in society. Ross added,

> The pretensions of the commercialized press to a priestly status
> have come to be so ridiculous that increasingly the public is indifferent
> to the so-called "invasions" of the traditional "freedom of the press"
> by government officials and to the newspapers' clamor to be carried
> in the mails for a pittance. Why should taxpapers meet postal deficits
> caused by hauling to readers for almost nothing thousands of tons of
> advertising circulars containing only a little tainted reading matter?

Perhaps the classic privileges should be withheld from newspapers which derive more than a third of their income from advertising. The "daily paper" would cost more to be sure, but then it might tell more truth![63]

The passions of Ross as a social critic and his interests in the contemporary developments of society were best reflected perhaps in *Changing America*, a collection of articles dedicated to "my irenic and catholic-minded co-laborer Albion W. Small." In his "The Suppression of Important News" he analyzed the problems of the daily press.

Ross suggested that the desire to give the public what it wants resulted in sensationalism, since a press that tried to cater to millions could not be expected to remain dignified: "To interest errand-boy and factory girl and raw immigrant, it had to become spicy, amusing, emotional, and chromatic. For these, blame, then, the American people."[64]

THE FAILURE OF THE DAILY PRESS

The problem of daily newspapers, however, was that they did not give the news, according to Ross, despite the fact that they utilized technological advancements in the pursuit of information, that more educated men and women had been drawn into journalism, that personal journalism had all but disappeared, that schools of journalism had been established "with high hopes." He listed and described three economic factors as contributing to the failure of the daily press.

First, the American press must be considered a capitalist enterprise. With rising costs for printing plants, staffs, and news agencies, large sums of money were necessary to establish and maintain newspapers. Editors were no longer owners of newspapers, because they did not have the capital. Instead, as Ross wrote,

More and more the owner of the big daily is a business man who finds it hard to see why he should run his property on different lines from the hotel proprietor, the vaudeville manager, or the owner of an amusement park. The editors are hired men, and they may put into the paper no more of their conscience and ideals than comports with getting the biggest return from the investment.[65]

The commercialization of the press meant that it was operated like any other business enterprise. Therefore,

> the paper is likelier to be run as a money-maker pure and simple—a factory where ink and brains are so applied to white paper as to turn out the largest possible marketable product. The capitalist-owner means no harm, but he is not bothered by the standards that hamper the editor-owner.[66]

Secondly, the growth of advertising was significant for any assessment of newspaper services. Ross referred to the major two functions of the press as those of providing news and selling advertising space: "one calls for good faith, the other does not. The one is the corner-stone of liberty and democracy, the other a convenience of commerce."[67] Since advertising contributed substantially to the income of the press and, thus, to its stability, concerns for subscribers as the second source of income remained less urgent. The results were, at least, a threat to the independence of news and editorial matter. But he warned, "When news-columns and editorial page are a mere incident in the profitable sale of mercantile publicity, it is strictly 'business-like' to let the big advertisers censor both.[68] On the other hand, Ross acknowledged the existence of critical judgment and good sense of individuals and did not propose the possibility of complete suppression of news and information by the press as a result of advertising pressures. He said that the "intelligence and the alertness of the reading public" helped regulate newspaper content also. But he warned, "The immunity enjoyed by the big advertiser becomes more serious as more kinds of business resort to advertising."[69]

Thirdly, the merger of newspapers with larger business interests and the acquisition of press properties by big business suggested the dangers of information control by large corporations. Ross was afraid that in such instances the press could easily become the mouthpiece for special interests which would try to influence public opinion:

> The magnate-owner may find it to his advantage not to run it as a newspaper pure and simple, but to make it—on the sly—an instrument for coloring certain kinds of news, diffusing certain misinformation, or fostering certain impressions or prejudices in its clientele. In a word, he may shape its policy by non-journalistic considerations.[70]

Ross went on to cite a number of cases to illustrate the power of economic interests over newspaper coverage and editorial decision-making. He talked about "kept newspapers," "killing important news," and "sacred cows" in an attempt to demonstrate the variety of ways in which press content was manipulated by owners and editors. He concluded,

> In view of their suppression and misrepresentation of vital truth, the big daily papers, broadly speaking, must be counted as allies of those whom—as Editor Dana reverently put it—"God has endowed with a genius for saving, for getting rich, for bringing wealth together, for accumulating and concentrating money."[71]

Even newspapers that had engaged in successful crusades against misconduct and corruption would cease to be effective. They would become valuable property and, therefore, remain guarded during future confrontations protecting their commercial investments. Thus, the results would be similar to those of other newspapers with purely commercial histories.

What could be done? Ross felt that one must "refrain from arraigning and preaching"; instead, he said,

> What is needed is a broad new avenue to the public mind. Already smothered facts are cutting little channels for themselves. The immense vogue of the "muck-raking" magazines is due to their being vehicles for suppressed news. Non-partizan leaders are meeting with cheering response when they found weeklies in order to reach their natural following. The Socialist Party supports two dailies, less to spread their ideas than to print what the capitalistic dailies would stifle. Civic associations, municipal voters' leagues, and legislative voters' leagues are circulating tons of leaflets and bulletins full of suppressed facts. Within a year five cities have, with the taxpayers' money, started journals to

acquaint the citizens with municipal happenings and affairs. In many
cities have sprung up private non-partizan weeklies to report civic information. Moreover, the spoken word is once more a power. The demand
for lecturers and speakers is insatiable, and the platform bids fair to
recover its old prestige. . . . Congressional speeches give vent to boy-
cotted truth, and circulate widely under the franking privilege. City
clubs and Saturday lunch clubs are formed to listen to facts and ideas
tabooed by the daily press.[72]

His own solution, however, was the establishment of endowed
newspapers. Ross felt that since the public was unable to recognize and pay for the truth, much could be gained for the idea of
democracy by turning away from the inadequate service of the
commercial media to public-owned newspapers: "Endowment is
necessary, and, since we are not yet wise enough to run a public-
owned daily newspaper, the funds must come from private
sources."[73] To prevent the control of such public newspapers by
individuals who might advocate a conservative, safe approach to
the printing of news and opinion, Ross suggested that the govern-
ing boards of such newspapers be selected from member of civic
and professional groups. He said,

> This could be done by letting vacancies on the governing board be
> filled in turn by the local bar association, the medical association,
> the ministers' union, the degree-granting faculties, the federated teachers,
> the central labor union, the chamber of commerce, the associated chari-
> ties, the public libraries, the non-partizan citizens' associations, the
> improvement leagues, and the social settlements. In this way the endow-
> ment would rest ultimately on the chief apexes of moral and intellectual
> worth in the city.[74]

Endowed newspapers would not play up crime and sensational
events or trivial occurrences, but give interesting, serious news
instead. They would not attempt to reach millions of readers, but
would typically be read by opinion leaders, for instance, like
teachers, preachers, and public figures. In addition, Ross saw the
duty of endowed newspapers as being corrective, thus helping to
keep the commercial press honest. He concluded that "the
endowed newspaper in a given city might print only a twentieth of
the daily press output and yet exercise over the other nineteen-

twentieths an influence great and salutary."[75] The idea of change through the introduction of corrective influences appeared also in connection with his discussion of the manipulation of news and information. At the time Ross suggested that more positive influences on the individual could be achieved through exposure to other life experiences. He said,

> The remedy for this sinister tendency is not the curbing of newspapers, but the strengthening of corrective influences. The pulpit addresses itself to the deeper parts of human nature rather than to the more easily awakened instincts. The teacher relies on organized information rather than on organized emotion to bring about the reforms he desires. The writer of a book more often addresses the reader's intelligence than the newspaper writer, so that the use of public libraries has a steadying effect.[76]

THE EFFECTS OF THE MEDIA

A few years later, Ross turned to the problem of the effects of motion pictures on children. In an address delivered to the National Motion Picture Conference in Chicago Ross attacked the failure to recognize that the needs of children are different from adult needs and should be recognized in the debates concerning the public showings of films. He was convinced that unregulated access would affect the minds of children and juveniles. Based upon his observations and his talks with parents and educators, Ross concluded that

> more of the young people who were town children sixteen years ago or less are sex-wise, sex-excited, and sex-absorbed than of any generation of which we have knowledge. Thanks to their premature exposure to stimulating films, their sex instincts were stirred into life sooner than used to be the case with boys and girls from good homes, and as a result in many the "love chase" has come to be the master interest in life.[77]

He was convinced that more exposure to certain types of films would result in even greater harm to society, and he advocated that society draw a line between films to be shown to children and to persons above 16 years of age. He advocated censorship for children's movies and the right of communities to bar from exhibition films which were not suitable for showing to children.

The concerns with the effects of propaganda were reflected in his treatment of the "wholesale manufacture of misconception." Ross argued that propaganda and censorship were the new methods of manipulating people and of winning political support. He observed, "To be obnoxious propaganda need not resort to falsehoods and misrepresentations; it may employ nothing but the truth, yet be anathema to the decent because under its fine professions it hides or suppresses the counter-balancing truth."[78] He listed a number of examples, including the use of newspapers as carriers of one-sided information for the benefit of large corporations, utilities, or politicians. To deflate unscrupulous propaganda, Ross advocated the widespread use of radio broadcasting. There were certain advantages over the use of newspapers to combat propaganda, among them the fact that "the spoken word can be more inflammatory than the written, and the human voice can stir emotion quicker than the printed page."[79] In addition, "a broadcasting station requires little capital, its chief asset is the 'cleared channel of the air' which has been granted it for a brief term on the ground of 'public interest, convenience and necessity'."[80]

In summary, Ross, too, explained communication as a necessary condition for the growth of society. He discussed economic and technological determinants of public communication systems and concentrated much of his commentary upon the effects of modern media on members of society. He warned that newspapers, in particular, may contribute to a loss of tradition and of a sense of history with their exclusive treatment of contemporary events. The danger of the modern press and its ultimate failure must be sought in the capitalist system which used newspapers as carriers of commercial messages or controlled them through mergers with business interests. Not unlike Bücher, he described the peculiar nature of the press as a public servant in its dissemination of news and opinion and as a salesman in its marketing of products. He advocated the establishment of publicly owned or endowed newspapers as possible solutions and a liberation from economic pressures. His discussion of communication effects, including the exposure of children and young adults to motion pictures, anticipated later mass-communication research areas that treated the effects of written, oral, or visual communication and the importance of studying children and mass communication. Ross provided a number of arguments in his attacks upon the abuses of the mass-media system to help strengthen ideas of a democratic system of mass communication in which access to truthful information, fairness, and the belief in freedom of expression are important concerns.

SUMNER AND HIS IDEA OF COMMUNICATION

William Graham Sumner (1840-1910) showed a great interest in economics and social problems from the beginnings of his academic career. His work centered on the ideas of individualism and laissez faire, as well as on the role of the "forgotton" man in society. In his writings he was influenced by Spencer, Gumplowicz, Ratzenhofer, and Lippert, whose *Culturgeschichte der Menschheit in ihrem organischen Aufbau* (1866/1867) was reflected in Sumner's most famous treatise, *Folkways*, published in 1906. He expressed an evolutionary view of social life and denied the possibility of social efforts to change the course of events:

> Spontaneous forces will be at work, compared with which our efforts are like those of a man trying to deflect a river, and these forces will have changed the whole problem before our interferences have time to make themselves felt.
>
> The great stream of time and earthly things will sweep on just the same in spite of us. . . . It will swallow up both us and our experiments. . . . That is why it is the greatest folly of which man can be capable, to sit down with a slate and pencil to plan out a new social world.[81]

He was convinced that any social progress must come gradually and be based upon the rather unconscious operations of social, economic, and intellectual forces.

Sumner considered language as the most important instrument of exchange among individuals and a condition which prepared the ground for mobility among people. He said, "The first and prime instrumentality for the exchange of anything between human beings is language. It might be called a tool without stretching that term out of all recognition; it is, at any rate, no organic product, but a societal one."[82] He went on to describe the gradual development of language in an evolutionary process that involved all members of society. The invention of writing established a major accomplishment in man's search for instruments that would overcome time and space. He spoke of "writing as a means for the preservation and transmission of ideas and culture across time and space. Literature discharges an important function in acquainting peoples with one another's characteristics; the novel has been highly effective in that way."[83] And he talked about the resulting cross-fertilization of culture contemplating the fact that civilization was actually a "function of numbers in contact."[84]

Intercommunication, according to Sumner, was seen in terms of the transmission of materials and ideas, and became an important function in the development of human civilization. He had pointed out earlier that "language is a product of the need of cooperative understanding in all the work, and in connection with all the interests, of life. It is a societal phenomenon."[85] With the rise of technology, communication improved and brought about the dissemination of ideas over large areas of the world; at the same time, progress also led to different forms of information retrieval from those of earlier days. Sumner commented upon the

> world-wide effects of the advances in the arts and sciences which
> have been made during the last hundred years. These improvements
> have especially affected transportation and communication; that is,
> they have lessened the obstacles of time and space, which separate the
> groups of mankind from each other and have tended to make the whole
> human race a single unit.[86]

In another connection he observed that guilds as forms of associations which brought about "accord and concord" were replaced by better modes of action: "Correspondence, travel, newspapers, circulars, and telegrams bring employers and capitalists the information which they need for the defense of their interests."[87] He added that employees were unable to use such information devices because of the lack of capital, but he suggested that the press could assist in the distribution of labor: "No newspapers yet report the labor market. If they give any notices of it—of its rise and fall, of its variations in different districts and in different trades—such notices are always made for the interest of the employers."[88]

As a matter of fact, Sumner saw in the advancements of society a need for the reorganization of industrial efforts on a worldwide scale. He said that "the immense increase in all facilities of transportation and communication has made it not only possible but necessary to organize industry in co-operative combinations which reach over state boundaries and embrace the whole globe."[89] He added that the direction of industrial growth forced consequences upon society which it could not ignore. Thus, he wrote, "If we use steam and electricity we must get space for their evolutions, and we must adjust our plans to their incidental effects. Organization on a grand scale is a necessary consequence of steam and electricity."[90] As result of this development was the loss of independence for the "little independent man." This, Sumner felt, was "as inevitable as the introduction of machinery and the consequences of machinery."[91] For him the communication of intelligence became a dominant cause and a reason for the reorganization of control into fewer, centralized areas, because the rise of communication provided the capabilities of "close, direct, and intimate action and reaction between the central control and the distributing agents."[92] Arguing from an economic point of view, Sumner suggested that "the highest degree of organization which is possible is the one which offers the maximum of profit; in it the economic advantage is the greatest."[93] And he added that other societal institutions, not just industrial concerns, would be subject to the same forces.

EFFECTS OF THE PRESS

The press, according to Sumner, was also a creation of the nineteenth century, together with industrialization and the reorganization of economic patterns in American society. Commenting upon the quality of the press and on its effects upon society, he concluded, "It is idle to deny that the worst papers are the most popular and make the most money."[94] He recognized, however, the dilemma of the press, torn between its responsibilities in a democracy and its potentials as a business investment. Sumner said,

> The result is that the press is, on the one side, an institution of indispensable social utility, and on the other side a foul nuisance. It exerts a tyranny which no one dare brave. One of the most remarkable facts, however, about the newspaper at this turn of the century is that a great newspaper becomes an entity independent of the opinion or will of its managers. It gets headway and drags them along with it. It has a reputation and policy and becomes subject to the law of consistency. Its managers are hampered by considerations, and obligations, and if they try to do justice to them all, they dare utter only colorless platitudes. If then they get a chance to "pitch into" something or somebody who has no power of defence they seize the opportunity to manifest freedom and independence. The result is blackguardism. The young century deserves pity when it accepts this bequest. What priestcraft was to the fourteenth century, presscraft is to the twentieth.[95]

Sumner's notions of the effectiveness of the press were tied up with a discussion of the relationship between the common man and societal institutions, like newspapers. He described the common man as a representative of a part of the masses which lives "by routine and tradition. It is not brutal, but it is shallow, narrow-minded, and prejudiced."[96] Since "thinking and understanding are too hard work," he suggested that the masses often "use routine, set formulae, current phrases, caught up from magazines and newspapers of the better class."[97] They also reacted to the press in ways that reinforced their prejudices; and the press, recognizing the needs of the common man, catered to his interests. Thus, the yellow newspapers thrive and displace all others because he likes them. The trashy novels pay well because his wife and daughters like them. The advertisements in the popular magazines are addressed to him. They show what he wants. The "funny items" are adjusted to his sense of humor. Hence all these things are symptoms. They show what he "believes in," and they strengthen his prejudices.[98]

In his discussion of symbols as means of suggestion, Sumner also talked about the effectiveness of illustrations, for instance. He said, "Illustrative pictures influence us. The introduction of them into daily newspapers is an important development of the arts of suggestion."[99] But he addressed himself mainly to language and to the power of "watchwords, catchwords, phrases, and epithets," which made up the apparatus of suggestion. Thus "Americanism," for instance became a symbol, a token which provided a "pass" for ideas and actions that were recommended, but could not be justified. Sumner felt that Americanism and patriotism, for instance, were a "duty laid upon us all to applaud, follow, and obey whatever a ruling clique of newspapers and politicians chooses to say or wants to do."[100] He concluded that symbols or tokens have a utility for suggestion, and that they carry "a coercion with them and overwhelm people who are not trained to verify assertions and dissect fallacies."[101]

The common man was a result of the evolution of democracy during the nineteenth century, according to Sumner, but his day of glory would be this century, when he will speak as a symbol for "the people" and when "newspapers bow down to him, flatter him, and treat him as the specimen type of 'the people.'"[102] He was convinced that the press, together with other institutions in society, such as universities and churches, had given way to the ideas of the common man for the worse of society. Sumner explained,

The newspapers have taken their cue from him, and our destiny has been settled without any reason or sense, without regard to history or political philosophy. That the press . . . and magazines could have so given up their functions and prostrated themselves before this organ of folly, for fear of falling out of sympathy with the man-on-the-curbstone, would have been incredible if we had not lived through it.[103]

He expressed his doubts about the usefulness of public discussions and newspaper presentations of issues that were extremely complicated and much too difficult to be dealt with by just about anyone who cared to comment upon them. "What is the use of education, learning, training, discipline, if the numbers can solve the questions? or if numbers hold the ultimate test by which to revise and verify results?"[104] And he warned that particularly newspapers were in no position to participate in reflection and debate, because they "are forced to catch everything as it flies. They have no time for quiet and sober reflection. They never finish anything. They never go deeply into anything and never go back to correct mistakes."[105] Still, common men made up the segment of society out of which flows "public opinion" as a life force. For Sumner, public opinion was "the basic force which underlies all [forms of societal self-regulation]."[106] It was defined as "a matter of feeling rather than of intellect; and the feeling is developed in connection with a more or less localized interest."[107] Thus, based upon sentiment and interest rather than on intellectual analysis, public opinion sought outlets not only in the political processes of modern times but also in the variety of mass communication media which reflected these interests and sentiments. Newspapers, too, helped create the type of man or woman who represented the educational efforts of a democracy. That is to say, Sumner saw the dangers of public schooling and mass communication in their contribution to achieve "big results on a pattern." He said,

> An orthodoxy is produced in regard to all the great doctrines of life. It consists of the most worn and commonplace opinions which are current in the masses. It may be found in newspapers and popular literature. It is intensively provincial and philistine. . . . The popular opinions always contain broad fallacies, half-truths, and glib generalizations of fifty years before.[108]

In summary, language, communication, and public opinion were described as elementary forces in society and the major concepts for an understanding of the evolutionary process in society, the preservation and transmission of culture, and the political and economic decision-making processes. Although he never addressed himself at length to these issues, there is an underlying assumption in many of Sumner's writings of the importance of these concepts. Sumner was not a social reformer like Small or Ross, who could be identified with the social movements of the late nineteenth and early twentieth century in the United States; however, in his assessment of the American press he sounded very much like any of the other authors, or like many of his contemporary press critics. Also, his appraisal of communication as a social process came close to the definitions of other writers of his time, including Small and Ross. Where he differed, however, was in his belief that inequality was inevitable and a sign of freedom and that social reform movements were based mostly upon the confusion and ignorance of their proponents. He continued to preach his doctrines in the face of a changing nation, in which social reforms shaped the political and economic agendas of the day, and thus proved his point, albeit in a strange way, that the power of symbols and the success of communication may bring about changes in the minds of people and thus changes in the political and economic structure of society.

NOTES

1. *The German Historical School in American Scholarship, A Study in the Transfer of Culture* (Ithaca: Cornell University Press, 1965), 232.

Albion W. Small, in *Origins of Sociology* (Chicago: University of Chicago Press, 1924) recalled a number of names of individuals who had spent some time at German universities "during the seventies, on the whole the most stimulating decade in German social science":

William G. Sumner (in the previous decade), Marburg and Göttingen, Social Science; Herbert B. Adams, History, Johns Hopkins, Heidelberg, 1876; John W. Burgess, Political Science, Columbia, Leipzig, Berlin, 1871-73; Richard T. Ely, Economics, Johns Hopkins and Wisconsin, Halle, Heidelberg, Geneva, and Berlin 1877-80; Henry W. Farnam, Political Economy, Yale, Strassburg, 1878; Frank J. Goodenow, Political Science, Columbia, Paris, and Berlin, 1879-82; Arthur T. Hadley, Economics, Yale, Berlin, 1878-79; George E. Howard, Sociology, Leland Stanford, Nebraska, Munich, and Paris, 1878-80; Edmund J. James, Political and Social Science, University of Pennsylvania, Halle, 1878-79;

Simon N. Patten, Economics, University of Pennsylvania, Halle, 1878; E.R.A. Seligman, Economics, Columbia, Berlin, Heidelberg, Geneva; William M. Sloane, History, Princeton and Columbia, Leipzig, 1876 Albion W. Small, Sociology, Chicago, Berlin, and Leipzig, 1879-81; Frank W. Taussig, Economics, Harvard, Berlin, 1879; William H. Tillinghast, History Assistant Librarian, Harvard, Berlin, 1878-80 [p. 326].

2. Roscoe C. Hinkle, Jr. and Gisela J. Hinkle, *The Development of Modern Sociology, Its Nature and Growth in the United States*, Studies in Sociology (New York: Random House, 1954), 2.

3. Ibid.

4. As quoted in Hinkle and Hinkle, 8-9.

5. "Concerning Three Articles in this Number of McClure's and a Coincidence that May Set Us Thinking," Editorial, *McClure's Magazine*, January, 1903, 336.

6. Louis Filler, *The Muckrakers* (University Park: Pennsylvania State University Press, 1976), p. 9.

7. Mable Dodge Luhan, *Movers and Shakers* (New York: Harcourt, Brace, 1936), 80-84.

8. "The Press and Public Opinion," *American Journal of Sociology* 5 (1899-1900), 372-382; also by Yarros, "A Neglected Opportunity and Duty in Journalism," *American Journal of Sociology* 22 (1916-1917), 211.

9. "A Laboratory Experiment in Journalism," *American Journal of Sociology* 11 (1905-1906), 297-311.

10. Frances Fenton, "The Influence of Newspaper Presentations Upon the Growth of Crime and Other Anti-Social Activity." *American Journal of Sociology* 16(1910-1911), 343.

11. "Is an Honest and Sane Newspaper Press Possible?" *American Journal of Sociology* 15 (1909-1910), 321-334. (written by "an independent journalist").

12. March 1908, 491-496.

13. March 1910, 303-311.

14. October 1906, 127-133.

15. November 1909, 586-593.

16. "Fifty Years of Sociology in the United States," *American Journal of Sociology*, 21 (1915-1916), 773.

17. "Review of *Bau und Leben des Sozialen Körpers*" by Schäffle, 2 (1896-1897), 310-315.

18. "The Scope of Sociology. Part II," *American Journal of Sociology* 5(1899-1900), 628, 629; and in "Part III," 5 (1899-1900), 778; "Part VI," 6 (1900-1901), 372; "Part VII," 6 (1900-1901), 491, 510. Also in "Some Contributions to the History of Sociology, Section XVII," *American Journal of Sociology*, (1924-1925), 177-194, which is devoted to Schäffle's contributions.

19. "The Scope of Sociology. Part VII," 522-23.

20. "General Sociology," *American Journal of Sociology* 18 (1912-1913), 205-206. In another article for the journal in the same year, Small elaborated on the concept of organism. He said,

The technical difference between the category 'organism' previous to 1850, and indeed for the most part long after Schäffle's *Bau und Leben* began to appear in 1875, and the role of the same idea since that time is that in the former period it was used in the most obvious popular sense, while in the latter it was elaborated and criticized and deliberately employed for what it was worth as a tool of analysis. [p. 450.]

Similar references to Schäffle are found in his *General Sociology* (Chicago: University of Chicago Press, 1905), 75-77.

21. "Some Contributions to the History of Sociology. Section XIX," *American Journal of Sociology* 30 (1924-1925), 329.

22. *General Sociology*, 619-620.

23. Albion W. Small and George E. Vincent, *An Introduction to the Study of Society* (New York: American Book, 1894), 246.

24. "The Bonds of Nationality," *American Journal of Sociology* 20 (1914-1915), 640.

25. Ibid.

26. *An Introduction*, 215.

27. Ibid., 216

28. Ibid., 217-218.

29. Ibid., 219.

30. Ibid., 223.

31. Ibid.

32. Ibid., 227-232.

33. Ibid., 224.

34. Ibid.

35. Ibid., 226.

36. Ibid., 133.

37. Ibid., 324.

38. Ibid., 325.

39. Ibid., 326.

40. Ibid.

41. Ibid., 329.

42. Ibid., 295.

43. Ibid.

44. Ibid., 329.

45. Ibid.

46. Ibid.

47. Ibid., 330.

48. *Principles of Sociology* (New York: D. Appleton-Century, 1938).

49. Ibid., 140.

50. "Moot Points in Sociology: VI," *American Journal of Sociology* 10 (1904-1905), 84.

51. "Moot Points in Sociology: IV," *American Journal of Sociology* 9 (1903-1904), 362.

52. Ibid., 361.

53. Ibid., 362.

54. "The Organization of Thought," *American Journal of Sociology* 22 (1916-1917), 318.

55. *Social Psychology* (New York: Macmillan, 1918), 231.

56. *Principles of Sociology*, 337.

57. *Social Psychology*, 352.

58. "Social Decadence," *American Journal of Sociology* 23 (1917-1918), 629-630.

59. *Social Psychology* ,86.

60. *Principles of Sociology*, 563.

61. Ibid.

62. Ibid., 564.

63. Ibid., 566.

64. "The Suppression of Important News," *Changing America. Studies in Contemporary Society* (New York: Century, 1912), 109.

65. Ibid., 112.

66. Ibid.

6. Ibid., 113.

68. Ibid., 114.

69. Ibid., 115.

70. Ibid., 116.

71. Ibid., 128-129.

72. Ibid., 130.

73. Ibid., 133.

74. Ibid., 134.

75. Ibid., 136.

76. "Social decadence," 630.

77. "What the Films are Doing to Young America," in *World Drift*, (New York: Century, 1928), 179.

78. *New-Age Sociology* (New York: D. Appleton-Century 1940), 483.

79. Ibid., 487.

80. Ibid., 488.

81. "The Absurd Attempt to Make the World Over," in *War and Other Essays*, edited by Albert G. Keller (New Haven: Yale University Press, 1911), 208-210.

82. William Graham Sumner and Albert G. Keller, *The Science of Society*, vol. 1 (New Haven: Yale University Press, 1934), 160.

83. Ibid., 161.

84. Ibid.

85. *Folkways, A Study of the Sociological Importance of Usages, Manners, Customs, Mores, and Morals* (Boston: Ginn, 1906), 134.

86. "Sociology," *War*, 187; this part was written originally in 1881.

87. *What Social Classes Owe to Each Other* (Caldwell, Idaho: Caxton Printers, 1974), 76; this part was written originally in 1883.

88. Ibid., 79.

89. "The Bequests of the Nineteenth Century to the Twentieth," *Yale Review* 22 (1932-1933), 736; this essay was originally written in 1901 and revised later; it was discovered a few months before publication in 1933.

90. Ibid.

91. Ibid.

92. Sumner, *The Challenge of Facts and Other Essays*, edited by Albert G. Keller (New Haven: Yale University Press, 1914), 85.

93. Ibid., 86.

94. "The Bequests of the Nineteenth Century to the Twentieth," in *Essays of William Graham Sumner*, edited by Albert G. Keller and Maurice R. Davie, vol. 1 (New Haven: Yale University Press, 1934), 233-234. This part and the following section on the news-

paper press did not appear in the first publication of the essay in the *Yale Review* cited above.

95. Ibid.
96. *Folkways*, 50.
97. Ibid., 48.
98. Ibid., 50-51.
99. Ibid., 176.
100. Ibid., 177.
101. Ibid.
102. Sumner, "The Bequests," *Yale Review* 744.
103. Ibid., 745.
104. Ibid., 748.
105. Ibid.
106. Sumner, *The Science*, 1927 edition, 727.
107. Ibid., 728.
108. Sumner, *Folkways. . .* , 631.

EPILOGUE

The selection of German and American scholarship represents but a small example of those works which may be regarded as the major sources of a history of communication and mass communication theory in Germany and the United States. Nevertheless, the writings of Schäffle, Knies, Bücher, Tönnies, Weber and those of their American colleagues Small, Ross, and Sumner offer considerable support for a study of society that places communication as a life process at the center of such scholarly endeavor.

They further suggest that an understanding of social communication must be based upon an investigation of symbolic behavior and the uses of language as they are affected by technological-economic developments and the rise of complex and sophisticated systems of public communication. The advancement of civilization created needs for new means of a rapid and efficient spread of knowledge, and it generated questions about supply and demand of information, production and consumption of news and opinion, and control over the media of dissemination. Thus, the discussion of communication in society emerged in a political-economic context which also served as a basis for press criticism. This perspective, however, should not be confused with a critical approach that represents a radically different ideological position.

Especially in the United States, in contrast to the abundant production and dissemination of material goods, there has been an inadequate production and dissemination of political—and in the widest sense—philosophical ideas. The encounter with Marxism, for instance, and the rise of scientific socialism remained a European experience, where Marxism confronted liberal democratic positions and seriously challenged the capitalist establishment. Instead, there has been a continuing reliance in the United States upon the power and influence of a democratic phase of capitalism and its ideology, which determined the boundaries of a critical assessment of the role and function of societal institutions, including the press. The social reform movement and the development of the social sciences in the United States must be viewed within a framework which could be described politically as a bourgeois-democratic system and philosophically as pragmatism or instrumentalism.

The bias of an economic interpretation of media activities remains also in its critical phase within these boundaries—even today. Any acknowledgment of Marxism or the reception of similar ideas as they may surface in an expressed concern for the welfare of the common man can be explained as a recognition of the usefulness of social and economic methods of analysis rather than an adoption of a Marxist position with its political consequences.

A realization of these conditions surrounding the development of mass communication studies is not only important for an understanding of the history of this field, but also significant for the construction of contemporary theories that take into account political and ideological realities. In particular, the treatment of news as a form of knowledge and as a commodity, and the definition of the press as a public service and a commercial agent provide the parameters for the study of the media. This includes an investigation of political and economic conditions which may lead to questions about the production and dissemination of cultural products as a form of domination and to the manipulation of public opinion as an example of legitimizing authority.

Specifically, ownership of the means of communication not only reflects economic power or political status, but also may determine definitions of education, democracy, and freedom of expression. In this way, it could affect the ability of the people to think critically about their political environment and to act responsibly in the conduct of their public and private affairs.

For instance, as education serves to support the political and economic system that encourages consumerism and stresses the value of material well-being, the mass media help reinforce these activities in their advertising and editorial functions. Similarly, democracy becomes an illusion of participation and access to decision-making processes through the rise of public opinion polls as news events. Finally, freedom of expression is confined by economic conditions of the media, the limited access to a forum of public discussion, and, perhaps most importantly, the inability to overcome the effects of an educational system that helps create and expand markets to encourage consumption of goods of all kinds.

A contemporary theory of mass communication must identify, describe, and analyze the effects of these economic-political determinants of social communication in an effort to develop an alternative prospective. In this context it seems necessary to confront the challenges of Marxism and the consequences of socialism.

The creation of publicly owned or endowed media, as has been suggested, may not be sufficient to redirect the function of the media. A more comprehensive approach would have to contemplate basic changes in the preparation of individuals to participate fully in their own affairs in order to help create conditions more favorable to their own development than currently possible. This also means a review of the definition of journalists to take into account their professional status as members of a political and intellectual group whose leadership as knowledge brokers and interpreters of the contemporary world may need protection from economic pressures. Such considerations would lead to questions of professional responsibility and freedom of expression as necessary conditions for the advancement of society.

BIBLIOGRAPHY

Aron, Raymond, *Main Currents in Sociological Thought*. Vol. II. Garden City, NY: Doubleday (Anchor), 1970.

Barth, Paul, "Spencer und Schäffle," *Viertels-jahresschrift für wissenschaftliche Philosophie u. Soziologie* (1904), 231-239.

Baumgarten, Eduard, Hrsg., *Max Weber Werk und Person*. Tübingen: J.C.B. Mohr (Paul Siebeck), 1964.

Bebel, August, "A. Schäffle: Aus meinem Leben," *Die Neue Zeit* 23 (1904-1905), 230-241.

Bendix, Reinhard, *Max Weber: An Intellectual Portrait*. NewYork: Doubleday (Anchor), 1962.

Bohrmann, Hans and Rolf Sülzer, "Massenkommunikationsforschung in der BRD. Deutschsprachige Veröffentlichungen nach 1960. Kommentar und Bibliographie," in Jörg Aufermann, Hans Bohrmann, und Rolf Sülzer, Hrsg., *Gesellschaftliche Kommunikation und Information*, Band 1, Frankfurt: Athenäum, 1973.

Bottomore, T. B., *Critics of Society: Radical Thought in North America*. New York: Pantheon, 1968.

Brenke, Else, "Schriften von Ferdinand Tönnies aus den Jahren 1875-1935," in *Reine und angewandte Soziologie. Eine Festgabe für Ferdinand Tönnies zu seinem achtzigsten Geburtstag*. Leipzig: Hans Burke Verlag, 1936.

Bücher, Karl, *Arbeit und Rhythmus*. Leipzig: B. G. Teubner, 1909.

—— *Die deutsche Tagespresse und die Kritik*. Tübingen: J.C.B. Mohr (Paul Siebeck), 1915.

—— "Die Presse," in *Handbuch der Politik*. Hrsg. von Paul Laband, et al. Berlin: Walther de Gruyter, 1914.

—— *Industrial Evolution*. New York: Henry Holt, 1901.

—— *Lebenserinnerungen*. Tübingen: Laupp'sche Buchhandlung, 1919.

—— "Die Presse," in *Handbuch der Politik*. Hrsg. von Paul Laband, et al. Berlin: Walther de Gruyter, 1914.

—— *Unsere Sache und die Tagespresse*, Tübingen: J.C.B. Mohr (Paul Siebeck), 1915.

—— "Ursprung und Begriff der Zeitung," in *Gesammelte Aufsätze zur Zeitungskunde*. Tübingen: Laupp'sche Buchhandlung, 1926.

—— "Volkswirtschaftliche Entwicklungsstufen," in Karl Bücher E. Heimann, E. von Philippovich, J. Schumpeter, *Grundriss der Sozialökonomik* I. Abteilung, 1. Teil, Tübingen: J.C.B. Mohr (Paul Siebeck), 1924.

—— "Zeitungsstatistik für das Deutsche Reich im Jahre 1885 und 1906," *Bulletin d l'Institut International de Statistique* XVII (1908).

—— "Das Zeitungswesen," in Paul Hinnebert, Hrsg., *Die Kultur der Gegenwart, ihre Entwicklung und ihre Ziele*. Berlin: B. G. Teubner, 1912.

—— *Zur Frage der Pressreform*. Tübingen: J.C.B. Mohr (Paul Siebeck), 1922.

Burckhardt, Jakob, *Griechische Kulturgeschichte*. Berlin: W. Spemann, 1898.

Cahnman, Werner, ed., *Ferdinand Tönnies: A New Evaluation.* Leiden: E. J. Brill, 1973.
————— and Rudolf Heberle, eds., *Ferdinand Tönnies, On Sociology: Pure, Applied, and Empirical.* Chicago: University of Chicago Press, 1971.
"Concerning Three Articles in This Number of McClure's and a Coincidence That May Set Us Thinking," Editorial, *McClure's Magazine* January 1903, 336.
Cunow, Heinrich, "Herr Dr. Albert D. F. Schäffle als Soziologe," *Die Neue Zeit* 9 (1890-1891), 492-498, 533-539, 561-570.
Dahrendorf, Ralph, *Pfade aus Utopia: Arbeiten zur Theorie und Methode der Soziologie.* München: Piper, 1967.
Dorfman, Joseph, "The Role of the German Historical School in American Economic Thought," *American Economic Review, Papers and Proceedings* 55 (May 1955), 17-18.
Dröge, Franz, *Wissen Ohne Bewusstsein—Materialien zur Medienanalyse.* Frankfurt: Athenäum, 1972.
————— and Winfried B. Lerg, *Kritik der Kommunikationswissenschaft.* Bremen: B. C. Heye, 1965. Reprinted from *Publizistik* 10:3 (1965), 251-284.
Dronberger, Ilse, *The Political Thought of Max Weber: In Quest of Statesmanship.* New York: Appleton-Century-Crofts, 1971.
Eisenstadt, A. S., "American History and Social Science," *The Centennial Review* 7 (1963), 255-272.
Enzensberger, Hans Magnus, *Einzelheiten 1. Bewusstseins-Industrie.* Frankfurt: Suhrkamp, 1962.
Fenton, Frances, "The Influence of Newspaper Presentations Upon the Growth of Crime and Other Anti-Social Activity," *American Journal of Sociology* 16 (1910-1911), 342-371, 538-564.
Filler, Louis, *The Muckrakers.* University Park: Pennsylvania State University Press, 1976.
Frankfurt Institute for Social Research, *Aspects of Sociology.* Boston: Beacon Press, 1972.
Gerth, H. H. and C. Wright Mills, *From Max Weber: Essays in Sociology.* New York: Oxford University Press, 1946.
Gollin, Gillian Lindt and Albert E. Gollin, "Tönnies on Public Opinion," in Werner J. Cahman, ed., *Ferdinand Tönnies: A New Evaluation.* Leiden: E. J. Brill, 1973, 181-206.
Gouldner, Alvin, *The Coming Crisis of Western Sociology.* New York: Basic Books, 1970.
Groth, Otto, *Die Geschichte der deutschen Zeitungswissenschaft, Probleme und Methoden.* München: Buchverlag Dr. Konrad Weinmayer, 1948.
————— *Die politische Presse Württembergs.* Stuttgart: Scheufele, 1915.
————— *Die unerkannte Kulturmacht: Grundlegung der Zeitungswissenschaft.* Vol. V. Berlin: Walter de Gruyter, 1960.
Hardt, Hanno, "The Development of Mass Communication as a Field of Study in Germany: An Introduction," Iowa City: University of Iowa School of Journalism, 1974. (unpublished)
Hawthorn, Geoffrey, *Enlightenment & Despair. A History of Sociology.* Cambridge: Cambridge University Press, 1976.
Heberle, Rudolf, "The Sociological System of Ferdinand Tönnies: 'Community' and 'Society,'" in Harry Elmer Barnes, ed., *An Introduction to the History of Sociology.* Chicago: University of Chicago Press, 1948.

Herbst, Jürgen, *The German Historical School in American Scholarship, A Study in the Transfer of Culture*. Ithaca: Cornell University Press, 1965.

Heuss, Theodor, "Max Weber in seiner Gegenwart," in Johannes Winckelmann, Hrsg., *Max Weber Gesammelte Politische Schriften*. Tübingen: J.C.B. Mohr (Paul Siebeck), 1958.

Hinkle, Roscoe C., Jr. and Gisela J. Hinkle, *The Development of Modern Sociology, Its Nature and Growth in the United States*. New York: Random House, 1954.

Holzer, Horst, *Gescheiterte Aufklärung? Politik, Ökonomie und Kommunikation in der Bundesrepublik Deutschland*. München: Piper, 1971.

Honigsheim, Paul, *On Max Weber*. New York: Free Press, 1968.

House, Floyd, "Review of *Soziologische Studien und Kritiken*, by Ferdinand Tönnies." *American Journal of Sociology* 32 (1926-1927), 124-126.

Hughes, H. Stuart, "The Historian and the Social Scientist," *American Historical Review* 66 (1960), 20-46.

"Is an Honest and Sane Newspaper Press Possible?" *American Journal of Sociology* 15 (1909-1910), 321-334.

Jaehrisch, Ursula, "Max Weber's Contribution to the Sociology of Culture," in Otto Stammer, ed., *Max Weber and Sociology Today*. New York: Harper & Row, 1971.

Jay, Martin, *The Dialectical Imagination. A History of the Frankfurt School and the Institute of Social Research, 1923-50*. Boston: Little, Brown, 1973.

Jöhlinger, Otto, *Zeitungswesen und Hochschulstudium*. Jena: Verlag von Gustav Fischer, 1919.

Kaufmann, M., *Socialism: Its Nature, Its Dangers and Its Remedies Considered*. London: Henry S. King, 1974.

Kirchner, Joachim, *Das Deutsche Zeitschriftenwesen: seine Geschichte und seine Probleme*. Wiesbaden: Otto Harrassowitz, 1962.

Knies, Karl, *Das Geld. Darlegung der Grundlehren von dem Gelde, insbesondere der wirtschaftlichen und der rechtsgiltigen Functionen des Geldes, mit einer Erörterung über das Kapital und die Ubertragung der Nutzungen*. Zweite verbesserte und vermehrte Auflage. Berlin: Weidmannsche Buchhandlung, 1885.

―――― *Die Politische Oekonomie vom Geschichtlichen Standpunkte*. Braunschweig: C. A. Schwetschke und Sohn, 1883; new and enlarged edition of *Politische Oekonomie vom Standpunkte der Geschichtlichen Methode*, 1853.

―――― *Die Statistik als selbstständige Wissenschaft: zur Lösung des Wirrsals in der Theorie und Praxis dieser Wissenschaft*. Kassel: Verlag der J. Luckhardt'schen Buchhandlung, 1850.

―――― *Der Telegraph als Verkehrsmittel. Mit Erörterungen über den Nachrichtenverkehr überhaupt*. Tübingen; Verlag der Laupp'schen Buchhandlung, 1857.

Knilli, Friedrich, *Deutsche Lautsprecher. Versuch zu einer Semiotik des Radios*. Stuttgart: Metzler, 1970.

Koszyk, Kurt, *Deutsche Presse im 19. Jahrhundert*. Berlin: Coloquium Verlag, 1966.

Lachmann, Ludwig M., *The Legacy of Max Weber*. Berkeley: Glendessary Press, 1971.

Lasalle, Ferdinand, *Die Feste, die Presse und der Frankfurter Abgeordnetentag*, in Otto Groth, *Die Zeitung*, Vol. III. Mannheim: J. Benscheimer, 1930.

Lazarsfeld, Paul, *Qualitative Analysis. Historical and Critical Essays*. Boston: Allyn and Bacon, 1972.

―――― and Anthony R. Oberschall, "Max Weber and Empirical Research," *American Sociological Review* 30: 2 (April 1965), 185-199.

Leigh, Robert D., ed., *A Free and Responsible Press. A General Report on Mass Communication: Newspapers, Radio, Motion Pictures, Magazines, and Books By the Commission on Freedom of the Press.* Chicago: University of Chicago Press (Midway Reprints), 1974.

Löbl, Emil, *Kultur und Presse.* Leipzig: Duncker & Humblot, 1903.

Luhan, Mable Dodge, *Movers and Shakers.* New York: Harcourt, Brace, 1936.

Macy, John, "Our Chromatic Journalism," *Bookman* 24 (October 1906), 127-133.

Marx, Karl and Friedrich Engels, *The German Ideology,* Part One with Selections from Parts Two and Three, edited by C. J. Arthur, New York: International Publishers (New World Paperbacks), 1970.

Mehring, Franz, "A. Schäffle," *Die Neue Zeit* 22 (1903-1904), 434-437.

Menger, Anton, *Neue Sittenlehre.* Jena: Gustav Fischer, 1905.

Mills, C. Wright, *The Sociological Imagination.* Harmondsworth, England: Penguin, 1970.

Mitzman, Arthur, *The Iron Cage: An Historical Interpretation of Max Weber.* New York: Alfred A. Knopf, 1970.

Mommsen, Wolfgang J., *Max Weber und die Deutsche Politik 1890-1920.* Tübingen: J.C.B. Mohr (Paul Siebeck), 1974.

Münster, Hans, "Ferdinand Tönnies und die Zeitungswissenschaft," *Zeitungswissenschaft* 5: 4 (1930), 224-228.

——— "Offene Antwort," *Zeitungswissenschaft* 5: 6 (1930), 321-322.

Muser, Gerhard, *Statistische Untersuchung über die Zeitungen Deutschlands 1885-1914.* Leipzig: Emmanuel Reinicke, 1918.

Oberschall, Anthony R., *Empirical Social Research in Germany, 1848-1914.* New York: Basic Books, 1965.

Palmer, Paul A., "Ferdinand Tönnies' Theory of Public Opinion," *Public Opinion Quarterly* 2 (1938), 584-595.

Parsons, Talcott, "Max Weber 1864-1964," *American Sociological Review* 30: 2 (April 1965), 171-175.

Paupié, Kurt, "Frankfurter Zeitung (1856-1943)," In Heinz-Dietrich Fischer, Hrsg., *Deutsche Zeitschriften des 17. bis 20. Jahrhunderts.* Pullach: Verlag Dokumentation, 1973.

Pennypacker, Samuel, "Sensational Journalism and the Remedy," *North American Review* 190 (November 1909), 586-593.

Pietilä, Veikko, *On the Scientific Status and Position of Communication Research.* Monograph No. 35. Tampere: Institute of Journalism and Mass Communication, 1977.

Prokop, Dieter, *Materialien zur Theorie des Films.* München: Hanser, 1971.

"Review of *Bau und Leben des Socialen Korpers,* by Albert Schäffle," *American Journal of Sociology,* 2 (1896-1897), 310-315.

Ross, Edward A., "Association," *American Journal of Sociology* 24 (1918-1919), 502-527.

——— "Moot Points in Sociology: Part II," *American Journal of Sociology* 9 (1903-1904), 105-123.

——— "Moot Points in Sociology: Part III," *American Journal of Sociology* 9 (1903-1904), 188-207.

——— "Moot Points in Sociology: Part IV," *American Journal of Sociology* 9 (1903-1904), 349-372.

——— "Moot Points in Sociology: Part VI," *American Journal of Sociology* 10 (1904-1905), 189-207.

—— *New-Age Sociology.* New York: D. Appleton-Century, 1941.

—— "The Organization of Thought," *American Journal of Sociology* 22 (1916-1917), 306-323.

—— *Principles of Sociology.* New York: D. Appleton-Century, 1938.

—— "Socialization," *American Journal of Sociology* 24 (1918-1919), 652-671.

—— *Social Control.* New York: Macmillan, 1916.

—— "Social Decadence," *American Journal of Sociology* 23 (1917-1918), 620-632.

—— "The Suppression of Important News," *Changing America, Studies in Contemporary Society,* New York: Century, 1912; reprinted from *Atlantic Monthly,* March 1910, 303-311.

—— "What the Films are Doing to Young America," *World Drift.* New York: Century, 1928.

Runciman, Walter G., *A Critique of Max Weber's Philosophy of Social Science.* Cambridge: Cambridge University Press, 1972.

Schad, Susanne Petra, *Empirical Social Research in Weimar Germany.* Paris-The Hague: Mouton, 1972.

Schäffle, Albert, *Abriss der Soziologie.* Hrsg. von Karl Bücher. Tübingen: Verlag der Laupp'schen Buchhandlung, 1906.

—— *Aus Meinem Leben.* 2 vols. Berlin: Ernst Hoffmann, 1905.

—— *Bau und Leben des Sozialen Körpers.* 4 vols. Tübingen: Verlag der Laupp'schen Buchhandlung, 1881.

—— *Das gesellschaftliche System der menschlichen Wirtschaft.* Vols. I & II. Tübingen: Verlag der Laupp'schen Buchhandlung, 1873.

—— *The Quintessence of Socialism.* New York: Humboldt, 1890.

—— *Review of Die Soziologische Erkenntnis,* by Ratzenhofer, *American Journal of Sociology* 4 (1898-1899), 528-543.

—— "Ueber die volkswirthschaftliche Natur der Güter der Darstellung und der Mittheilung," *Zeitschrift für die gesammte Staatswissenschaft* Heft 1 (1873), 1-70.

Schippel, Max, "Schäffles Lebensbild," *Sozialistische Monatshefte* (1905), 1009-1015.

Schleswig-Holsteinische Volkszeitung, Kiel, 29. Juli, 1932.

Scott, William, *The Development of Economics.* New York: Century, 1933.

Small, Albion, "The Bonds of Nationality," *American Journal of Sociology* 20 (1914-1915), 629-683.

—— "A Decade of Sociology," *American Journal of Sociology* 11 (1905-1906), 1-10.

—— "Dr Albert Schäffle," *American Journal of Sociology* 9 (1903-1904), 708-709.

—— "Fifty Years of Sociology in the United States," *American Journal of Sociology* 21 (1915-1916), 721-864.

—— "General Sociology," *American Journal of Sociology* 18 (1912-1913), 200-214.

—— *General Sociology.* Chicago: University of Chicago Press, 1905.

—— "Material for the Idea 'Democracy,'" *American Journal of Sociology* 25 (1919-1920), 257-297.

—— *Origins of Sociology.* Chicago: University of Chicago Press, 1924.

—— "The Present Outlook of Social Science," *American Journal of Sociology* 18 (1912-1913), 433-469.

—— "Review of *Industrial Evolution,* by Karl Bücher," *American Journal of Sociology* 7 (1901-1902), 286-287.

—— "The Scope of Sociology: Part II," *American Journal of Sociology* 5 (1899-1900), 617-647.

————— "The Scope of Sociology: Part III," *American Journal of Sociology* 5 (1899-1900), 778-813.

————— "The Scope of Sociology: Part VI," *American Journal of Sociology* 6 (1900-1901), 324-380.

————— "The Scope of Sociology: Part VII," *American Journal of Sociology* 6 (1900-1901), 487-531.

————— "The Scope of Sociology: Part IX," *American Journal of Sociology* 10 (1904-1905), 26-46.

————— "The Sociologist's Point of View," *American Journal of Sociology* 3 (1897-1898), 145-170.

————— "Some Contributions to the History of Sociology: Part X," *American Journal of Sociology* 29 (1923-1924), 305-324.

————— "Some Contributions to the History of Sociology: Part XII," *American Journal of Sociology* 29 (1923-1924), 455-479.

————— "Some Contributions to the History of Sociology: Part XV," *American Journal of Sociology* 29 (1923-1924), 707-725.

————— "Some Contributions to the History of Sociology: Part IVII," *American Journal of Sociology* 30 (1924-1925), 177-194.

————— "Some Contributions to the History of Sociology: Part XVIII," *American Journal of Sociology* 30 (1924-1925), 302-310.

————— "Some Contributions to the History of Sociology: Part XIX," *American Journal of Sociology* 30 (1924-1925),, 310-336.

————— "Some Contributions to the History of Sociology: Part XXIII," *American Journal of Sociology* 30 (1923-1924), 479-488.

————— "The Vindication of Sociology," *American Journal of Sociology* 15 (1909-1910), 1-15.

————— and George Vincent, *An Introduction to the Study of Society*. Chicago: American Book, 1894.

Spengler, Joseph J. and William R. Allen, eds., *Essays in Economic Thought: Aristotle to Marshall*. Chicago: Rand McNally, 1960.

Sumner, William Graham, "The Absurd Attempt to Make the World Over," *War and Other Essays*. Edited by Albert G. Keller. New Haven: Yale University Press, 1911.

————— "Bequests of the Nineteenth Century to the Twentieth," Yale Review XXII (1932-1933), 732-754.

————— *The Challenge of Facts and Other Essays*. Edited by Albert G. Keller. New Haven: Yale University Press, 1914.

————— *Essays of William Graham Sumner*. 2 vols. Edited by Albert G. Keller and Maurice R. Davie. New Haven: Yale University Press, 1934.

————— *Folkways, A Study of the Sociological Importance of Usages, Manners, Customs, Mores, and Morals*. Boston: Ginn, 1906.

————— "Mores of the Present and Future," in *War and Other Essays*. Edited by Albert G. Keller, New Haven: Yale University Press, 1911.

————— "Sociology," in *War and Other Essays*. Edited by Albert G. Keller, New Haven: Yale University Press, 1911.

————— "The State and Monopoly," in *Earth-Hunger and Other Essays*. Edited by Albert G. Keller. New Haven: Yale University Press, 1913.

————— *What Social Classes Owe to Each Other*. Caldwell, Idaho: Caxton Printers, 1974.

——— and Albert Galloway Keller, *The Science of Society*. Vol. I. New Haven: Yale University Press, 1934.

———, Albert Galloway Keller, and Maurice R. Davie, *The Science of Society*, Vol. IV. New Haven: Yale Univeristy Press, 1927.

Taubert, Rolf, "Die Hilfe (1894-1943)," in Heinz-Dietrich Fischer, Hrsg., *Deutsche Zeitschriften des 17. bis 20 Jahrhunderts*. Pullach: Verlag Dokumentation, 1973.

Tebbel, John, *The Media in America*. New York: Thomas Y. Crowell, 1974.

Thomas, W. I., "The Psychology of the Yellow Journal," *American Mazagine* March 1908, 491-496.

Thon, O. *"The Present Status of Sociology in Germany: Part I."* Translated by Albion Small. *American Journal of Sociology* 2 (1896-1897), 567-588.

——— "The Present Status of Sociology in Germany: Part II." Translated by Albion Small. *American Journal of Sociology* 2 (1896-1897), 718-736.

Tönnies, Ferdinand, "Die Bedeutung der Presse für die öffentliche Meinung," *Der Weg zur Freiheit 8:* 17 (1938) 257-260.

——— *Community and Society (Gemeinschaft und Gesellschaft)*. Translated and edited by Charles P. Loomis. New York: Harper & Row (Torchbooks), 1963.

——— *Einführung in die Soziologie*. Stuttgart: Ferdinand Enke, 1931, as reported by E. G. Jacoby, "Three Aspects of the Sociology of Tönnies," in Werner Cahnman, ed., *Ferdinand Tönnies: A New Evaluation*. Leiden: E. J. Brill, 1973.

——— "Einteilung der Soziologie," *Zeitschrift für die gesamte Staatswissenschaft* 79: 1 (1925). Translated in Werner Cahnman and Rudolf Heberle, eds., *Ferdinand Tönnies, On Sociology: Pure, Applied, and Empirical*. Chicago: University of Chicago Press, 1971.

——— "Führeraufgaben im Werden der öffentlichen Meinung," *Deutsche Presse* 17 (Jan.-Juni 1927), 267-279.

——— *Kritik der öffentlichen Meinung*. Berlin: Verlag von Julius Springer, 1922.

——— "Macht und Wert der Öffentlichen Meinung," *Die Dioskuren: Jahrbuch für Geisteswissenschaften* 2 (1923), 72-95. Selections from it translated in Werner Cahnman and Rudolf Heberle, eds., *Ferdinand Tönnies, On Sociology: Pure, Applied, and Empirical*. Chicago: University of Chicago Press, 1971.

——— "Mein Verhältnis zur Soziologie," in Richard Thurnwald, Hrsg, *Soziologie von Heute*. Leipzig: C. L. Hirschfeld, 1932. Translated in Werner Cahnman and Rudolf Heberle, eds., *Ferdinand Tönnies, On Sociology: Pure, Applied, and Empirical*. Chicago: University of Chicago Press, 1971.

——— "Offene Antwort," *Zeitungswissenschaft* 6: 1 (1931), 1-2.

——— "The Present Problems of Social Structure," *American Journal of Sociology* 10 (March, 1904-1905), 569-588.

——— "Reform der Presse," *Ethische Kultur* 33 (1925), 26-27.

——— *Schriften der deutschen Gesellschaft für Soziologie, 1. Serie: Verh.d.dtsch. Soziologentage*. Band 1, Verhandlungen des Siebten Deutschen Soziologentages. Tübingen: J.C.B. Mohr (Paul Siebeck), 1931.

——— "Statistik und Soziographie," *Allgemeines Statistiches Archiv* 18 (1929), in Werner Cahnman and Rudolf Heberle, eds., *Ferdinand Tönnies, On Sociology: Pure, Applied, and Empirical*. Chicago: University of Chicago Press, 1971.

——— "Zur Theorie der Öffentlichen Meinung," *Schmoller's Jahrbuch für Gesetzgebung, Verwaltung und Volkswirtschaft* 40: 4 (1916), 2012.

Vincent, George, "A Laboratory Experiment in Journalism," *American Journal of Sociology* 11 (1905-1906), 297-311.

von Wiese, Leopold, *Schriften der deutschen Gesellschaft für Soziologie, 1. Serie: Vehr.d. dtsch.Soziologentage.* Band 1, Verhandlungen des Siebten Deutschen Soziologentages. Tübingen: J.C.B. Mohr (Paul Siebeck), 1931.

Ward, Lester, *Pure Sociology. A Treatise on the Origin and Spontaneous Development of Society.* New York: Macmillan, 1919.

Weber, Karl, "Zur Soziologie der Zeitung," in *Festgabe Fritz Fleiner zum Siebzigsten Geburtstag.* Zürich: Polygraphischer Verlag, 1937.

Weber, Marianne, *Max Weber, Ein Lebensbild.* Tübingen: J.C.B. Mohr (Paul Siebeck), 1926.

Weber, Max, *Gesammelte Aufsätze zur Soziologie und Sozialpolitik,* Tübingen: J.C.B. Mohr (Paul Siebeck), 1924.

—— "Politik als Beruf," in Johannes Winckelmann, Hrsg., *Max Weber Gesammelte Politische Schriften.* Tübingen: J.C.B. Mohr (Paul Siebeck), 1958.

—— *Schriften der deutschen Gesellschaft für Soziologie, 1. Serie: Verhandlungen der deutschen Soziologentage.* Band 11, Verhandlungen des Zweiten Deutschen Soziologentages. Frankfurt: Sauer/Auvermann, KG 1969. (1913).

Wilson, Francis G., *A Theory of Public Opinion.* Chicago: Henry Regnery, 1962.

Winckelmann, Johannes, Hrsg., *Max Weber, Staatssoziologie.* Berlin: Duncker & Humblot, 1966.

Wirth, Louis, "The Sociology of Ferdinand Tönnies," *American Journal of Sociology* 32 (1926-1927), 412-422.

—— Review of *Soziologische Studien und Kritiken: Dritte Sammlung,* by Ferdinand Tönnies. *American Journal of Sociology* 36 (1930-1931), 682.

Woodward, C. Vann, "History and the Third Culture," *Journal of Contemporary History* 3: 2 (1968) 23-35.

Wright, Charles R., *Mass Communication. A Sociological Perspective,* New York: Random House, 1975.

Yarros, Victor S., "A Neglected Opportunity and Duty in Journalism," *American Journal of Sociology* 22 (1916-1917), 203-211.

—— "The Press and Public Opinion," *American Journal of Sociology* 5 (1899-1900), 372-382.

INDEX OF NAMES

ABOUT THE AUTHOR

Hanno Hardt is Professor of Journalism at the University of Iowa; he has also been teaching at the universities of Berlin, Munich, Münster, Mainz (Germany), and Salzburg (Austria) as a visiting professor. His most recent publication (with Elke Hilscher and Winfried B. Lerg), *Presse im Exil. Ein Beitrag zur Kommunikationsgeschichte des Exils, 1933-45*, deals with the emigration of German journalists after Hitler's rise to power.